Community Work and Social Action

COMMUNITY WORK AND SOCIAL ACTION

Dr. Nandan K. Mandal

CENTRUM PRESS
NEW DELHI-110002 (INDIA)

CENTRUM PRESS
H.O.: 4360/4, Ansari Road, Daryaganj,
New Delhi-110002 (India)
Tel: 23278000, 23261597, 23255577, 23286875
B.O.: No. 1015, Ist Main Road, BSK IIIrd Stage,
IIIrd Phase, IIIrd Block, Bengaluru-560085 (INDIA)
Tel: 080-41723429
Email: centrumpress@gmail.com
Visit us at: www.centrumpress.com

Community Work and Social Action

First Edition, 2011

ISBN 978-93-81293-65-2

PRINTED IN INDIA

Printed at Tarun Offset, Delhi

Contents

Preface

Social workers specializing in social action and community development help community organizations and agencies help themselves. They contribute to the grassroots approach by joining other disciplines to bring about social change and community development and providing services to reduce poverty and economic and social dependency. During this era of community fragmentation, social alienation, and economic degeneration of the poor and the middle class, the need for skilled professionals in social and community development has never been greater.

The Social Action Model is a theory of social work practice. The social action model is key to sociopolitical empowerment for work with oppressed groups, communities, and organizations. The model strives to reallocate sociopolitical power so that disenfranchised citizens can access the opportunities and resources of society and, in turn, find meaningful ways to contribute to society as valued human beings.

Community Social work action uses psychoanalytical theory, group work and community work to settle the existing problems which are created either by state or by capitalist class. Anti capitalists' movement, human rights movements showed the inability of social work methods and processes to affect existing system because in these movements radical/critical approach of social work practiced.

Whatever view one has about the nature of community development, it is clear that it is distinct from social capital. Social capital is a prerequisite for community development processes. Without social capital, community development processes could not operate. There would be no family, neighbourhood and community networks; people would not trust each other; there would not be reciprocal relationships and so on. Where there is sufficient social capital to support community development processes the community development process will also generate social capital which can then be used in other community development processes. Community development is one way of producing social capital. There are many other ways and places including workplaces, sporting events, religious activities, schools and carnivals.

Models and techniques for community practice have been with us for some time and social work history is rich with community oriented practices, and providing alternative field placement opportunities along with the more traditional individual agency-based field placements, is a responsible way to reflect this domain of practice. Community development programs are on the cutting edge of social work practice, and it is encouraging to see innovative schools of social work developing field-training experiences that include alternative models. The community oriented model that is the focus of the following study exposes students to a wide array of challenges that result in them being better prepared as social work practitioners, policy makers, administrators, educators and researches, within the spectrum of community practice. This paper is the result of this two-year study in which the writer completed dissertation research requirements. This involved the writer in an intermittent-active role as will be discussed later.

This book re-examines the concept of community work and social action in the Indian and abroad context and attempts to integrate participatory and rights-based concerns with social work practice and community work.

—Editor

1

Introduction

COMMUNITY WORK

What is community work? How has it developed in the UK? What is it's current state? We review thinking and practice in the field of community work, and question the direction it is currently taking. The term community work has a relatively short history in the United Kingdom. Nonetheless, the number of full-time practitioners who were described as being engaged in community work by the early 1980s was roughly equivalent to youth work or adult education. Then there appeared to be some 5,365 community workers, 60 per cent of which were employed in the voluntary sector. Since then there has been no substantial survey of community workers-and there have also been fundamental changes in the economic and institutional context in which they operate.

In this piece we explore: the emergence of community work in the UK; the impact of anti-poverty initiatives such as the Community Development Project in the late 1960s and early 1970s; the shape of work in the 1980s-here focusing upon the categorisation and definition of community work advanced by David Thomas in his book *The Making of Community Work* (1983); and the state of practice in the 1990s and at the turn of the century.

THE EMERGENCE OF COMMUNITY WORK

In the late 1950s and early 1960s accounts of practice and theoretical explorations began to appear that viewed community workers as a distinct occupation. Prior to this there were separate groups of workers such as community centre wardens, secretaries of councils of social services and development workers on new housing estates, who did not possess a common occupational identity.

As Thomas (1983: 25) has argued, the main orientation was to the educational. Not unexpectedly-given the process-focus of many of the key figures, and the institutional location of much of the funding and work. The *Younghusband Report* (1959) on social work was a significant turning point.

It specifically drew on the North American division of social work into casework, group work and community organization, describing the latter as: primarily aimed at helping people within a local community to identify social needs, to consider the most effective ways of meeting these and to set about doing so, in so far as their available resources permit. The first major collection of material (Kuenstler 1961) took up the notion of 'community organization', but it was the terms 'community development' and 'community work' that became popular-and tended to merge.

The term 'community development' was adopted by many U.K. workers and projects for work that focused on work with local neighbourhood groups to set and meet their own needs. The changes were symbolized in two initiatives-the setting up a study group by the Gulbenkian Foundation in 1966 (the first report appeared in 1968) to look at the nature and future of community work in the UK; and the development of the Community Development Projects by the Home Office as part of an anti-poverty strategy. We will look at both in turn.

Community Work and Social Change

The Gulbenkian Report was actually focused around training but inevitably spread its net much wider. Community work was taken to include:

- helping local people to decide, plan and take action to meet their own needs with the help of available outside resources;

- helping local services to become more effective, usable and accessible to those whose needs they are trying to meet;
- taking account of the interrelation between different services in planning for people;
- forecasting necessary adaptions to meet new social needs in constantly changing circumstances.

From this the committee concluded that community work had in it aspects of direct neighbourhood work, closer relations between services and people, inter-agency coordination, and planning and policy formulation. In a crucial section they argued: This community work function should be a recognised part of the professional practice of teachers, social workers, the clergy, health workers, architects, planners, administrators and others. In the modern conditions of social change it is also a necessary full time professional task.

The educationalists on the committee had argued for the conceptualization of community work as part of education-especially adult education. Their case rested on a belief that as an intervention it was fundamentally an educational or learning process, in fulfilment of which the use of specialist community workers was only one strategy. Thus, the advancement of specialist workers-and the emphasis on the role of workers in making services more effective, and in planning, signalled a significant movement away from the educational position. Further, this report needs to be considered in conjunction with other shifts, especially in social work with the move to generic workers recommended by the Seebohm Report (HMSO 1968). There did appear to be a possibility that community work might become a key element of social work (mirroring the three strands of practice in the North American literature-casework, groupwork and community organization). Thomas argues that:

The most profound effect of the demise of the educational influence was that the process goals of community work were not developed beyond the rudimentary expression they were given in the texts of the 1950s and 1960s... The educational aspects of intervention... have remained rooted in two narrow orthodoxies... The first... was that process goals became associated in the minds of the new practitioners of the 1970s only with changes in individual or personal development. The second orthodoxy was to identify process goals with the rhetoric of 'raising political consciousness'... The educational goals of community work embrace both these... but they are also much wider.

The opportunity was also lost of developing community work within community centres and the definition of community work continued to be tied to the particular issues of the day.

In Scotland, the position was a little different. Following the Alexander Report (SED 1975) and the establishment of a new local government structure community education services were formed in most regions. While a considerable amount of community work remained in social service departments in a number of regions, there has been a significant lobby for community development within community education (PCEO 1992). Significantly, bearing in mind our earlier comments concerning community associations, the linking of adult education with youth and community work, has meant that the educative core of community development has been asserted. The process is educational. It is about people in communities creating opportunities for growth and change and deliberate movement towards the ends which they determine and in process of doing so increase their critical awareness, knowledge, skills and attitudes.

THE COMMUNITY DEVELOPMENT PROJECTS

During the 1960s and early 1970s there was a growing recognition of the extent to which poverty remained a major feature of UK society. There had also been a fairly substantial series of debates around the significance and importance of people's participation in various aspects of government activity-perhaps the best known being the Skeffington Report on planning. Following the efforts of the Democratic administration in the United States of America to wage a 'War on Poverty', the UK government sought a similar, but cheaper, initiative.

Self-help and resident participation were seen to be possibilities for the improvement of inner city situations. The result, in 1969, was the launch of the Community Development Projects programme.

It was the largest action-research project ever funded by government. The avowed intention was to gather information about the impact of existing social policies and services and to encourage innovation and co-ordination. The projects had a strong and explicit research focus and an emphasis on social action 'as a means of creating more responsive local services and of encouraging self help'. The projects were initially based in 12 areas of social deprivation. These were neighbourhoods of 3,000 to 15,000 people. Each project involved a small group of professional workers and researchers. The emphasis in CDPs on research meant that they produced a range of important material both about the nature of community work and about the social, political and economic condition of particular areas. Workers in many of the projects came to reject the analysis and strategies of the original project proposals. They sought to organise and research around larger questions of inequality and deindustrialisation rather than more localized concerns around community organization. There was often a desire to bring about a much stronger link between the struggles of the workplace and those of the neighbourhood and community; and to develop means by which groups can join together in things like federations to better influence decision making on a city-wide, regional and national basis. As Loney (1983: 23) comments, the community workers who entered the field in the late 1960s and early 1970s frequently rejected the traditional (educational) models of community work. They replaced the process-orientated 'non-directiveness of Batten and Batten (1967) with a commitment to organizing and a readiness to take up oppositional positions. By 1974 the Home Office had largely given up on the projects and they were wound up in 1976.

In some respects, the optimism and enthusiasm with which community work and 'participation' were greeted in the early 1970s and late 1960s waned with the realisation that many of the issues the work sought to confront were not resolvable at the local level-a realisation that was underlined by the widespread public expenditure cuts after the oil crisis of 1974. There was a considerable growth in the political awareness of community workers in the mid to late 1970s and this has been reflected in the adoption by workers of very different ideological stances. This is sometimes represented by the contrasting of so called social work or community development traditions of practice, with political action traditions: The former focused on the community as a social unit or organism, and was concerned with so called 'soft' issues such as social disorganisation and the need to build up networks and resources. The 'political action tradition' identified the community as a political unit, and emphasised 'hard' issues such as oppression and powerlessness. People associated themselves with each tradition, and each was thought to have its own particular organising styles and methods.

Three further dynamics were also at work: a more general movement away from associational and community group activity (perhaps best articulated in more recent years in the work of Robert Putnam); the rise of managerialism; and the coming to power of politicians who stressed market solutions. All can be seen in developments during the 1980s.

Community Work in the 1980s

In the early 1980s another report sponsored by the Calouste Gulbenkian Foundation (and written by David Thomas) suggested that community work had three major aspects: First, to help people take action on specific issues of importance to them. These issues will almost invariably involve the influence of resources, either those held, for example, by local authorities, or to be found within communities themselves. I have referred to this as the distributive aspect of community work. It is equivalent to the conventional category of 'product goals' familiar in community work literature. Influence on the distribution of resources will be terminal goals for the people involved, but I have argued that we should see them also as instrumental in contributing towards: secondly, the development of political responsibility; and thirdly, that of communal coherence.

In a sense these five approaches are far broader than 'community work'-especially the last, service extension. As Thomas argues: The correct relationship is that community work is a contribution to each of these approaches and, perhaps more importantly, we need to be aware of the range of other contributions that are possible and desirable, and whose value may have been obscured by the attention given to community work. Here, especially, we need to consider youth work, adult education, planning, public health and social work. Social workers, in particular following the Barclay Report (NISW 1982) and the emphasis on community care began to explore the potential of 'community-based' approaches.

The nature of community work had shifted. While some workers still had the freedom, and were disposed, to encourage opposition to the social and economic policies of the Conservative government in Britain-and their impact on local communities (especially with regard to the closure of heavy industries, engineering works and mines upon local communities); the context in which many were employed had changed. The language of managerialism had spread through many local authorities recasting much of the work in terms of meeting organizational objectives rather than local community needs. Most particularly, the focus was upon the more effective use of resources and the efficiency of services-especially with regard to housing and care. There was a significant shift away from locating workers in local neighbourhoods in order to sustain and develop local groups and associational life.

In many respects we have a clearer picture of local activity in Scotland than in England from this time. This is largely due to Alan Barr's (1991) detailed account of practice in Strathclyde. He brought out a number of significant elements. However, two things in particular stand out. The first is the emphasis on community development and process that the workers studied still had (in contrast with the context in which they were working). This may flow, in part, from the particular cultural, political and social situation in Scotland and the focus that community education provides. That said, the work was located in a social work department; and it is likely that a number of community workers in other parts of the UK would have assented to these concerns at this time. The second, and endearing, feature of this research is that it brings out a great deal of the routine day-to-day activities that go to make up jobs such as ours. One of the significant features here is the relatively low amount of face-to-face work undertaken by senior workers as compared to their assistants.

Community Work in the 1990s

By the early 1990s the position of community development work had become a little battered and activity was reduced (Popple 1995: 30). The squeeze on public expenditure; moves to curtail the activities of local authorities (and even to abolish some-such as the Greater London Council); continued high levels of unemployment and poverty; and movements into community care had all acted to alter the face of the work. As Butcher (1992) argued at the beginning of the decade, 'community work' was going through considerable change and redefinition.

By the mid-1990s it was clear that community work approaches were being further harnessed to the development of centrally planned initiatives such as community care; and have become less the province of the traditional concerns of community organization and development. Where people have been able to hang on to some of these concerns-as perhaps has been the case in a number of the rural community initiatives-the emphasis was arguably less on fostering democracy than on facilitating enterprise, holding onto local services such as post offices and pubs, and on developing social provision such as housing. There has also been a flurry of interest in rural work and in children's work.

Instead of looking to community work as an organizing idea, a number of people started to talk of community practice (and this is certainly reflected in the North American literature-see, for example, Hardcastle and Powers 2004). In other words, various areas of work can be seen to have a 'community dimension' and that we need to do is look at the ways in which ideas of 'community' permeate public and social policies and can be used to create alternatives. A further shift in the rhetoric of community development emerged in the mid-1990's with the turn to 'capacity building'. Skinner (1997: 1-2) defines capacity building as follows: Development work that strengthens the ability of community organizations and groups to build their structures, systems, people and skills so that they are better able to define and achieve their objectives and engage in consultation and planning, manage community projects and take part in partnerships and community enterprises. It includes aspects of training, organizational and personal development and resource building, organized in a planned and self-conscious manner, reflecting the principles of empowerment and equality.

The language and direction of 'capacity-building' fitted in with moves toward a greater concern with economic development and planning-although a number of those interested in promoting (such as Eade 1997) are aware of some of its limitations. It was deeply inscribed with a technicist orientation-and was a long way from the more radical concerns of community workers in the early 1970s.

The radical tradition has kept alive. Cooke and Shaw (1997) argued for the re-etablishment of the value of and direction of radical community work-but freedom of movement remained limited for many practitioners-and much of the writing remained caught up in the theoretical concerns of the early 1970s.

Community Work Today

State-sponsored community work remains largely locked into the mix of care, economic development and service delivery improvement work that developed during the 1980s and 1990s. However, three particular areas of state-sponsored work did, to some limited extent, bring a stronger emphasis upon community-based organization and group-functioning in England. First, the emergence and growth of tenant management organizations has led to some attention being given to the cultivation of local groups and the deepening of their capacity to develop and run their own organizations. However, this has not been without tensions (ODPM 2002). In particular local authorities have tended to see tenant management organizations as extensions of their management activity whilst those involved are more likely to see themselves as community activists. They have also tended to see them as rivals. The result was that those employed to facilitate the development of tenant's management organizations and cooperatives often slipped into either representing the view or policies of the local authority to the group or advising them on the technicalities of housing finance funding. The enhancement of local group life was commonly sidelined into a series of courses on 'how to chair a committee' and such like.

Second, the *New Deal for Communities* Programme in England-part of the government's strategy to 'tackle multiple disadvantage in the most deprived neighbourhoods' -has involved an emphasis upon local community involvement.. However, results from the interim evaluation of the initiative indicate that there is only patchy evidence of increased participation in local networks, neighbourliness and involvement in local groups. In contrast, there does appear to have been a significant increase in the trust invested by local residents in local institutions. As the evaluators stressed, community involvement and engagement takes time.

Third, the *Sure Start* programme, originally announced in 1998 and aimed at increasing the quality and availability of child care in selected areas in England, improving the health and well-being of children, and providing support for parents initially involved a significant emphasis upon community development and involvement. Some interesting and apparently successful locally-based work emerged. A strong case was made for this by Norman Glass and others involved in the development of the programme on the grounds that:... it was necessary, in the case of early years at any rate, to involve local people fully in the development and management of the programme if it was to take root and not simply be seen as another quick fix by middle-class social engineers. "What works" is important, but "how it works", at least in this policy area, is equally, if not more, important. (Glass 2005)

If people 'owned' programmes it was argued, then they would both be more likely to address relevant needs and to engage people. However, the community development orientation also contributed to the effective abolition of the programme.

Community development takes time. Disadvantaged communities have to be persuaded to participate, and their natural suspicion leads them to hang back until there is something to show. So the "local" Sure Start programmes have always been behind schedule, and-a mortal sin under New Labour-underspent.

The governments desire to rapidly extend the programme as part of a larger strategy around child care and parenting involved the establishment of large numbers of children's centres within what was termed a 'children's trust approach' and the development of interdisciplinary professional teams. The patient, and it was argued, ultimately rewarding business of community development and full participation did not fit in with such a model.

The main carrier of a concern to cultivate community coherence and local group life in England and Wales at least, were churches and religious groups. The numbers of youth workers employed by local churches had increased significantly during the 1990s and alongside it there had also been a noticeable emphasis placed upon community development. In part this was linked to the need to encourage better use of church buildings and facilities-but there was also a strong theological argument for attention to community life beyond that of the church. A number of Methodist churches, for example, used a community centre model around which to base their activities. Within, and associated with, mosques there developed a significant range of welfare and other networks and services.

In Scotland, the picture was a little different. The community education tradition remained reasonable strong and vocal-adopting, in significant part, the language of community learning. In a Scottish Executive paper this was defined as 'informal learning and social development work with individuals and groups in their communities. The aim of this work is to strengthen communities by improving people's knowledge, skills and confidence, organisational ability and resources'. The book continued, 'Community learning and development makes an important contribution towards promoting lifelong learning, social inclusion and active citizenship'. There is a real sense in which the educational role of community development had not been lost.

One further important element came into play in terms of debates about policy-social capital. Significant press attention was given to Putnam's arguments around the diminution of social capital in the USA (and the impact this had upon people's health, education and happiness). It also encouraged some important debates within academic and policy circles. While there has been some exploration of what a concern with deepening social capital might mean in terms of work in communities it has been, on the whole, rather disappointing. Part of the problem is that it entails policymakers and practitioners entertaining and making sense of issues within a markedly different frame of reference than that which dominates discussion and policy today. The work involved is long-term, dependent upon process and concerned more broadly with flourishing and happiness.

SOCIAL ACTION FOR RURAL COMMUNITY IN INDIA

SARC is a non-governmental, non-profit making, non-political development organization initiated by a group of pioneering youth having diverse expertise of Sambalpur region and later on joined by academician, development protagonists & professionals from different capacity; conceptualizing a substantial commitment to work for the upliftment of downtrodden & socially excluded-marginalized community of western part of Orissa, India.

We need funding support for implementation of four nos. of Day Care cum Counselling Center in Naxal affected area of Sambalpur District of Orissa, India.

Title of the Project: "Day Care cum Counseling Centre for the Children and Adolescent of Naxal Affected Area (Care, Protection & Rehabilitation) of Sambalpur District in Orissa."

Need of the Project: Orissa is one of the most affected state by Maoist since last decade. The region being underdeveloped, unapproachable and remote, it has further aggravated the situation. Another factor is that it is one of the states where majority of the tribal population are inhabited in forest and hilly villages, because of which the tribals of several areas are not able to mingle with the mainstream of development. There are several factors such as lack of access to communication, lack of education and lack of livelihood opportunities leading to grooming of Maoists in the region.

The amalgamations of these factors influenced severely the way of life of the tribal populations in Orissa in general and Sambalpur district in particular. The fringe villages of Sambalpur district is inhabited by several diverse and unique tribal populations such as Oram, Munda, Kisan, Goand having majority of the population.

The baseline data indicate that some of the tribals even in the age of globalization and after 6 decades of independence has not entered into the arena of development. It is needless to mention here that certain inhabitation still are not connected with the all weather roads, do not have access to safe drinking water, no access to education, health, and electricity, still in many cases they are not even able to obtain two square of meal a day. These are also some the reasons basing on which the Maoist misled the innocent tribal communities. Due to these factors they are not able to keep pace with the mainstream of development.

The proposed locations of the project area namely-Chakliabahal, and Tikiba comes under Integrated Tribal Development block of Jamankira under Sambalpur District of Orissa comprising of 18 villages of 2 Gram Panchayats with a population of 5,578. The ethnic composition implies that over 71% of population belongs to ST and SC category, 15% backward communities and 14% General respectively. From socio economic point of view the female literacy of the 2 Panchayats is below 30% and more than 90% of the people obtain their livelihood from minor forest produces and partly from agriculture. The dropout rate among the school going children is very high. Over the last six decades though India has achieved substantial socio-economic progress, a large chunk of the proposed area is still illiterate, uneducated, malnourished, and lack social infrastructure, productive assets and employment.

Objectives: To change the lives of the under privileged children and Adolescent in Naxal affected four villages by developing their fullest potential for making them a healthy, productive and responsible member of the society. Justification of the Project: On one hand there is certain nature of under development of tribals, and inability to enter into the arena of development, entitlement and ignorance and on the other hand these mixed feeling of tribal population has been capitalized by the several forces. One of such forces is the extremist group such as maoist. Through their alternative thinking in the name of under development they influence tribals and drag them into the unconstitutional mechanism.

It is due to this dycotomy, tribal populations as a whole are misdirected by the Maoists movement. They are becoming instrumental in their fight against the state or government missionaries through unlawful means. It is further widening the gap between the state lead development and unlawful activity of social development, i.e. Maoists movement.

Victims: The tribal populations who are in vicious circle of Maoists movement are not able to come into field of development. Generation to generation they are falling into the trap of the movement. Several villagers those who are even trying to come out of Maoists clutches are not able to do so, due to lack of education, awareness and employment opportunities.

Adolescent which account of 22.8% of the population according to the planning commission projection often been perceived as a group of adult mental process and a transition from socio-economic dependence towards relative independence. Adolescent has been often been perceived as a group of people with problems, disturbances and a rebellious streak in them. This opportunities is favourable for the extremists to influence the adolescent to drag them into the pray of moist and ultimately engaged them in unlawful activities against state/Development. In the circumstances the proposal Day Care cum Counseling

Center not only provide security to the 0-6 years child for the working & ailing mother but also give right direction to the Adolescent by developing their special and distinct need for making them a healthy, productive and responsible member of the society. By giving proper counseling in a climate of positive stimulation and a condignly environment, adolescent not only can grow off healthy and responsible member of society but also not fall in to the pray of moist.

Child and Victimization: Maoists movement for their nafed strategy, recruit innocent children and there by children's are falling into trap of the movement. They are breeding the children since the childhood towards the movement, against the state as a result of these the child is deprived from getting basic health, education and recreation.

Child and Education: Since there is no potential education facility for the tribal children they are following the path of Maoists in the several villages of Sambalpur mainly in Jamankira, Jujumura and Naktiduel Blocks. Due to lack of education and livelihood opportunities they are following the traditional tribal livelihood practices by collecting minor forest produces or remain as an unemployed. This reduces the traditional livelihood practice of tribals ultimately developing the insecurity crisis in their life due to fear of Maoists movement. The poor functioning of Schools and Anganbadi centres has aggravated the situation more.

Strategy:

1. In search of livelihood in hilly and tribal regions, the parents are either going to forest, leaving their children and adolescent behind in the villages, for their subsistence.
2. Lack of education facilities, Counseling facility, lack of Pre School, Aganbadi centers and other educational facilities are leading to aimless life of children's and adolescent in the tribal area.
3. Education is a lifeline for the all round development of the community which is not available to the children and adolescent of the movement area.

4. Childrens especially Maoist affected area are undernourished due to lack of sufficient food and livelihood opportunities, non functioning of Aganbadi centres and Schools, due to fear of the movement. Parents do not send their children to schools with the fear that children may be trafficked by the naxalites into their works. So neither they are willing to send their children to school nor putting them into mainstream of development.

Approaches: Social Action for Rural Community (SARC) mission is to make a positive change with the lives of the disadvantage children and our vision is a society where each and every child, adolescent and young persons are supported to realize their potential. The organisation has been working in these areas since last ten years to keep pace with the social development process. SARC work as a catalyst to change the lives of village children and give them a better future through interventions that engage young children as well their parents and community. SARC strategy ensures that young children's and adolescent survive and thrive that they are physically, mentally and emotionally healthy and intellectually curious and prepare them for going to formal schooling without any fear.

SARC will establish 4 nos of Day Care cum Counseling Centers in naxalite affected village of Jamankira Block. The day care cum counseling center will be run from 9 AM to 4 PM besides conducting daily counseling for the adolescent in time of need special adolescent counseling season will be held on every Monday from 2 PM to 4 PM by the foster mother cum counsellor on life skill education, cycology counseling on seven types, namely (i) Physical/health related (food & nutrition, psycho-somatic ailments, general health, physical exercise, etc.); (ii) Familial (understanding, sharing and security within the family); (iii) Financial (cost of education, health, recreation, etc.); (iv) Psychological (nervousness, lack of confidence, anxiety, etc.); (v) Social (friendship, sharing relationship with friends/ teachers and coping with sexual drives); (vi) Emotional (anger/ aggression, depression, loneliness, insecurity and feeling of guilt); and (vii) Academic (concentration, time-management, examination phobia, memory, study habits, etc.). Besides this quarterly sensitization camp for parents and adolescent will organize to address the need of the family on health, education and livelihood opportunities.

The day care cum counseling center will be in the following villages:

1. Rakhibahal, Po. Tikiba, Block. Jamankira
2. Goelmunda, Po. Fasimal, Block. Jamankira
3. Kulunda, Po. Chakuliabahal, Block. Jamankira
4. Hatisal, Po. Chakuliabahal, Block. Jamankira.

SARC believes that a few years of life from conception up to the age of 5 or 6 is the most crucial period of human life where the fastest and most critical change takes place in human brain and body. When the foundations of the health, intellect, personality and social adjustment are laid to enable every individual to grow to his/her full potential and become a healthy productive and responsible member of society. The child's basic needs at this stage must be met and failure to do so can lead to permanent and sometimes unalterable damages. The basic objective of the project is to meet the cognitive, social, emotional and physical needs of most vulnerable young children and adolescent in the naxal affected area. The above needs of the young child can be met through a clean and healthy environment, adequate and appropriate nutrition and loving and stimulating care, providing recreational facilities.

They will be assessed by the clinical psychologists and counselors who are trained on women and child development. It is clear that the family alone can no longer be expected to provide fully that is needed for the development of the child and especially in the movement area the state and society has a bigger role to play in the development of the child. SARC has also noticed that with the decrease in no.s of joint family system and the increasing number of nuclear family especially in the tribal families, working women need support in terms of quality, substitute care for day care services, which are not only required by working mothers but also women belonging to poor families. Poor Women require support and relief for child care as she has the struggle to cope with burden of activities within and outside the home.

To make the programme more successful from the planning stage community participation will be ensured.

Expected Outcome:

- The child parents will be relieved for child care and they can engage for income generation activity.
- The parental care and support towards the children will be increased.
- The girl child who were engaged in care of their younger siblings will go to school for schooling.
- Malnutrition will be reduced and all the childrens will be immunized.
- The percentage of children mainstreaming in the formal schooling will be increased.
- The drop-out rate will be reduced.
- Health of child will be improved and regularly monitored.
- Prevent disruptive deviations and removed confusion in the life of adolescent.
- The adolescent does not fall into the trap of moist movement.
- The adolescent gain positive mental health and overcome stresses and strains of everyday life.
- Childrens I.Q will be accessed and remedial actions will be taken.
- A peaceful environment will be created among the families of the villages and no. of people falling into the hands of the movement will be decreased.

2

Theory and Practice of Community Development

COMMUNITY DEVELOPMENT

Since the late nineteenth century, 'the use of the term community has remained to some extent associated with the hope and the wish of reviving once more the closer, warmer, more harmonious type of bonds between people vaguely attributed to past ages'. Before 1910 there was little social science literature concerning 'community' and it was really only in 1915 that the first clear sociological definition emerged. This was coined by C. J. Galpin in relation to delineating rural communities in terms of the trade and service areas surrounding a central village. A number of competing definitions of community quickly followed. Some focused on community as a geographical area; some on a group of people living in a particular place; and others which looked to community as an area of common life. Beyond this there are issues around the way 'community' appears in political discourse. For some it might mean little more than a glorified reworking of the market. For others, it may be a powerful organizing ideal (such as those concerned with advancing the communitarian agenda). Here we will focus on under standings within social theory-and ask why should educators be interested in them?

People talk about community development in many different ways. Neighbourhood and Community Centre Coordinators have described community development as:

- planning services
- servicing self help groups
- running support and social action groups
- building community networks
- participating in inter-agency meetings
- undertaking needs assessment
- increasing people's skills
- resourcing the community to meet needs
- improving quality of life
- defining priorities
- working towards social justice
- empowering individuals and communities.

Several uses of Community Development

People use the term community development in many different ways. Three of the principal uses are outlined in the table. They are contrasted with direct service.

A COMMUNITY DEVELOPMENT PROCESS

There are many approaches to community development and many community development definitions. For example:

The West Yorkshire Community Work Training Group: The West Yorkshire Community Work Training Group gives a systematic description of a community development process. The steps in the process are seen simultaneously from the point of view of the group of people in the community development process and the community development worker:

1. Group: Vaguely dissatisfied but passive.

   Worker: Simulates people to think through why they are dissatisfied and with what.

2. Group: Now aware of certain needs.

   Worker: Simulates people to think about what specific changes would result in these needs being met.

3. Group: Now aware of wanting changes of some specific kind. Worker: Stimulates people to consider what they

might do to bring about such changes by taking action themselves.

4. Group: Decide for themselves to meet some needs.

   Worker: Stimulates people to consider how best they can organise themselves to do what they now want to do.

5. Group: Plan what to do and how to do it.

   Worker: Stimulate people to consider and decide in detail what to do, who will do it, and when and how they will do it.

6. Group: Act according to the plans.

   Worker: Stimulate people to think through any unforseen difficulties or problems they may encounter.

7. Group: Evaluate the result of what they have achieved.

   Worker: Assists people to reflect on what they have achieved, how they achieved it. What they learnt from this and what they might do next.

8. Restart the process.

   This community development process could be used with a small group of people, a street, a neighbourhood or a whole community.

Susan Kenny in Developing Communities

Development in Australia (1994) does not define community development. She discusses the nature of community development in terms of principles and processes. She sees the principles of community development as:

- objectivity and impartiality
- social justice
- citizenship and human rights
- empowerment and self-determination
- collective action
- tolerance of diversity
- working for change and involvement in conflict

- liberation and participatory democracy
- accessibility of human services.

Kenny notes community development has been "identified as: a job or profession in itself; an important component of all human service work; a method or approach in social or economic development; a philosophical and intellectual approach to the world; and a political activity".

Community Development Outcomes

Community development processes are open-ended and can lead to many different outcomes:

- individuals developing self-esteem and confidence
- people participating in social activities to overcome social isolation
- increased participation in political and citizenship activities
- practical outcomes such as a changed bus route or a new pedestrian crossing
- government funding for new or additional services.

THE CONNECTION WITH SOCIAL CAPITAL

Whatever view one has about the nature of community development, it is clear that it is distinct from social capital. Social capital is a prerequisite for community development processes. Without social capital, community development processes could not operate. There would be no family, neighbourhood and community networks; people would not trust each other; there would not be reciprocal relationships and so on.

Where there is sufficient social capital to support community development processes the community development process will also generate social capital which can then be used in other community development processes. Community development is one way of producing social capital. There are many other ways and places including workplaces, sporting events, religious activities, schools and carnivals.

Low Social Capital

If there is no or low social capital in the group, neighbourhood or community, it will not be possible for those people to work together for the common good. If there is no social capital present the causes may be:

- the human capital required for social capital's core building blocks is absent e.g. self-esteem, trust, communication skills
- there are inadequate levels of material well-being-people are struggling for survival
- there is inadequate physical infrastructure-such as places to meet, public spaces, telephones, newspapers
- the human, economic and physical infrastructure prerequisites are present but there have been no opportunities to develop the networks and interconnections between people.

Where there is insufficient social capital to support a community development process, the community development worker may need to:

- undertake activities that develop the essential human capital prerequisites, e.g. self-esteem, communication skills
- work to increase the material well-being of the group through advocacy, social policy development and material assistance
- work to develop the physical infrastructure-meeting rooms, public spaces, etc
- undertake activities through which people can make interconnections with each other in a safe environment.

HIGH SOCIAL CAPITAL

Where there are high levels of social capital people will:

- feel they are part of the community
- feel useful and be able to make a real contribution to the community

- will participate in local community networks and organisations
- will pull together for the common good in floods and bush fires they
- will welcome strangers
- all will help out with something but no one will do everything.

Community development processes will be much easier to develop with high levels of social capital than with low levels of social capital.

THE STRUCTURE OF THE COMMUNITY DEVELOPMENT SUBJECT

This chapter describes and analyses the development of the community development subject within one particular Australian-based social work course over a ten-year period. This course involves two years of study for a Bachelor of Social Work (BSW) following the completion of two earlier years of university education. The social work degree is also offered to Distance Education students in either a two-year full-time, or four-year part-time framework, and since 2004 to BSW students based in Singapore. Some students also undertake a combined four-year Bachelor of Arts/BSW degree, or combined Bachelor of Health Sciences/BSW degree.

Community development subject is a compulsory final year subject involving twelve weeks of two hour lectures for on-campus students. Distance education students receive a workbook containing all the material used in the lectures, and also attend a compulsory workshop in February. The Singapore-based students also receive the workbook and participate in weekly tutorials plus a compulsory workshop in February. There is, however, little if any community development content in the accompanying direct practice subjects such as working with individuals, working with families and groups, cross-cultural social work, fieldwork skills and practicum, etc. Overall, the community development subject appears to occupy a small, if not marginal, place within the curriculum.

This marginalization arguably duplicates the equally marginal position of community development in the AASW's Practice Standards for SocialWorkers document, whereby community development warrants only a two word mention in a thirty-one-page publication. Both the professional social work association and the university appear to place community development outside the mainstream of social work practice. Social work seems to be defined narrowly as direct practice with individuals or groups, and community development is constructed as a specialist activity that is assumed to be of interest to only a small minority of students and graduates.

APPROACHING THE THEORY OF COMMUNITY

It is helpful to begin by noting that community can be approached as a value. As such it may well be used to bring together a number of elements, for example, solidarity, commitment, mutuality and trust. It comes close to the third of the ideals that were inscribed on many of the banners of the French Revolution – fraternity (the others, as you will most likely remember, were liberty and equality). Socialists such as William Morris talked similarly of 'fellowship':

Fellowship is heaven, and lack of fellowship is hell; fellowship is life, and lack of fellowship is death; and the deeds that ye do upon the earth, it is for fellowship's sake ye do them. Community can also be approached as a descriptive category or set of variables. In practice the two are entwined and often difficult to separate. Here we will initially explore community in three different ways. As:

Place. Territorial or place community can be seen as where people have something in common, and this shared element is understood geographically. Another way of naming this is as 'locality'. This approach to community has spawned a rich literature – first in 'community studies' and more recently in locality studies (often focusing on spatial divisions of labour).

Interest. In interest or 'elective' communities people share a common characteristic other than place. They are linked together by factors such as religious belief, sexual orientation, occupation or ethnic origin. In this way we may talk about the 'gay community', the 'Catholic community' or the 'Chinese community'. Development in what might be called the sociology of identity and selfhood have played an important role in 'opening out the conceptual space within which non-place forms of community can be understood'. 'Elective groups' and 'intentional communities' (ranging, according to Hoggett *op cit* from cyber-communities to car-boot enthusiasts) are a key feature of contemporary life.

Communion. In its weakest form we can approach this as a sense of attachment to a place, group or idea (in other words, whether there is a 'spirit of community'). In its strongest form 'communion' entails a profound meeting or encounter – not just with other people, but also with God and creation. One example here would be the Christian communion of saints – the spiritual union between each Christian and Christ (and hence between every Christian). Another is Martin Buber's interest in meeting and 'the between'.

There is, of course, a strong possibility that these different ways of approaching community will also overlap in particular instances. Place and interest communities may well coincide – for example in the case of places where many of those who live there work in the same industry – such as was the case in 'mining villages'. Willmott (1989) argues that it is legitimate to add a third understanding of community – that of attachment – as communities of place or interest may not have a sense of shared identity.

Anthony P. Cohen's (1982; 1985) work around belonging and attachment is a great help in this respect. He argues that communities are best approached as 'communities of meaning'. In other words, '"community" plays a crucial symbolic role in generating people's sense of belonging'. The reality of community, Cohen argues, lies in its members' perception of the vitality of its culture. "People construct community symbolically, making it a resource and repository of meaning, and a referent of their identity'. This, and the above discussion, leads us to three key questions:

- How is one community or communion marked off from another?

- What sort of social networks or systems are involved in a particular grouping or encounter?
- What norms or 'habits' are involved?

Boundary and Community

Cohen argues that 'community' involves two related suggestions that the members of a group have something in common with each other; and the thing held in common distinguishes them in a significant way from the members of other possible groups. Community, thus, implies both similarity and difference. It is a relational idea: 'the opposition of one community to others or to other social entities'. This leads us to the question of boundary – what marks the beginning and end of a community?

Cohen's argument is that boundaries may be marked on a map (as administrative areas), or in law, or by physical features like a river or road. Some may be religious or linguistic. However, not all boundaries are so obvious: 'They may be thought of, rather, as existing in the minds of the beholders'. As such they may be seen in very different ways, not only by people on either side, but also by people on the same side. This is the *symbolic* aspect of community (or communion) boundary and is fundamental to gaining an appreciation of how people experience communities (and communion). An obvious example of this is the sorts of ritual people connect with in terms of religious observance, for example, the rites of worship, the objects involved and the actions of the priest, imam or rabbi.

Indeed, it is very significant that the notion of community recurs in major religions:... the Christian ideal of the communion of saints and the congregation and the Eucharist as forms of community; the centrality of *umma* or community in Islamic traditions and contemporary practice and theology; community is prominent theme in Judaism, and in Buddhism. (Confucianism is not, of course, a religion, but neo-Confucianism is closely intertwined with Buddhism and with traditional religious cults of the family and ancestors, and Confucian norms of family and community life are politically significant in many contemporary contexts.

Each has expression has its own symbols and markers of boundaries defining who is 'in communion' or 'in community', and who is not. The defining of a boundary places some people within, and some beyond the line. The definition of 'community' or 'communion' can, thus, become an exclusionary act. The benefits of belonging to a particular group are denied to non-members. A very obvious example of this is the growth of 'gated communities' in the USA and UK. A physical barrier is erected to keep out, in this case, those who are poor or who are seen as a threat.

Community as Network and Local Social System

As Lee and Newby (1983) point out, the fact that people live close to one another does not necessarily mean that they have much to do with each other. There may be little interaction between neighbours. It is the nature of the relationships between people and the social networks of which they are a part that is often seen as one of the more significant aspects of 'community'.

When people are asked about what 'community' means to them, it is such networks that are most commonly cited. 'For most of us, our deepest sense of belonging is to our most intimate social networks, especially family and friends. Beyond that perimeter lie work, church, neighbourhood, civic life, and [an] assortment of other "weak ties"'. As well as helping us to build a sense of self and individuality, such informal relationships 'also enable us to navigate our way around the demands and contingencies of everyday living'.

In a very influential study, Bott argued that the immediate social environment of urban families was best considered, 'not as the local area in which they live, but rather as the network of actual social relationships they maintain, regardless of whether these are confined to the local area or run beyond its boundaries'. For many social scientists, the idea of 'network' was attractive because it could be mapped and measured. Writers like Stacey (1969) gave up on community as a 'non-concept' and instead explored local social systems. The 'connectedness' (or density) (and other qualities) of social networks help explain or, at least describe, key aspects of people's experiences.

An example of what analysing networks can tell us is provided by Wenger's study of the support received by older people in North Wales. She looked at the changing composition of networks using three criteria: the availability of close kin; the level of involvement of family, friends and neighbours; and the level of interaction with voluntary and community groups. As a result she identified five types of support network. The commonest form was the second followed by the first – and tended to be the most 'robust' in terms of providing people with informal support.

Wenger on Support Networks for Older People

Wenger identified five types in her study:

- *the local family-dependent support network*. This mainly relied on close kin, who often shared a household or lived locally.
- *the locally integrated support network*. This typically consisted of local family, friends and neighbours.
- *the local self-contained support network*. Usually restricted in scale and containing mainly neighbours, this form had relatively little kin involvement.
- *the wider community-focused support network*. Involving a high level of community activities, this form also typically entailed a high number of friends and kin.
- *the private restricted support network*. Characterized by an absence of close kin, aside from a spouse in some cases, this 'type' also meant few friends or neighbours.

The nature of the networks within in particular place or grouping is, thus, of fundamental importance when making judgments about 'communities' – and the extent to which people can flourish within them. Humans are social animals. Connection and interaction both widen and deepen what we can achieve, and makes possible our individual character. It may even emerge as 'communion'. There are strong forces working against the formation and health of local social systems. Increasingly we operate across significant distances (for example, via letters, the telephone and the internet) when dealing with financial matters such as banking, shopping and the payment of bills. The various forces linked to globalization (commodification, marketization and the corporatization) have led to significant shifts in the locus of power. Governments (whether local or national) have become increasingly market-driven. 'It is not just that governments can no longer "manage" their national economies', Colin Leys comments, 'to survive in office they must increasingly "manage" national politics in such a ways as to adapt them to the pressures of trans-national market forces'. This has entailed two particular dynamics: a growing centralization in key areas of policy making in many countries (with local agencies having to meet to centrally-determined targets with regard to the way in which they work and the outcomes they achieve); and a hugely increased presence of commercial enterprises in local services with the obvious consequence of an erosion of democracy and the notion of there being public goods.

The combined impact of this movement is a drive towards encouraging people to view themselves as consumers of services (rather than participants) and an associated move towards individualization from more collective concerns. In this situation, as Zygmunt Bauman has commented, we may well look longingly at the notion of 'community-it is the 'kind of world which is not, regrettably, available to us- but which we would dearly love to inhabit and which we hope to repossess'. However, in a world where market ideologies have become dominant and infused all areas of life, we have increasingly lost a sense of working together to make change.

Insecurity affects us all, immersed as we all are in a fluid and unpredictable world of deregulation, flexibility, competitiveness and endemic uncertainty, but each one of us suffers anxiety on our own, as a private problem, an outcome of personal failings and a challenge to our provide *savoir-faire* and agility. We are called, as Ulrich Beck has acidly observed, to seek biographical solutions to more systematic contradictions; we look for individual salvation from shared troubles. That strategy is unlikely to bring the results we are after, since it leaves the roots of insecurity intact; moreover it is precisely this falling back on our individual wits and resources that injects the world with the insecurity we wish to escape.

It was this over-focus on private troubles (as against public issues) that was a central feature of C. Wright Mills' work-and his argument that we to retain an appreciation of both, and the relationships between them, retains its power.

Community-Norms and Habits

Whether people are disposed to engage with one another is dependent upon the norms of a particular society or community – and the extent to which individuals make them what de Tocqueville, writing in the first half of the nineteenth century, called 'habits of the heart' (1994: 287) – and this leads us back to our initial discussion of community as a value. To judge the quality of life within a particular community we, need to explore what shared expectations there are about the way people should behave – and whether different individuals take these on.

Three linked qualities appear with some regularity in discussions of communal life:

Tolerance – an openness to others; curiosity; perhaps even respect, a willingness to listen and learn.

Reciprocity – Putnam (2000) describes generalized reciprocity thus: 'I'll do this for you now, without expecting anything immediately in return, and perhaps without even knowing you, confident that down the road you or someone else will return the favour'. In the short run there is altruism, in the long run self-interest.

Trust – the confident expectation that people, institutions and things will act in a consistent, honest and appropriate way (or more accurately, 'trustworthiness' – reliability) is essential if communities are to flourish. Closely linked to norms of reciprocity and networks of civic engagement, social trust – trust in other people – allows people to cooperate and to develop. Trusting others does not entail us suspending our critical judgment – some people will be worthy of trust, some will not. One of the fascinating things about these qualities is that in a very important sense such expectations do not need to be imposed upon people. As Matt Ridley put it, 'Our minds have been built by selfish genes, but they have been built to be social, trustworthy and cooperative'. He continues:

> Humans have social instincts. They come into the world equipped with predispositions to learn how to cooperate, to discriminate the trustworthy from the treacherous, to commit themselves to be trustworthy, to earn good reputations, to exchange goods and information, and to divide labour... Far from being a universal feature of animal life, as Kropotkin believed, this instinctive cooperativeness is the very hallmark of humanity and what sets us apart from other animals.

To this extent, the cultivation of reciprocity, honesty and trust is less about building alien institutions and structures, than creating the conditions for their emergence. Self-interest may bring people together, but in interaction something else emerges. 'Feelings and ideas are renewed, the heart enlarged, and the understanding developed, only by the reciprocal action of men one upon another'.

Fostering Community-Social Capital

Here I want to suggest that a sense of belonging and the concrete experience of social networks (and the relationships of trust etc. that are involved) can bring significant benefits. However, as we have seen, the sense of attachment and quality of social networks varies greatly between the different 'communities' that people name. It could be argued that we should be focusing on enhancing the quality of social networks etc. rather than the creation or strengthening of 'community'. As a way of appreciating the possibilities here I want to look at the idea of social capital – and Putnam's (2000) impressive exploration and compilation of evidence concerning its health and benefits. From there I want to return to the idea that in meeting with others there is the possibility of communion – and that this is, for many, a highly desirable goal. The notion of social capital is a useful way of entering into debates about civil society – and it is central to the arguments of Putnam and others who want to 'reclaim public life'. This is how Putnam introduces the idea:

> Whereas physical capital refers to physical objects and human capital refers to the properties of individuals, social capital refers to connections among individuals – social networks and the norms of reciprocity and trustworthiness that arise from them. In that sense social capital is closely related to what some have called "civic virtue." The difference is that "social capital" calls attention to the fact that civic virtue is most powerful when embedded in a sense network of reciprocal social relations. A society of many virtuous but isolated individuals is not necessarily rich in social capital.

In other words, interaction enables people to build communities, to commit themselves to each other, and to knit the social fabric.

Putnam marshals an impressive amount of material to demonstrate that:

Public spaces in high social-capital areas are cleaner, people are friendlier, and the streets are safer. Traditional neighbourhood "risk factors" such as high poverty and residential mobility are not as significant as most people assume. Places have higher crime rates in large part because people don't participate in community organizations, don't supervise younger people, and aren't linked through networks of friends.

Economic prosperity. A growing body of research suggests that where trust and social networks flourish, individuals, firms, neighbourhoods, and even nations prosper economically. Social capital can help to mitigate the insidious effects of socioeconomic disadvantage.

Health. There appears to be a strong relationship between the possession of social capital and better health. 'As a rough rule of thumb, if you belong to no groups but decide to join one, you cut your risk of dying over the next year *in half*. If you smoke and belong to no groups, it's a toss-up statistically whether you should stop smoking or start joining'. Regular club attendance, volunteering, entertaining, or church attendance is the happiness equivalent of getting a college degree or more than doubling your income. Civic connections rival marriage and affluence as predictors of life happiness.

Francis Fukuyama (1999) raises some useful questions around the 'Putnam thesis' and Ladd (1999) is very critical of the approach – disputing the interpretation much of the evidence. However, that was prior to the marshalling of evidence in *Bowling Alone* (Putnam 2000). The book is a powerful argument for the cultivation of social networks and the norms of reciprocity, trustworthiness and truthfulness they entail. It also draws attention to some of the downsides of such networks – they can be oppressive and narrowing. It is, therefore, important to work for tolerance and the acceptance, if not celebration, of difference.

Fostering Community-Communion

Elizabeth Frazer suggests that given the sorts of conditions we have been discussing, the experience of community 'will be both euphoric and fleeting'. However, there is a significant 'pay-off':

On occasion or at such times members experience a centred and bounded entity that includes the self as such; they engage in exchanges and sharing that are personalized; the orientation to each other and to the whole engages the person and, as some are tempted to put it, his or her soul. It is from such occasions that 'the spirit of community' or 'sense of community' is achieved. Here I think we have the 'pay-off' of community... In the relation of community concrete patterns of material social relations are felt to be transcended... [T]he aspiration to community is an aspiration to a kind of connectedness that transcends the mundane and concrete tangle of social relationships.

This moment of transcendence or connection has been explored by various writers – but for me Martin Buber's work around encounter and community has been the most suggestive. For Buber encounter (*Begegnung*) has a significance beyond co-presence and individual growth. He looked for ways in which people could engage with each other fully – to meet with themselves. The basic fact of human existence was not the individual or the collective as such, but 'Man with Man' (Buber 1947). As Aubrey Hodes puts it:

When a human being turns to another as another, as a particular and specific person to be addressed, and tries to communicate with him through language or silence, something takes place between them which is not found elsewhere in nature. Buber called this meeting between men the sphere of the between.

Encounter (*Begegnung*) is an event or situation in which relation (*Beziehung*) occurs. We can only grow and develop, according to Buber, once we have learned to live in relation to others, to recognize the possibilities of the space between us. The fundamental means is dialogue. 'All real living is meeting' he once wrote.

Such meeting isn't just between two people. Buber believed that in such encounters the eternal could be glimpsed. In speech and silence there was great possibility. In dialogue, a person is present to another (and the other), they are attentive and aware-listening and waiting. In the stillness of this 'in-between world' they may encounter what cannot yet be put into words.

EDUCATION AND COMMUNITY

The case for community as an aim of education (or at least the cultivation of social networks and the associated concern with reciprocity, trust and tolerance) is strong. Indeed, we may follow Dewey and argue that working so that all may share in a common life is *the* aim of education. We may also join with Buber and seek to educate so that people may meet each other as truly human. There is also an interesting question of ends and means. Can we educate for community without being in community? Certainly, this has been a key question within debates around schooling for community. In the last few years the idea of community has been the subject of renewed focus among those advancing the communitarian agenda (e.g. Etzioni 1995). For educators there are a number of implications as James Arthur (2000) has noted. One of the strongest questions here has been the tendency of political communitarians to plough a fairly authoritarian furrow. Our problem in this context is the sheer scale of the task at hand. Increased centralization in many areas of government, globalization and the insinuation of market-thinking into many areas of social life undermine the quality of local social systems and obstruct communion. However, the direction we must take is clear. As Zygmunt Bauman has argued we need to work to 'gain control over the conditions under which we struggle with the challenges of life'. For the most of us 'such control can be gained only *collectively*'.

Social Capital

The notion of social capital is said to have first appeared in Lyda Judson Hanifan's discussions of rural school community centres. He used the term to describe 'those tangible substances [that] count for most in the daily lives of people'. Hanifan was particularly concerned with the cultivation of good will, fellowship, sympathy and social intercourse among those that 'make up a social unit'. It took some time for the term to come into widespread usage. Contributions from Jane Jacobs (1961) in relation to urban life and neighbourliness, Pierre Bourdieu (1983) with regard to social theory, and then James S. Coleman (1988) in his discussions of the social context of education moved the idea into academic debates.

However, it was the work of Robert D. Putnam that launched social capital as a popular focus for research and policy discussion. 'Social capital' has also been picked up by the World Bank as a useful organizing idea. They argue that 'increasing evidence shows that social cohesion is critical for societies to prosper economically and for development to be sustainable'. In this piece we explore the idea of social capital, review some of the evidence with regard to the claims made about it, and assess its significance for educators.

Social Capital for Starters

For John Field the central thesis of social capital theory is that 'relationships matter'. The central idea is that 'social networks are a valuable asset'. Interaction enables people to build communities, to commit themselves to each other, and to knit the social fabric. A sense of belonging and the concrete experience of social networks (and the relationships of trust and tolerance that can be involved) can, it is argued, bring great benefits to people.

Trust between individuals thus becomes trust between strangers and trust of a broad fabric of social institutions; ultimately, it becomes a shared set of values, virtues, and expectations within society as a whole. Without this interaction, on the other hand, trust decays; at a certain point, this decay begins to manifest itself in serious social problems... The concept of social capital contends that building or rebuilding community and trust requires face-to-face encounters.

There is now a range of evidence that communities with a good 'stock' of such 'social capital' are more likely to benefit from lower crime figures, better health, higher educational achievement, and better economic growth. However, there can also be a significant down side. Groups and organizations with high social capital have the means (and sometimes the motive) to work to exclude and subordinate others. Furthermore, the experience of living in close knit communities can be stultifying-especially to those who feel they are 'different' in some important way.

Defining Social Capital

Bourdieu:'Social capital is the 'the aggregate of the actual or potential resources which are linked to possession of a durable network of more or less institutionalized relationships of mutual acquaintance and recognition'.

Coleman:'Social capital is defined by its function. It is not a single entity, but a variety of different entities, having two characteristics in common: they all consist of some aspect of a social structure, and they facilitate certain actions of individuals who are within the structure'.

Putnam:'Whereas physical capital refers to physical objects and human capital refers to the properties of individuals, social capital refers to connections among individuals – social networks and the norms of reciprocity and trustworthiness that arise from them. In that sense social capital is closely related to what some have called "civic virtue." The difference is that "social capital" calls attention to the fact that civic virtue is most powerful when embedded in a sense network of reciprocal social relations. A society of many virtuous but isolated individuals is not necessarily rich in social capital'.

The World Bank: 'Social capital refers to the institutions, relationships, and norms that shape the quality and quantity of a society's social interactions... Social capital is not just the sum of the institutions which underpin a society – it is the glue that holds them together'.

The three thinkers that most commentators highlight in terms of developing a theoretical appreciation of social capital are Pierre Bourdieu, James Coleman and Robert Putnam. Bourdieu wrote from within a broadly Marxist framework. He began by distinguishing between three forms of capital: economic, cultural and social. A basic concern was to explore the processes making for unequal access to resources and differentials in power-and the ways in which these fed into class formation and the creation of elites. He understood social capital to be 'the aggregate of the actual or potential resources which are linked to possession of a durable network of more or less institutionalized relationships of mutual acquaintance and recognition'. The possession of social capital did not necessarily run alongside that of economic capital, but it still was, in his view, an attribute of elites, a means by particular networks held onto power and advantage. In Field's word, he 'presumed that social capital generally functions to mask the naked profit-seeking of its holders, and is therefore inimical with the open democratic society that he espoused in his journalism and political activism'.

James Coleman's (1988) contribution to the development of the notion of social capital was to theorize it in a way that illuminated the processes and experiences of non-elite groups. In other words, he argued that those living in marginalised communities or who were members of the working class could also benefit from its possession. Drawing upon a base of rational choice theory James Coleman (1990, 1994) looked to social capital as part of a wider exploration of the nature of social structures. He argued that social capital was defined by its function. 'It is not a single entity, but a variety of different entities, having two characteristics in common: they all consist of some aspect of a social structure, and they facilitate certain actions of individuals who are within the structure' (Coleman 1994).

However, as Portes (1998), Foley and Edwards (1999) and others have pointed out, a number of problems flow from defining social capital by its function. In particular, the same 'outcome' could flow from very different processes. However, Coleman's explorations were to highlight the possibility that different institutions and social structures were better suited to the cultivation of reciprocity, trust and individual action than others. Like other social investigators he highlighted the role of the family and kinship networks, and religious institutions in the creation of social capital. He believed that changes in both spheres were problematic. They were less able to socialize in appropriate ways; ties appeared to be looser and weaker. It is interesting to compare Coleman's and Bourdieu's contributions to thinking about social capital. John Field brings out some interesting dimensions:

Bourdieu's treatment of social capital is somewhat circular; in summary it boils down to the thesis that privileged individuals maintain their position by using their connections with other privileged people. Coleman's view is more nuanced in that he discerns the value of connections for all actors, individual and collective, privileged and disadvantaged. But Coleman's view is also naively optimistic; as a public good, social capital is almost entirely benign in its functions, providing for a set of norms and sanctions that allow individuals to cooperate for mutual advantage and with little or no 'dark side'. Bourdieu's usage of the concept, by contrast, virtually allows only for a dark side for the oppressed, and a bright side for the privileged.

It was into this situation that Robert Putnam's work on social capital exploded. Returning to commentators such as de Tocqueville, and drawing on some of the debates around, and insights from, Coleman's contribution, he looked to the significance of association and civic community. He wrote from a background in political science and, as such, brought out some important dimensións. Based, initially, on a detailed study of Italian political institutions he argued for the significance of social capital and the quality of civic life in the cultivation of democratic society. He then turned his attention to social capital in the United States-first in an influential article (Putnam 1995) then in a major study: *Bowling Alone*. In the latter Putnam discussed social capital as follows:

> Whereas physical capital refers to physical objects and human capital refers to the properties of individuals, social capital refers to connections among individuals – social networks and the norms of reciprocity and trustworthiness that arise from them. In that sense social capital is closely related to what some have called "civic virtue." The difference is that "social capital" calls attention to the fact that civic virtue is most powerful when embedded in a sense network of reciprocal social relations. A society of many virtuous but isolated individuals is not necessarily rich in social capital.

Robert Putnam's ability to draw upon a wide range of theory, to synthesize and write for a wider audience, and to catch the public mood in the United States would have been enough to encourage a wider embrace of the notion of social capital. However, when this was added to the depth and range of data he and his team were able to access and analyse with regard to social capital in the United States it was not surprising that *Bowling Alone* became a powerful focus for debate.

Putnam-why Social Capital is Important

First, social capital allows citizens to resolve collective problems more easily... People often might be better off if they cooperate, with each doing her share....

Second, social capital greases the wheels that allow communities to advance smoothly. Where people are trusting and trustworthy, and where they are subject to repeated interactions with fellow citizens, everyday business and social transactions are less costly.... A third way is which social capital improves our lot is by widening our awareness of the many ways in which our fates are linked... When people lack connection to others, they are unable to test the veracity of their own views, whether in the give or take of casual conversation or in more formal deliberation. Without such an opportunity, people are more likely to be swayed by their worse impulses....

The networks that constitute social capital also serve as conduits for the flow of helpful information that facilitates achieving our goals.... Social capital also operates through psychological and biological processes to improve individual's lives. ... Community connectedness is not just about warm fuzzy tales of civic triumph. In measurable and well-documented ways, social capital makes an enormous difference to our lives.

Types of Social Capital: Those concerned with social capital have looked to the density of social networks that people are involved in; the extent to which they are engaged with others in informal, social activities; and their membership of groups and associations. Their big worry is that in the USA, for example, there has been a significant decline in the active membership of associations (like PTAs, football teams and community groups) and a corresponding increase in individualized leisure activities (most especially watching television). For example, there has been drop in the number of people involved in league (team) bowling and a growth in individual bowling. The result is that social capital is weakened.

Bridging, Bonding and Linking Social Capital

Michael Woolcock, a social scientist with the World Bank (and Harvard) has helpfully argued that many of the key contributions prior to *Bowling Alone* failed to make a proper distinction between different types of social capital. He distinguished between:

Bonding social capital which denotes ties between people in similar situations, such as immediate family, close friends and neighbours.

Bridging social capital, which encompasses more distant ties of like persons, such as loose friendships and workmates.

Linking social capital, which reaches out to unlike people in dissimilar situations, such as those who are entirely outside of the community, thus enabling members to leverage a far wider range of resources than are available in the community.

The Putnam team looked to whether social capital is *bonding* (or exclusive) and/or *bridging* (or inclusive). Putnam suggested that the former may be more inward looking and have a tendency to reinforce exclusive identities and homogeneous groups. The latter may be more outward-looking and encompass people across different social divides.

Bonding capital is good for under-girding specific reciprocity and mobilizing solidarity... Bridging networks, by contrast, are better for linkage to external assets and for information diffusion.... Moreover, bridging social capital can generate broader identities and reciprocity, whereas bonding social capital bolsters our narrower selves.... Bonding social capital constitutes a kind of sociological superglue, whereas bridging social capital provides a sociological WD-40.

These were not seen as either-or categories to which social networks can neatly assigned – 'but "more-or-less" dimensions along which we can compare different forms of social capital. However, Putnam did not really look at linking social capital nor did he come to grips with the implications of different forms of social capital i.e. that 'different combinations of the three types of social capital will produce different outcomes.

THE DECLINE OF SOCIAL CAPITAL IN THE USA

Putnam demonstrated that on a range of indicators of civic engagement including voting, political participation, newspaper readership, and participation in local associations that there were serious grounds for concern. It appeared that America's social capital was in decline. First in the realm of civic engagement and social connectedness he was able to demonstrate that, for example, over the last three decades of the twentieth century there had been a fundamental shift in:

***Political and civic engagement*:** Voting, political knowledge, political trust, and grassroots political activism are all down. Americans sign 30 percent fewer petitions and are

40 percent less likely to join a consumer boycott, as compared to just a decade or two ago. The declines are equally visible in non-political community life: membership and activity in all sorts of local clubs and civic and religious organizations have been falling at an accelerating pace. In the mid-1970s the average American attended some club meeting every month, by 1998 that rate of attendance had been cut by nearly 60 percent.

Informal social ties: In 1975 the average American entertained friends at home 15 times per year; the equivalent figure (1998) is now barely half that. Virtually all leisure activities that involve doing something with someone else, from playing volleyball to playing chamber music, are declining.

Tolerance and trust: Although Americans are more tolerant of one another than were previous generations, they trust one another less. Survey data provide one measure of the growth of dishonesty and distrust, but there are other indicators. For example, employment opportunities for police, lawyers, and security personnel were stagnant for most of this century-indeed, America had fewer lawyers per capita in 1970 than in 1900. But in the last quarter century these occupations have boomed, as people have increasingly turned to the courts and the police.

He went on to examine the possible reasons for this decline. Crucially, he was able to demonstrate that some favourite candidates for blame could not be regarded as significant. Residential mobility had actually been declining for the last half of the century. Time pressure, especially on two-career families, could only be a marginal candidate. Some familiar themes remained though:

- *Changes in family structure* (i.e. with more and more people living alone), are a possible element as conventional avenues to civic involvement are not well-designed for single and childless people.
- *Suburban sprawl* has fractured the spatial integrity of people's. They travel much further to work, shop and enjoy leisure opportunities. As a result there is less

time available (and less inclination) to become involved in groups. Suburban sprawl is a very significant contributor.

- *Electronic entertainment*, especially television, has profoundly privatized leisure time. The time we spend watching television is a direct drain upon involvement in groups and social capital building activities. It may contribute up to 40 percent of the decline in involvement in groups.

However, generational change came out as a very significant factor. A "long civic generation," born in the first third of the twentieth century, was passing from the American scene. 'Their children and grandchildren (baby boomers and Generation X-ers) are much less engaged in most forms of community life. For example, the growth in volunteering over the last ten years is due almost entirely to increased volunteering by retirees from the long civic generation'.

Subsequently, there has been some evidence appearing linked to working patterns-with only one third of British workers, for example, working 'normal hours'. Halpern (2009a) comments, 'A consequence of our modern service economy appears to be that the majority of people now work part-time or do shift work, leading to a 'de-synchronisation' of our leisure and social activities'. One study, by Matt Clark and associates (forthcoming but quoted by Halpern), found that 'even controlling for levels of working hours, those who do shift work end up spending substantially less time in social and participative activities'.

Some Critiques and Developments of the Bowling Alone Thesis

Francis Fukuyama (1999) raised some useful questions around the 'Putnam thesis' and the late Everett C. Ladd (1999) was very critical of the approach – disputing the interpretation much of the evidence in Putnam's original (1995) article. Ladd's argument was that American civic life was not so much in decline but rather 'churning'. Some organizations had lost members, others had sprung up in their place. He believed that 'the individualism at the heart of the country's conception of citizenship gave Americans no alternative but to cooperate with one another' (Lenkowsky 2000). Lenkowsky continues:

This being so, ebbs and flows in organizational membership should be seen as stemming not from any broad disaffection with civic groups or public life per se but from uncertainty about how best to work together during changing times. The very concern sparked by Putnam's lament was itself, Ladd suggested, a sign of America's still abundant supply of social capital.

However, Ladd was writing prior to the marshalling of evidence in *Bowling Alone* (Putnam 2000). In many respects, Ladd's central thesis was undermined by the data assembled by Putnam. Four more recent contributions have shed new light on the interpretation put on the data.

From Membership to Management in American Civic Life

First, Theda Skocpol has powerfully demonstrated that one of the most significant changes lies in the changing shape of associational life. In particular she questions the over-focus in the work of Putnam and others on the workings of local groups and associations. 'American civic voluntarism', she writes, 'was never predominantly local and never flourished apart from national government and politics'. Social capital theorists have tended to examine 'all forms of social connectedness at once'. Rather than there being some major generational shift, she suggests, a 'confluence of trends and events sparked a shift from membership mobilization to managerial forms of civic organizing'. She continues:

After 1960 epochal changes in racial ideals and gender relationships delegitimated old-line US membership associations and pushed male and female leaders in new directions. New political opportunities and challenges drew resources and civic activists toward centrally managed lobbying. Innovative technologies and sources of financial support enabled new, memberless models of association building to take hold. And finally, shifts in American class structure and elite careers created a broad constituency for professionally managed organizing... The most privileged Americans can now organize and contend largely among themselves, without regularly engaging the majority of citizens. There may well have been a decline in social capital, but these shifts are perhaps more significant and have led to 'fraying' of vital links in US associational life.

Community Participation

A second significant contribution has come from those theorists exploring the realities and experiences of family and work life. Here, the work of Ann Bookman (2004) is of interest. She argues that we need to extend our appreciation of what constitutes community participation-especially if we are interested in what women do. Bookman has drawn attention to the informal connections formed to help with family care-and which do not register with many social capital commentators. New forms of "social capital"-just as important as money in the bank-are developing among working families in both urban and suburban environments. These new relationships are binding us together and reshaping our communities in a literal and social sense.

Bookman charts the ways in which working families reach out to each other and to community-based programmes to address the issues they face-especially around caring for children and relatives. In addition she draws attention to the impact of what she describes as the 'stalled gender revolution'-and the extent to which women are still expected to shoulder disproportionate responsibilities for care, community engagement and domestic functioning.

Hybrid Associations

Third, as Robert J. Sampson and his associates on the Project on Human Development in Chicago Neighborhoods, have shown in their multi-cohort study, while traditional associations like close relationships with neighbours are declining, other 'hybrid' associations are beginning to be significant. One of these is the non-profit organization which is an important site of collective action.

Social Capital and Inequality

Last, there has been some significant discussion with regard to the relationship between social capital and inequality. As Wilkenson and Pickett (2009) put it, 'does inequality create low levels of trust, or does mistrust create inequality?'. Putnam (2000) viewed community and inequality as 'mutually reinforcing', with casual arrows running in both directions. However, commentators such as Eric Uslaner (2002) along with Bo Rothstein have argued that it is inequality that affects trust rather than the other way around.

While we can see that there have been some significant changes in the ways that people engage with local institutions and networks, we need, thus, to be careful of arguing for an overall decline. There may well have been a movement, as Skocpol (2003) put it, away from active membership toward professionalization and management in civic life. There may also have been a decline in involvement in local associations and groups, and in national membership organizations and fellowship groups-but whether this adds up to a significant diminution in social capitals another matter. At present, the balance of evidence as far as the USA, UK and other Anglo-Saxon countries, as well as France, are concerned is that there has been a broadly similar decline (Halpern 2009b). In other countries, such as in Scandinavia, trust levels have remained relatively high and even increased. As Bo Rothstein (1998) has argued, this can in part be explained by differing moral and political logics in societies. Thus, while in the USA and UK there has been a significant shift towards privatisation and individualism, this can be contrasted with a less egotistic and more mutual or 'solidaristic individualism' in some societies.

Social Capital and Concrete Benefits Associated

While the jury may be out over aspects of the arguments around decline, Putnam's assessment of the benefits of what he defines as social capital remains an important reference point. He is able to demonstrate that:

- Child development is powerfully shaped by social capital. Trust, networks, and norms of reciprocity within a child's family, school, peer group, and larger community have far reaching effects on their opportunities and choices, educational achievement, and hence on their behaviour and development.

- In high social-capital areas public spaces are cleaner, people are friendlier, and the streets are safer. Traditional neighbourhood "risk factors" such as high poverty and residential mobility are not as significant as most people assume. Places have higher crime rates in large part because people don't participate in community organizations, don't supervise younger people, and aren't linked through networks of friends. As Sampson and his associates have also shown those communities with 'collective efficacy'-the confidence to intervene born of higher rates of social capital-are characterized by lower crime rates.
- A growing body of research suggests that where trust and social networks flourish, individuals, firms, neighbourhoods, and even nations prosper economically. Social capital can help to mitigate the insidious effects of socioeconomic disadvantage. The growing presence of non-profit organizations in some areas as one aspect of this. Another is the quality of the networks in the 'underground economy of the urban poor'.
- There appears to be a strong relationship between the possession of social capital and better health. 'As a rough rule of thumb, if you belong to no groups but decide to join one, you cut your risk of dying over the next year *in half*. If you smoke and belong to no groups, it's a toss-up statistically whether you should stop smoking or start joining'. Regular club attendance, volunteering, entertaining, or church attendance is the happiness equivalent of getting a college degree or more than doubling your income. Civic connections rival marriage and affluence as predictors of life.

Many of these findings have been underlined by subsequent explosion in studies around happiness and well-being. The World Bank (1999) has also brought together a range of statistics to make the case for the social and economic benefits of social capital. For example they argue that there is evidence that schools are more effective when parents and local citizens are actively involved. 'Teachers are more committed, students achieve higher test scores, and better use is made of school facilities in those communities where parents and citizens take an active interest in children's educational well-being'. They also indicate some negative impacts, for example, when disgruntled local elites joined together to close health clinics in Uttar Pradesh. Child mortality rates soared as a result.

ORGANIZATIONS OF SOCIAL CAPITAL

The idea of looking at social capital in firms and organizations was, as Cohen and Prusak (2001) said, relatively new. This may be because of the way in which the dominance of more mechanistic and system-oriented conceptions of organizational activity have 'masked their deeply social nature. A number of those concerned with organizational development, like Cohen and Prusak, have become increasingly suspicious of the 'people, processes, technology' mantra, 'ceaselessly intoned as a summary of the sources of organizational effectiveness'. There has, of course, been a significant embracing of the notion of human capital-but those writing about it rarely approach the social nature of organizations-and often fall prey to a tendency to draw upon theories and metaphors that derive financial and physical notions of capital. The argument of those concerned with social capital is that when harnessed it generates economic returns. More particularly, the benefits claimed include:

Better knowledge sharing, due to established trust relationships, common frames of reference, and shared goals. Lower transaction costs, due to a high level of trust and a cooperative spirit (both within the organization and between the organization and its customers and partners). Low turnover rates, reducing severance costs and hiring and training expenses, avoiding dis-continuities associated with frequent personnel changes, and maintaining valuable organizational knowledge. Greater coherence of action due to organizational stability and shared understanding.

Given the relative infancy of the application of social capital to organizational life there is little sustained or substantial research that can support attention to the notion within organizations. It certainly isn't *the* key to success, but it is part of the fabric of organizational life-and the need to engage with it is, arguably, growing. The increasing complexity of organizations and the scale of informational activity; globalization; external and internal volatility; and what Cohen and Prusak call 'the challenge of virtuality' (work carried out over a distance of time and space) all contribute here.

Social Capital and Informal Education

Robert Putnam's discussion of social capital, in particular, provides informal educators with a powerful rationale for their activities. After all the classic working environment for the informal educator is the group, club or organization. The evidence and analysis also provides a case against those who want to target work towards those who present the most significant problems and tie informal educators' activities to the achievement of specific outcomes in individuals. Several points need underlining here.

First, from the material marshalled by Putnam and others we can see that the simple act of joining and being regularly involved in organized groups has a very significant impact on individual health and well-being. Working so that people may join groups – whether they are organized around enthusiasms and interests, social activity, or economic and political aims – can make a considerable contribution in itself. Encouraging the development of associational life can also make a significant difference to the experience of being in different communities. Here we might highlight the case of schooling. Educational achievement is likely to rise significantly, and the quality of day-to-day interaction is likely to be enhanced by a much greater emphasis on the cultivation of extra-curricula activity involving groups and teams.

Second, informal education's long standing concern with association and the quality of life in associations can make a direct and important contribution to the development of social networks (and the relationships of trust and tolerance that is usually involved) and the strengthening of democracy. Informal educators interest in dialogue and conversation, and the cultivation of environments in which people can work together, take them to the heart of what is required to strengthen and develop social capital and civic society. Their ethical position also demands they attend to the downsides of networks – in particular, the extent to which they are oppressive and narrowing. A focus on tolerance and the acceptance, if not the celebration, of difference is required. There is a place for bridging, bonding and linking social capital.

Third, there is a strong argument here against those who wish to concentrate the bulk of resources on groups and individuals who present the strongest social problems (currently the received thinking among many policy makers). If we follow Putnam's analysis through then we can see that, for example, crime can be reduced, educational achievement enhanced and better health fostered through the strengthening of social capital. Significantly this entails working across communities – and in particular sustaining the commitment and capacities already involved in community organizations and enthusiast groups, and encouraging those on the cusp of being actively involved. The majority of the people we are talking about here cannot be classified as suffering from multiple disadvantage, will not be engaged in criminal activity, and will be (or have been) engaged with education systems and/or the world of work. In other words, open and generic work needs to be afforded a far higher priority – and so-called 'issue-based' work needs to be more closely interrogated as to the benefits it brings.

Notion of Social Capital and its Some Issues

To conclude it is worth highlighting four key issues with regard to the notion of social capital. The way in which the notion of social capital is used by the central writers Bourdieu, Coleman and Putnam while offering some important insights, and a focus for data collection and analysis, is not as yet rich theoretically. This may simply mean that more work needs to be done, or imply that the concept itself is problematic.

First, while the notion of social capital clearly has some utility we need to be aware of the dangers of 'capitalization'. As Cohen and Prusak (2001) have commented, not everything of value should be called 'capital'. There is a deep danger of skewing our consideration of social phenomenon and goods towards the economic. The notion of capital brings with it a whole set of discourses and inevitably links it, in the current context, to capitalism.

Second, there has been a tendency not to locate exploration properly within a historical framework. Coleman and Putnam do analyse data and material over time-but fail to fully contextualize it. Skocpol (2003), by placing her work within historical analysis, has been able to show just how some of the important assumptions made by Putnam, for example, need to be questioned.

Third, much of the main work undertaken around social capital has failed to properly address the gender dimension of social capital. As we saw in the work of Skocpol (2003), Bookman (2004) and others, the way in which women engage and create local networks, and have to manage caring often falls beneath the radar of social capital researchers and theorists. To give him his due, Putnam does address gender in terms of changing patterns of local involvement-but does not theorize it substantially, nor does he really connect with the sorts of concerns that Bookman has been subsequently voicing around the way in which we think about networks of caring, for example.

Fourth, much of the discussion of social capital has treated it as a 'good thing'. Bourdieu, at least, was interested in the notion as a way of explaining how some were able to access resources and power, while others were not. However, the scale of local surveillance that can be involved, the possible impacts around what is deemed acceptable behaviour, and the ways in which horizons may be narrowed rather than expanded are not unambiguously 'good things'.

In terms of developing social analysis it might well be that those theorists who have explored individualization and globalization within society have something more to offer than social capital theorists. That said, though, some of the empirical work that has been done linking involvement in associational life and participation in social networks to the enhancement of educational achievement, the promotion of health and the reduction of crime is of great significance. Social capital researchers, and Robert Putnam in particular, has done us a great service. While aspects of his argument and research will continue to be disputed over the coming years, his central message is surely true. Interaction enables people to build communities, to commit themselves to each other, and to knit the social fabric.

Idea of Community Development

The idea of community development grew, in large part, out of the activities of colonial administrators. We examine this legacy and the theory and practice that emerged. We also look to the body of overlapping ideas, including community participation, community organization and community work that has run alongside the notion of community development.

Like many of the terms around the community work and community education field, the notion of 'community development' is beset with difficulties. In this piece we suggest that it is perhaps best used to describe those approaches that look to cultivate mutual aid, local networks and communal coherence. In many respects as a body of thinking and practice it links strongly to more recent concerns around the cultivation of social capital.

The Colonial Legacy

The notion of community development owes a great deal to the efforts of colonial administrators. After the Second World War the British Colonial Office became concerned with 'community development'. Mayo (1975) suggests that administrators 'concocted' the term out of their attempts to develop 'basic education' and social welfare in the UK colonies. For example, a 1944 report, *Mass education in the colonies*, placed an emphasis on literacy training and advocated the promotion of agriculture, health and other social services through local self help (Midgley et al 1986). This was a set of concerns similar to those surrounding the interest in rural development and educational 'extension' in North America in the first two decades of the century. Community development was defined in one UK government publication as: active participation, and if possible on the initiative of the community, but if this initiative is not forthcoming spontaneously, by the use of techniques for arousing and stimulating it in order to achieve its active and enthusiastic response to the movement.

The concern with community development was, in part, a response to the growth of nationalism, and, in part an outcome of a desire to increase the rate of industrial and economic development. The notion began to feature strongly in United Nations documents during the 1950s-and these drew extensively on the British literature and experiences in Africa and India. Three important elements were identified:

- a concern with social and economic development.
- the fostering and capacity of local co-operation and self-help.
- the use of expertise and methods drawn from outside the local community.

Within this there does appear to be a certain contradiction. Community development emphasizes participation, initiative and self help by local communities but is usually sponsored by national governments as part of a national plan. While from one side it can be seen as the encouragement of local initiative and decision making, from the other it is a means of implementing and expediting national policies at the local level and is a substitute for, or the beginning of, local government.

The focus on the social and economic, local and global, also helps to situate debates about community development-and the disillusionment with its achievements that was widespread in many Southern countries by the 1970s. Many governments, particularly in Africa, failed to provide adequate financial support but nevertheless extolled the virtues of self-help. Community development was soon recognized by the people to amount to little more than a slogan which brought few tangible benefits.

However, we should not forget in this process is that community development had also spawned a growing literature. Workers were not only able to draw on the extensive American literature of community organization-there were now various guides and discussions arising specifically out of the experience of 'developing' countries, for example, Batten's (1957) classic textbook *Communities and their Development.*

It is not without significance that while the community organization literature became broadly located in social work, the community development literature had far more an 'educational' hue. Yet, we do need to take some care here-just because a discourse found expression in North American social work does not mean that it was not informed by educational thinkers. However, the institutional location of the work, combined with the orientation of its proponents is important. Batten, for example, who wrote a string of influential books (e.g. 1957; 1965; 1967) was based at the University of London Institute of Education. As we will see when we come to look at the experience of community work in the United Kingdom this educational orientation was to wane there also in the late 1960s.

The Move away from Education

To make sense of the notion of community development it is helpful to situate it alongside other strands of community work practice. Here it is useful to consider Thomas' (1993) discussion of the five main strands or approaches that characterized community work in the early 1980s. He talked about:

Community Action: Community action was seen as focusing on the organisation of those adversely affected by the decisions, or non-decisions, of public and private bodies and by more general structural characteristics of society. The strategy aims to promote collective action to challenge existing socio-political and economic structures and processes, to explore and explain the power realities of people's situations and, through this twin pronged approach, develop both critical perspectives of the status quo and alternative bases of power and action.

Community Organisation: Community organization, according to Thomas, involves the collaboration of separate community or welfare agencies with or without the additional participation of statutory authorities, in the promotion of joint initiatives.

Community Development: Community development was seen as emphasizing self-help, mutual support, the building up of neighbourhood integration, the development of neighbourhood capacities for problem-solving and self-representation, and the promotion of collective action to bring a community's preferences to the attention of political decision-makers.

Social Planning: This orientation/approach was presented as being concerned with the assessment of community needs and problems and the systematic planning of strategies for meeting them. Social planning comprises the analysis of social conditions, social policies and agency services; the setting of goals and priorities; the design of service programmes and the mobilisation of appropriate resources; and the implementation and evaluation of services and programmes.

Service Extension: This is a strategy that seeks to extend agency operations and services by making them more relevant and accessible. This includes extending services into the community, giving these services and the staff who are responsible for them a physical presence in a neighbourhood.

In Britain the notion of community development became associated for some with shifts within community work towards more radical approaches (following the experiences of workers within the Community Development Projects of the early 1970s). In particular this involved a movement away from what could be described as an informal education perspective, into what would be better labelled social action. However, the radicalism of many of the workers attracted into the work in the late 1960s and early 1970s in many northern countries was not to last.

The waning of key social movements, the increased influence of managerialism, and more general economic and political shifts around marketization and globalization meant that there was in many countries, a gradual drift into a policy orientation and a focus on the implementation of social care and regeneration initiatives. In other words, there was a significant movement into approaches to what people described as 'community development' that looked to what Thomas described as social planning and service extension.

In some places there were countervailing forces to this movement away from education and from mutual aid and community. In Scotland, for example, the developing professional and political interest in community education kept a stronger focus on more locally-based and associational work. In a similar way the experience of non-formal education programmes in some countries retained an interest in the ways in which local people understood their situation and reflected more of a 'bottom-up' approach to policy formation.

Capacity Building of Community Development

Some of the classic concerns of community development found expression in the early 1990s in the notion of 'capacity building'. There was an interest in developing the ability of local groups and networks to function and to contribute to social and economic development. On the whole, though, the idea of capacity building often remained associated with a technicist and economistic viewpoint-a concern with competencies, 'investing' and so on. There were those that looked to the 'bottom-up' and more convivial aspects of traditional community development.

A few contributions also emerged that had a more thorough theoretical basis. Eade's (1997) approach, for example, and that of development agencies such as Oxfam, was linked into certain fundamental beliefs, for example: 'that all people have the right to an equitable share in the world's resources, and to be the authors of their own development; and that the denial of such rights is at the heart of poverty and suffering'. Strengthening people's capacity to determine their values and priorities, and to act on these, is the basis of development.

Capacity building is an approach to development rather than a set of discrete or pre-packaged interventions. So while there are certain basic capacities (social, economic, political and practical) on which development depends, Oxfam seeks to support organisations working for sustainable social justice.

From this flow a number of implications. That:

- capacity building must not be seen in isolation.
- all have capacities that may not be obvious to outsiders and it may take time to discover these.
- if it is to be inclusive, interventions must take into account different and sometimes negative, ways in which the impacts will be experienced.
- flexibility is important but this must not be at the expense of a loss of direction with regard to wider processes of social and economic transformation.
- capacity building is not 'doing development' on the cheap or against the clock. Nor is it risk-free.

The problem was that many of those interested in capacity building located it within a particular paradigm. It was capacity-building within a particular set of policy parameters. There was not often a disposition to build capacity that might oppose or fail to the 'importance' of state interests and priorities.

Community Participation and Debates

In the late 1960s there was some exploration of different models of participation and their relationship to community development. Since then concern around popular and community participation in key agencies such as the United Nations has been part of the discourse of community development. As Midgley et al have noted, the notion of popular participation and that of community participation were interlinked. The former was concerned with broad issues of social development and the creation of opportunities for the involvement of people in the political, economic and social life of a nation, 'the latter connotes the direct involvement of ordinary people in local affairs'.

As such community participation can be seen as linking with older concerns with associational democracy and the like. In some countries the notion of community participation has reappeared in discussions around the need to bring some local services and facilities more directly into the control of local people. For example the 2005 election manifesto for the British Labour Party argued for 'new opportunities for communities to assume greater responsibility or even ownership of community assets like village halls, community centres, libraries or recreational facilities'.

This concern with local control and networks had some roots in the debates that emerged around social capital in the late 1990s and early 2000s. Significant press attention was given in the United States and the UK to Robert Putnam's arguments around the diminution of social capital in the USA (and the impact this had upon people's health, education and happiness). It also encouraged some important debates within academic and policy circles.

While there has been some exploration of what a concern with deepening social capital might mean in terms of work in communities it has been, on the whole, rather disappointing. Part of the problem is that it entails policy makers and practitioners entertaining and making sense of issues within a markedly different frame of reference than that which dominates discussion and policy today. The work involved is long-term, dependent upon process and concerned more broadly with flourishing and happiness. State intervention is largely short-term, looking to outcomes and interested in economic growth and efficiency.

Along with Thomas and others we argue here that there is some merit in restricting the notion of community development to those approaches that focus on the cultivation of local democracy, mutual aid, local networks and communal coherence. Economic development and the quality and appropriateness of state and other services may well form a part of this attention-but are not the foci around which activity revolves.

Over the next few years it will be interesting to see how more convivial notions of community development fare. There are strong forces for continuing centralization and marketization in many states. At the same time, it appears that many of the older policy imperatives such as the focus on economic growth are not cutting it in terms of people's feeling of well-being. There appears still to be some yearning after community and a feeling that something has been lost in many countries. Whether this can be turned into significant activity is an open question.

Community Education

Broadly, we can approach community education as 'education for community within community'. In other words, something called 'community' is not just the place or context in which education is to occur, fostering community is also a central concern. The process of becoming part of an existing social network in order to encourage dialogue and learning is sometimes labelled as informal education in UK discussions or as community education in Scottish debates. For example, CeVe (Scotland) have defined community education as:..a process designed to enrich the lives of individuals and groups by engaging with people living within a geographical area, or sharing a common interest, to develop voluntarily a range of learning, action and reflection opportunities, determined by their personal, social, economic and political needs.

However, this particular definition does not put 'education for community' at the centre of the work (although some practitioners may interpret it to do so)-and this dilutes the concept somewhat.

Community education in its stronger sense has parallels in the tradition of community organization in the USA, sozial padagogik in Germany, animation in France and socio-cultural work in Belgium. Furthermore, it links up with the thinking and practice of those who have worked for community-based, and democratic schooling-and for child-centred education. If approached in many Southern countries, then our focus would most likely be non-formal education or community participation. It could be seen as close to the Latin American tradition of popular education or the French tradition of la vie associative with its emphasis on association.

Different practice traditions have arisen in various contexts-but there are some important points of contact and exchange.

They have not grown in isolation. For example, in recent years the work of Paulo Freire has been influential in each. We can also draw lines historically-for example from Rousseau through key thinkers in the social pedagogy tradition to Dewey and then on through Lindeman and others to community organization and informal education. Each tradition of practice provides a way to the others-and it is perhaps most helpful to think of them as always existing in relation to one another.

COLONIALISM AND DEVELOPMENT OF EDUCATION

We explore in more detail the colonial nature of community education (and community development) and some important themes for practitioners in community organization and community participation.

The Indebted South

The vast majority of countries in the South have remained locked into positions in the international economic order which impose constraints on national decision-making of a quite different magnitude from those which affect most countries in the North. In the 1980s these inequalities in power and influence were brought into sharper focus by a global recession and a widespread debt crisis among developing countries. A study covering 107 developing countries, of which forty-one were categorized as 'least developed countries', found that between 1980 and 1990 there were significant falls for most 'developing countries' in gross domestic product, public expenditure and private consumption per head. The latter decreased in 81 percent of the least developed countries and in 64 percent of other developing countries.

The United Nations (2000) reports that more than 2.8 billion people, close to half the world's population, live on less than the equivalent of $2/day. More than 1.2 billion people, or about 20 percent of the world population, live on less than the equivalent of $1/day. South Asia has the largest number of poor people (522 million of whom live on less than the equivalent of $1/day). Sub-Saharan Africa has the highest proportion of people who are poor, with poverty affecting 46.3 percent or close to half of the regions' population (United Nations Briefing).

Debt service (the amount of money paid in interest and other charges on loans) increased to claim a greater share of export earnings in 87 percent of the least developed countries and in 84 percent of the other developing countries during the 1980s. For a number of states in Latin America, and for some in Africa, difficulties in repaying international loans had already started in the 1970s, with the 1973 oil price rises bringing the first major shock to more fragile economies.

Debt Increases and Decreases

Sub-Saharan Africa: For every $1 received in aid grants in 1999, the countries in the region paid back $1.51 in debt service. They owe $231 billion to creditors, that is $406 for every man, woman and child in Africa. Sub-Saharan countries spend over twice as much on debt service as on basic health care. They spend 6.1 % of GNP on education and spent 5.0 % of GNP on debt service. If Africa's debt were cancelled it could almost double its spending on education.

In sub-Saharan Africa, GDP per capita had grown at over 3 percent a year between 1965 and 1973 but had stagnated between 1973 and 1980. Between 1980 and 1988 it fell by about 25 percent. More recent figures (United Nations 2000) reveal that the top fifth (20 percent) of the world's people who live in the highest income countries have access to 86 percent of world gross domestic product (GDP). The bottom fifth, in the poorest countries, has about one percent. In 1998, for every $1 that the developing world received in grants, it spent $13 on debt repayment (United Nations Briefing).

Education in the South

Between 1950 and 1970, the numbers of those enrolled in schools rose dramatically on a global level, and literacy levels rose, though not as rapidly as had been hoped. Rural communities, and especially rural women, still missed out on educational opportunities. None the less, the hope was that access to education would deliver many benefits: for the nation, a skilled work force to contribute to economic development, national unity and social cohesion, and in some countries, popular participation in politics. For the individual, it promised an escape from poverty, greater social prestige and mobility, and the prospect of a good job, preferably in town. In practice these hopes were often unfulfilled, particularly among the least privileged social groups, but they remained powerful aspirations.

In many countries of the South the debt crisis of the 1980s ended an era of unprecedented growth for education. Countries severely affected by the economic crisis, often compounded by military and political conflict, saw the numbers of children enrolling in school fall, and a marked increase in dropout rates among children who do start school. They saw a decline in opportunities for young people and adults to participate in education. More recently, the situation has generally improved in a number of countries-although, most significantly, not in sub-Saharan Africa. The United Nations (2000) reports that worldwide:

The number of children in school has risen significantly, from 599 million in 1990 to 681 million in 1998. (However, there are major regional disparities-school enrolments went down in sub-Saharan Africa-from 60 percent in 1980 to 56 percent in 1996). Since 1990, some 10 million more children go to school every year, which is nearly double the 1980-90 average. East Asia, the Pacific, Latin America and the Caribbean are close to achieving universal primary education.

The number of out-of-school children decreased from 127 million in 1990 to 113 million in 1998. In Latin America and the Caribbean, for example, the number of out-of-school children was halved, from 11.4 million in 1990 to 4.8 million in 1998. (There are significant gender differences, however. Girls represent 60 percent of out of school children. In a similar fashion attendance tends to be lower in rural areas).

The number of children in pre-school education has risen by 5 percent in the past decade. Some 104 million children were enrolled in pre-primary establishments in 1998. The number of literate adults doubled from 1970 to 1998 from 1.5 billion to 3.3 billion. Today, 85 percent of all men and 74 percent of all women can read and write.

Some 87 percent of young adults (15-24 years olds) are literate worldwide. Despite progress in actual numbers, illiteracy rates remain too high: at least 875 million adults remain illiterate, of which 63.8 percent are women – exactly the same proportion as 10 years ago. United Nations Briefing-education

Given the scale of indebtedness and the lack of internal funds for education and social programmes, Southern countries have become particularly dependent on assessments and perspectives made by key international and national agencies in the north. Here the various reviews and policy analyses undertaken or sponsored by the World Bank have been particularly influential.

As King (1991) argued, the agency map of educational priorities became much more clearly profiled, but this often happened without a corresponding local attempt to analyse national educational requirements. The sheer comprehensiveness of the Bank's analysis of national education systems, and indeed the thoroughness of many of the education missions of other agencies, can sometimes suggest that there is nothing more for the local agencies to say. This is an exaggeration, of course, but it points to an imbalance between the weight of the external analysis of a country's educational needs and the country's own diagnosis. On some debates about education, the signals broadcast from the agency perspective are so powerful it is difficult to hear the local voices at all.

The problem is that the views of the Bank are borne of a particular perspective and their views on economies and on the education sector are open to considerable debate. The Bank's research insights and opinions are not ordinary research findings but are one significant part of a series of conditions and negotiations about loans to education in the South. Second, there is frustration at the sheer visibility and influence of the polices. Third, there is much indignation that the major Bank polices in education seem to rest so heavily on the work of foreign, Northern scholars and agency staff. The pervasive influence is relatively recent and borne of the economic crisis facing many Southern countries. One reason for the power of the Bank in this area is because their reports are easily available, cheap and well presented. This in a situation where there is relative little literature which looks across a continent or region.

The Question of Colonialism

Discussion of the dominance of external visions of education inevitably brings us to questions of colonialism and imperialism. *Colonialism* in its most traditional sense involves the gaining of control over particular geographical areas and is usually associated with the with the exploitation of various areas in the world by European powers from about 1500 on. It is often used interchangeably with 'imperialism'. (Imperialism-as the extension of state power and dominion either by direct territorial acquisition or by gaining political and economic control of other areas-of course, has a longer history). Colonialism commonly involves the settlement of the controlling (often western) population in a territory; and the exploitation of local economic resources for metropolitan use. It has taken many forms ranging from models of assimilation e.g. France and Portugal where the occupying power has sought make the colony more formally part of their system and culture; to more segregational approaches such as that adopted by Britain.

Neo-colonialism is usually taken as referring to the economic situation of former colonies post-independence. Here the basic argument runs something like the following. Political de-colonization did little or nothing to alter the economic balance between states and the power of western (and now eastern) capital. International law, institutions such as the World Bank (and banks in general), corporate property rights and the operation of world markets has left control in the hands of the elites in the former metropolitan powers.

Under neo-colonialism, as under direct colonial rule, the relationship between the centre and the periphery... is said to involve the export of capital from the former to the latter; a reliance on Western manufactured goods and services which thwarts indigenous development efforts; further deterioration in the terms of trade for the newly independent countries; and a continuation of the process of cultural Westernization which guarantee the West's market outlets elsewhere in the world the operations of transnational corporations in the Third World are seen as the principal agents of contemporary neo-colonialism since these are seen as exploiting local resources and influencing international trade and national governments to their own advantage.

The linkage of economic change and education; and the interest of the World Bank in such developments would appear to support the thesis that education initiatives can be the agent of colonialism. This is certainly the case for schools, argues Carnoy:... schools are *colonialistic* in that they attempt to impose economic and political relationships in the society *especially* on those children who gain least (or lose most) from those relationships. Schools demand the most passive response from those groups in society who are the most oppressed by the economic and political system, and allow the most active participation and learning from those who are least likely to want change. While this is logical in preserving the status quo, it is also a means of colonializing children to accept unsatisfactory roles. In its colonialistic characterization, schooling helps develop colonizer-colonized relationships between individuals and between groups in society. It formalizes these relationships, giving them a logic that makes reasonable the unreasonable.

This echoes the sorts of arguments put forward by Gandhi and Kenyatta with regard to schooling. It is also in this way that Freire characterizes colonialism as the culture of silence. The colonial element in schooling (or in informal and non-formal education initiatives) being the attempt to silence particular ways of speaking about the world. To this extent one class or group could be said to colonize another. Sometimes the term domestic or internal colonialism is used to describe such exploitative relationships between the 'centre' (the metropolis) and the 'periphery' (the satellite) of particular societies or nation states. There have been problems around such usage-especially as colonialism has tended to be used in relation to the exploitation of majority populations by minority groups. However, as a metaphor it remains a highly suggestive one-especially as it dramatizes the links with imperial powers.

As well as direct economic and political arrangements, colonialism also involves powerful cultural forces, in particular, language. Fanon (1952) has written graphically of the experience of being colonized by language. To speak... means above all to assume a culture, to support the weight of a civilization". An especially pernicious aspect of this is the way in which this entails taking on a restricting and demeaning sense of self. One of Fanon's main targets was the extent to which 'blackness' in French (or English for that matter) was associated with sin and evil.

In an attempt to escape the association of blackness with evil, the black man dons a white mask, or thinks of himself as a universal subject equally participating in a society that advocates an equality supposedly abstracted from personal appearance. Cultural values are internalized, or "epidermalized" into consciousness, creating a fundamental disjuncture between the black man's consciousness and his body. Under these conditions, the black man is necessarily alienated from himself. (Poulos 1996)

With the work of Said (1985), Spivak (1990) and others we now have a powerful set of under standings concerning the discourses of colonialism and the way in which it is imposed upon institutions and draws people into its net. (This body of literature is sometimes, confusingly, described as *post-colonial* theory. The 'post' here can be variously taken as a historical period after colonialism; as being concerned with those writers who opposed, and hence looked beyond, colonialism; and as somehow linked with the discourse of post-modernism or post-modernity. Education systems, in their different forms, are key carriers and promoters of the discourses of colonialism. They are also potentially significant weapons in the countering of such discourses.

INFORMAL AND NON-FORMAL EDUCATION PROGRAMMES

Many of the adult (and non-formal) education programmes associated with 'post-independence' governments looked to combat 'colonial mentalities' and to further a commitment to the emerging nation state. Another overt example of an anti-colonialist programme was Cuba's *Schools in the Countryside* initiative which had as one of its objectives, 'to eliminate economic, political and cultural dependence on the United States'. Certainly, as writers such as Fordham (1993) have shown, non-formal education initiatives became associated with work that was self-consciously 'relevant' to the needs of disadvantaged groups. A number of those involved as educators were concerned with reducing poverty, increasing equity and about greater equality in the distribution of power and resources, but were constrained by political circumstance. Education is not politically neutral. It is an active supporter and faithful reflector of the status quo in society.

If the status quo is predominantly unequal and unjust, and it is increasingly so, education will be increasingly unequal and unjust and there will be no place for non-formal education to improve the conditions of the poor. If, however, society is moving in an equalitarian direction, then non-formal education can and will flourish. Torres (1990:129) in his study of the politics of non-formal education in Latin America similarly argues that many popular education programmes have had a clear emphasis on social mobilization and political development.

Churches, unions and groups within social movements have been involved in such initiatives-and there has, in some at least, been a concern to resist unwarranted state intervention into civic life. However, not all informal and non-formal educational initiatives have been so focused on social and political justice. Indeed, it could be said that many have been rather more concerned with creating conditions for capitalist advancement. Often this has been wrapped up with a desire to stimulate economic growth and development, but it can end up either advantaging investors (frequently from the former colonial powers) or having little impact on growth. The case of literacy programmes is instructive in this respect.

Literacy Programmes

Literacy has become associated in the minds of some policy makers with development. Here I do not need to go into debates about functional literacy and absolute literacy. However, we do need to recognize that during the 1980s and 1990s, political conflicts as much as economic problems have sharpened awareness of the issues in non-formal education. Literacy is seen as a political issue by many governments. High illiteracy figures are often regarded as revealing failures in their education systems. Governments of all political persuasions have, therefore, made at least sporadic efforts to promote literacy among adults, sometimes with substantial funding from international organizations.

They frequently made significant use of non-formal programmes. In the 1970s there was a fairly widespread belief that literacy was a sound economic investment which would lead to increased productivity. In the recessionary climate of the 1980s, the short-term returns on literacy were called into question, and generally speaking the long-term rewards of education received less attention. Furthermore, with high levels of unemployment, there are usually sufficient literate candidates for the shrinking numbers of jobs requiring literacy.

What is more, the outcomes of government-sponsored literacy programmes and campaigns have been extremely mixed. Literacy work has largely taken two forms. Short campaigns involving mass mobilization have been one method. Literacy programmes involving ongoing work over a period years, either nationally or targeting selected communities or regions, have been the other. In societies undergoing major political change, 'revolutionary governments' have been generally more able to mobilize people both to teach and to learn.

In countries where there is little popular identification with the regime, especially under authoritarian governments, efforts at literacy promotion may be regarded with suspicion or even contempt. It is in these circumstances that non-governmental literacy initiatives have become a focus of interest. It could be argued that greater community involvement and organization may generate challenges to the government-demands for democracy, land reform, and greater access to services such as education. However, one of the key outcomes of such literacy programmes, Youn gman (2000) argues, is that they, and the aid that sustains them, work to legitimate capitalist development and social inequality.

Youn gman's study of the National Literacy Programme in Botswana (1978-1987) argued that it was promoted by the state in terms of the modernization of society and the extension of educational opportunity. Aid providers were attracted by its concern with equity.

However..., the programme in fact served to reproduce the class, gender and ethnic inequalities within society. Furthermore, at the political level it constituted a strategy of state legitimation by demonstrating a welfare concern for providing the rural areas with social services. Ideologically, the programme planners in 1979 adopted a narrow and conservative conception of literacy, and consciously reject conscientization or mobilization approaches that might have empowered the learners: 'the political element in the [Freire] method was not seen as being appropriate to Botswana. There was also a negative response to a somewhat militant campaign'. The overall consequences of the National Literacy Programme, and therefore of the aid which sustained it, was to legitimate Botswana's capitalist development and social inequality.

King (1991) in his excellent survey of the area draws out three key further trends around literacy in the South A move from a concern with literacy alone to a concern with the schooling-literacy interrelationship. In some of the literature there has been an assumption that as people become more literate they will encourage their children to go to school. There has been little or no research done of this-and indeed the reverse process may be more relevant. What has been of particular concern to the World Bank and others was that the ability of primary schooling to attract and hold its clienteles was faltering. For as long as primary school enrolments were rising as a percentage of the population then it was possible to believe that over the course of a generation illiteracy would been eliminated.

In Africa there is now evidence of declining participation in schooling (this may be one of the impacts of droughts, economic disruption and wars). A further factor in some places has been the levying of fees as the income from taxes and aid has decreased. There have also been worries around the quality of primary schooling in a number of states-particularly those that are poor. Lacking textbooks, adequate facilities and teachers the idea of a full primary education is rather remote.

The reassertion of achievable measures of school and adult literacy. In looking at the achievements of both primary schooling and literacy work a basic question is posed: what is the level of basic education for all, including adults, that should be set as a minimum in order to retain elementary literacy skills? There has been an increased interest in the setting of standard measures of performance and here the World Bank has been active. This shift along with the others is sometimes referred to as the 'new realism'.

A move from the campaign literature to the analysis of literacy realities. This is evident in the third of our trends. There are still very few detailed and textured studies of work in particular countries or regions. There does seem to have been a shift in the literature however, to more grounded discussions of literacy-and less of the rhetorical, exhortorary material.

Street (2001) has assembled a collection of case studies of more recent literacy initiatives which underline a number of the above concerns and that reveal some of the issues around the discourse of non-formal education and literacy.

The conclusion must inevitably be that while some informal, non-formal and popular education programmes have had a concern to combat colonialism and 'colonial mentalities' others have effectively worked in the opposite direction. The particular power of non-formal education (and things like community schooling) in this respect isn't just the content of the programme, but also the extent to which it draws into state and non-governmental bodies various institutions and practices that were previously separate from them; and perhaps resistant to the state and schooling.

The state often has a significant influence in these organizations-often through the nature of the funding it provides. International aid has a similar impact. Community groups may become part of state education and welfare systems and various activities can become part of school and institutional life. By wrapping up activities in the mantle of community there is a sleight of hand. By drawing more and more people into the professional educator's net there is the danger a growing annexation of various areas of life (a particular them of Illich's work). Under this guise concerns such as skilling and the quietening of populations can take place.

Community Organization

We explore this north American tradition of community practice. We also identify some historical and current themes in community organization theory and practice. It is difficult to point to particular moments in time and say this is where the concerns that we now label community work, community development, community organization or community participation began. We can certainly look to the activities of social reformers and philanthropists in the nineteenth century, for example, the Jewish Board of Guardians or the settlements such as Toynbee Hall in the UK and Hull House in North America. The mutual aid activities of churches and chapels, the YMCA and various working class organizations are also of significance. We could turn to the concern of some colonial administrations to develop local organizations so that some of their work may be undertaken.

In Germany we might examine the tradition of social work practice known as sozial padagogik (social pedagogy). In France we could turn to the activities of animateurs who came into being at the end of the nineteenth century with the establishment of compulsory education and what became known as the popular education movement. Their task was and is, basically, to promote access to education and cultural/leisure facilities. We could go on listing elements like this. However, we can pinpoint with some accuracy when the actual terms came into use. Central to this effort is the growing attention to the idea of 'community' in the early decades of the twentieth century in North America.

Lindeman on Community

The aim of community life is to bring about amicable relations between men and groups of men (1921: 1)

An ideal community should furnish to its human constituents:

1. Order, or security of life and property through the medium of an efficient government.
2. Economic well-being, or security of income through an efficient system of productive industry.
3. Physical well-being, or health and sanitation through public health agencies.
4. Constructive use of leisure time, or recreation though public health agencies.
5. Ethical standards, or a system of morality supported by the organized community.
6. Intellectual diffusion, or education through free and public institutions within the reach of all.
7. Free avenues of expression, or means by which all the elements of the community might freely express themselves; free newspapers and public forums.
8. Democratic forms of organization, or community-wide organization through which the entire community might express its thought and see that its will is done.
9. Spiritual motivation, or religious associations which might diffuse throughout all forms of community organization the religious or spiritual motive.

In many respects, Lindeman's list parallels contemporary concerns. The disposition to self determination and democracy was common to a number of North American thinkers (mostly associated in one way or another with John Dewey). Along with Lindeman two other figures cast a significant shadow over our practice today: Mary Parker Follett and Grace Coyle.

THE IMPORTANCE OF THE GROUP

Follett, who was later to work with Lindeman, emphasized

creative social experience (1918; 1924). She believed that such experience is the basis of state structure and that moves had to be made to strengthen group life. In particular she argued for the provision of citizen training through free group association, for adult and worker's education and for neighbourhood education. 30). She drew on work undertaken in North American settlements and on the development of community centres in some schools in Boston (the latter looking remarkably like what we have come to know as community schools). Her ideas were enthusiastically taken up in other countries like the UK. Early pioneers of the community association and centre movement were deeply influenced by her work.

Coyle was also interested in the methods of democratic leadership in small groups and in group relations. She was a settlement worker and then joined the staff of the Industrial Women's Department of the YWCA. She began the first sustained programme for group workers in 1923 (Reid 1981) and later went on to draw together a number of formulations concerning group process in an influential book *Social Process in Organized Groups* (Coyle 1930). There followed a series of articles and debates which sought to examine group work as a method and its place within social work in North America.

Again what became known as social group work (and Coyle's work in particular) was taken up by key figures in the United Kingdom-especially in youth work. Here an interesting contrast appears-and one that remains today and causes some confusion. In the UK youth work became associated with education departments in the state system whereas elsewhere in Europe and North America it tends to be seen as an aspect of social work. In a similar way while UK social work was, and is, narrowly defined and very casework dominated, in the 1920s and 1930s USA social work became characterized by three strands: casework, group work and community organization.

Community Organization

Lindeman's book was the first to appear on what became known in North America as community organization. He later was to write what has become one of the classic texts of adult education but his immediate background was as an organizer of boys' and girls' clubs in Michigan (the forerunner of what are now known in the USA as 4-H clubs); and then a lecturer at the YMCA College in Chicago.

His involvement in the YMCA movement and his interest in rural community life show through strongly in his book. Lindeman stressed his belief that the his goals for community could never be completely met and there was always need for compromise. He defined community organization as: those phases of social organization which constitute a conscious effort on the part of a community to control its affairs democratically, and to secure the highest services from its specialists, organizations, agencies, and the institutions by means of recognized interrelations.

Here we can see the sort of sequence that appears with some regularity in books about community organization and community work. What also emerges is a broad notion of community organization as furnishing a working relationship between the democratic process and the specialist: 'the democratic process expresses itself or is personified in the total community membership. The Specialist expresses himself, or is personified in the division of labour which produces highly skilled persons and agencies, organizations and institutions, which are equipped to do one thing effectively'. Here too, a sound warning about impatience and the slowness and stuttering progress that such work can involve.

With the second half of the 1940s came a number of classic texts on community organizing. A further generation of texts-perhaps the best of which was Ross (1955) further popularized practice. Ross saw community organization as: a process by which a community identifies its needs or objectives, orders (or ranks) these needs or objectives, develops the confidence and the will to work at these needs or objectives, finds the resources (internal and/or external) to deal with these needs or objectives, takes action in respect to them, and in so doing extends and develops co-operative and collabourative attitudes and practices in the community.

He appears to have dual aims:

- the achievement of certain community identified goals; and
- the development of co-operative and collabourative attitudes and practices.

The tension between these goals can be significant and, the definition is dependent on having some agreement as to what is meant by community.

Ross, like Lindeman, was writing with a background of significant involvement in the YMCA movement (although this time in Canada). However, by the time he was writing 'specialist' workers had, he argued, developed a 'distinctive pattern of work which can be utilized in a wide variety of settings to deal with any one of a number of problems'.

ROTHMAN ON COMMUNITY ORGANIZING

Locality development: typifies the methods of work with community groups used by settlement houses and in 'colonial' community development work. A major focus is on the process of community building. Working with a broad, representative cross section of the community, workers attempt to achieve change objectives by enabling the community to establish consensus via the identification of common interests. Leadership development and the education of the participants are important elements in the process. In this approach great store is set by the values of both participation and leadership.

Social action: is employed by groups and organizations which seek to alter institutional policies or to make changes in the distribution of power. Civil rights groups and social movements are examples. Their methods may be, often are, abrasive, and participation is the value most clearly articulated by those who use this approach. Both leadership and expertise may be challenged as the symbolic 'enemies of the people'.

Social planning: is the method of community organization traditional to health and welfare councils although its scope and arena were enlarged in the 1960s to encompass city planners, urban renewal authorities and the large public bureaucracies. Effort is focussed primarily on task goals and issues of resource allocation. Whereas the initial emphasis of this approach was on the co-ordination of social services, its attention has expanded to include programme development and planning in all major social welfare institutions. Heavy reliance is placed on rational problem solving and the use of technical methods such as research and systems analysis. Expertise is the cherished value in this approach, although leadership is accorded importance as well.

These elements are drawn in a fairly extreme way. There is considerable overlap between the elements-but the focus on difference is useful in that it points attention to dimensions such as process, the role of the plan, and the tension between the state and dominant groups and those who believe themselves to be excluded.

Community Participation

In the late 1960s there was a series of debates around 'participation'. While 'participation' may be a vague term its advocates often rely on two key arguments about its value. It: makes for justice in decision-making-people have some say in, and influence on, collective decisions has an educative value. Through participation people learn (Beetham 1992). These interests became formalized in a number of United Nations reports including *Popular Participation in Development* (1971) and *Popular Participation in Decision Making for Development* (1975).

According to Midgley et al (1986) the notion of popular participation and that of community participation are interlinked. The former is concerned with broad issues of social development and the creation of opportunities for the involvement of people in the political, economic and social life of a nation, 'the latter connotes the direct involvement of ordinary people in local affairs'. One United Nations document (1981) defined community participation as:

The creation of opportunities to enable all members of a community to actively contribute to and influence the development process and to share equitably in the fruits of development. This is a very general definition and raises as many questions as it answers.

As with other traditions of community intervention the theoretical base for the work is relatively patchy. There is material around the context and the specific problems within different societies; and there is a long standing tradition of writing around political theory. However, much of what is written around process remains at the level of 'practice wisdom' and is not worked into a wider ranging framework.

In recent years there have been some useful developments in thinking around the notion of community participation. This has both involved a critique of 'participatory techniques' when used in the service of unjust and often illegitimate interests and some more optimistic explorations of participatory approaches that link into more transformational political forms. In many respects, as various contributors to Cooke and Kothari (2001) underline, it is still necessary to approach state-sponsored community participation initiatives with some care.

Claims to participation can often be little more than the wish to consult within a narrow policy framework. There can be a sharp contrast with the level of involvement expected within more associational forms of democracy or even those approaches concerned with the cultivation of social capital. There is certainly a gap between such approaches and what can be seen in some of the more rigorous developments in participatory governance (Hickey and Mohan 2004).

3

Community Based Social Work

This is another training document in the series of community mobilizing methods for results other than a physical construction such as a communal water supply, clinic or school. The product or output is a programme of services for vulnerable members of the community, many of whom can help themselves if only they are provided with a relatively small amount of help and encouragement.

What is Social Work?

The profession of Social Work is an odd mixture of many things. It is usually practised by government civil servants in the west (Europe and North America) while many international NGOs have social workers on their staff. The clientele of social work are often called the vulnerable, i.e people whose special conditions or circumstances put them in positions of weakness or vulnerability in comparison with the mainstream of a society. Generally they include members of society who need some help. Typically, these include those with physical or mental disabilities, persons who are not able to work for a living or not able to care for themselves. In special cases, these may include battered women (those who have been physically or emotionally assaulted – e.g by their spouses –and can not escape dangerous situations on their own), frail elderly persons, children without parents to support them, or who are being mistreated, The tasks of a social worker mainly include administration and counselling, along with a little bit of medical (usually psychological) intervention and advocacy.

The social worker provides her or his clients with little bits of wisdom, advice, information, counselling, as needed. Every case is different. The government (or NGO) social worker in a western country (Europe and North America) provides services that are usually provided by elders and family members in other countries. Social work services are too expensive for governments in the least developed countries. The word "social" is a bit misleading because, in the west, where it is mainly practised, the social worker does not work with a whole society, or even with a community or a group in a social context. The social worker usually handles "cases," and a case is usually about an individual or lately increasingly, a family. This is even more ironical because where social work is taught, usually in a university in a department or a school of social administration or social work, often (where they are small) they are attached to sociology departments.

Such schools or departments, in turn, are then usually also where community development (like much of the material on this web site) is also taught. Community development, in contrast, is an activity aimed at social institutions, such as communities or groups, rather than at individuals. One of the many motivating facts pushing the development of this web site is that the empowerment of communities is important and highly needed in low income countries. Limiting the training of community workers to those who are studying in universities, limits the available number of potentially capable community workers; this should be taught to middle school level students (after they have been working out in the real world and have some life experience).

This document will not teach you how to become a social worker (any more than the water module will teach you how to become a civil engineer), but will help you in initiating and developing a community based social work (CBSW) programme. The training on this web site is aimed at community workers who do not have to be educated to university level.

Where is CBSW Appropriate?

Rich countries can usually provide social work services (on

an individual or family basis, not community based), and poor countries rely on the advice, experience and knowledge of elders and family members. So where would it be appropriate to place a community based social work programme? Community based social work services are needed where they can not be provided by elders and families, but where there is not enough finance available to provide it on an individual basis. The situation which comes to mind most readily is where there are large displaced or refugee populations, in camps, in poor countries. Further to that, after the emergency is over, those same refugees may return home. Their lives will have been interrupted, losing many family members, including elders and family members, thus the need for social work services remains. So long as there is enough funding available for a professional social worker to supervise the community based work, keeping it up to required standards, the community itself can supply the energy, time and interest in making it work.

Apart from refugee situations, wherever there is a large disaster that results in the removal of elders and family members, and/or which disrupts the normal and traditional social organization, are included among situations where it would be appropriate to set up a community based social work programme. Post disaster situations would be included in these.

Where there are large refugee populations, the basic services, food, water, shelter, elementary medical, are usually provided, often by UN agencies and international NGOs. Finance is not unlimited, however, so there may only be a token attempt at providing social work services, if any at all. This is a good situation in which to consider organizing a community based social work programme.

Community Perceptions

When a child is a witness to atrocities that destroy her world, she is affected. To watch your family members and/or neighbours being shot or bombed produces immense trauma if you are a child. In many cases, the experience results in the child withdrawing into herself, refusing to talk, and/or refusing to respond to daily interactions. The child who is traumatized by the same events which lead to refugee or displaced communities, may display behaviour that is often misinterpreted by her remaining family or care givers. Sometimes she is deemed as mentally retarded, and beyond recovery. Sometimes she is seen as affected by evil spirits. Sometimes her condition is seen as a punishment for previous misdeeds by her family members. In all these cases, there is much shame and secrecy associated with her behaviour. All too often her care givers do not understand that she is reacting to the terrible events of the disaster or civil war, and they do not know that the condition can be reversed by a few simple interventions.

Many times such children are hidden (even tied up) in darkened rooms away from public view. They can not dress or clean themselves, and often are found in their own filth and in poor health, hungry, dirty, sick, weak and helpless. Public announcements do not get the message across. Hands on intervention is needed to assess each child.

If they are traumatized by atrocious events, and not retarded or otherwise disabled by other factors, they can show remarkable changes, learning to dress themselves, clean themselves and feed themselves. This requires patience, love and care, extended over several weeks and months. A stimulus or two in the form of a doll, and perhaps later a ball, are effective and useful tools for the job. Here is a situation, repeated hundreds of thousand times around the world, where a community based social work programme is appropriate. This is a typical or classic situation for CBSW.

A single, university educated, professional social worker can appraise the situation, prescribe appropriate interventions, and monitor. Community mobilizers can work with the community members to identify hidden and suffering children, recruit community level social workers, arrange for their training and supervision, organize CBOs to manage and operate the CBSW programme at community level, and ensure an effective flow of information. Local residents, on a volunteer basis or with some incentives, can provide the care and stimulation to the children in need, and keep the mobilizers informed about changing conditions and further needed training.

This is only one of many kinds of situations involving vulnerable refugees or displaced persons in communities disrupted by (but surviving) disasters caused by natural or human made events.

The PHC Principles

The "Primary Health Care" (PHC) policy promoted by WHO (UN World Health Organization), has several basic principles, perhaps the best known one being that prevention is better than cure. Another, that is particularly applicable here to community based social work, is the idea that resources should not be spent on expensive cures for a few people.

Underlying this is a public health policy in support of the greatest good for the greatest number. With a limited budget available, that means to concentrate on a few common diseases, to provide elementary training to persons educated at low levels, and reaching the most rural and remote patients. This gave rise to the popular (but slightly inaccurate) concept of "The Barefoot Doctor." If the PHC policy is transferred to the need for social services, then the idea is to give elementary training to persons without university level education, concentrating on the most common and easily treated conditions, and relying on a referral system for more complicated diseases or conditions.

The goal in community based social work, then, is to organize a cadre of community members who can be given low level training (i.e not requiring university education) to treat a limited number of social conditions of vulnerable community members. Their interventions will not be as flexible or a sophisticated as those of social workers with university level education and extensive social work training, but they will be able to reach a wider proportion of the population than if only highly skilled and relatively costly professionals are employed.

"The greater good for the greater number."

Structure

Where you have a population of refugees or others who have had severe disruptions in their community lives, where they are able to access support for their immediate needs (food, shelter, water, housing) but no social welfare. Where you may have a professional social worker or two for a population too large for them to reach everybody. Where you have a situation conducive to organizing voluntary community groups.

There you have the basis for CBSW. The professional social workers need to make a needs analysis to determine the limited number of conditions that can be addressed by community workers with low level training. They then need to train and to supervise the training of a cadre of community workers who have access to the client community or communities. Both the needs assessments and the training would not be once-off, but ongoing. They and the community workers (mobilizers) need to identify, recruit, and train community members, as community leaders of the programme, as practitioners of social work interventions in their communities, and as monitors of the changing situations in their respective communities.

Members of the community groups conduct the social work interventions. They need to be supported with training and guidance by the mobilizers and (more indirectly by) the professional social workers. What results in effect is like a social work pyramid, with the professional social worker(s) at the apex, possible social work trainers (temporary or long term) supervised by the social workers, mobilizers, community leaders and managers of the community groups (CBOs) and community and CBO members who conduct most of the interventions.

Training and Support

In general, community mobilizers should never be trained once-and-for-all, but need regular support, encouragement, and a forum in which to ask questions that arise in the field. In CBSW this is even more a requirement. First, mobilizers without formal training (the main audience for this web site) need continued support and professional inputs.

Second, the tragedies witnessed in CBSW require field workers to meet with their colleagues to share experiences and to be re-energised and re-infused with enthusiasm and positive attitudes. A CBSW programme as described above needs a routine and predictable forum for getting mobilizers together to share experiences, to ask questions arising from the field, and to obtain inputs from more highly trained and educated social workers. A training unit could be an answer to this need. How it is to be set up depends upon available finances and circumstances.

An initial training programme for the mobilizers could use the first six training modules from this web site. They can be printed and handed out in the training programme. They can be easily adapted to developing a CBSW programme. The training for social work, in contrast, needs to be defined and generated by the professional social workers, after they make their initial appraisal of the situations, and will be modified as new information comes in.

COMMUNITY PRACTICE

Community Practice is a branch of social work in the United States that focuses on larger social systems and social change, and is tied to the historical roots of United States social work. The field of community practice social work encompasses community organizing, social planning, human service management, community development, policy analysis, policy advocacy, evaluation, mediation, electronic advocacy and other larger systems interventions. In the field of social work, community practice is often contrasted with direct practice social work, in which social workers work directly with individuals solving micro-level problems. Community Practice has been referred to in the past as Macro Practice, though Community Practice is now the standard term in the United States.

Community Practice has considerable overlap with many other applied social sciences, such as urban planning, economic development, public affairs, rural sociology and nonprofit management. Community Practice social workers typically have a Masters in Social Work (MSW). There are several MSW programs in the United States that offer Community Practice Concentrations, while many other MSW programs offer specializations in one or several types of community practice, such as social services administration or policy analysis. The professional group of community practitioners is the Association for Community Organization and Social Administration (ACOSA), which publishes the leading journal in the field, The Journal of Community Practice.

TRAINING GROUND FOR SOCIAL WORK STUDENTS

Providing services to communities while providing education and training for social work practice in communities is at the core of this paper. These activities are discussed and reviewed in the context of social work in communities. Social work field placements (internships) in communities can provide positive learning experiences for students and excellent services to communities. The Winslow Project, a two-year community-focused placement for two group of first year master of social work (M.S.W.) Students is described and the results of this project are discussed. In order to fulfill a commitment to the community concept, students need a well-defined concept of group and community practice in order to provide the range and quality of services that are required for social work practice in the 21st's century global community paradigm. Providing social work intervention practices in the community is paramount to the further development of social work as a profession. It will also provide support and encouragement for communities to provide these supportive services within the community context. Social work history is rich with the type of models necessary for this to occur.

In this chapter, a study related to social work field instruction and community practice is discussed. The field placement experience is an important cornerstone of the graduate social work experience. Through these internships, students are able to relate their classroom education to practical applications. Traditionally most schools of social work utilize agency based individual placements as the primary field training for their students.

Community social work has the potential for being neglected in these types of restrictive placements, as well as in the classroom, and even in the generalized arena or domain of practice methodology. To fulfill a commitment to the community concept, social work students need a well-defined concept of group and community practice in order to provide the range and quality of services that are required for social work practice in the 21st's century global community paradigm.

Field Training: An Overview

The type and quality of field experience in social work and other disciplines is an important area of study, relative to skill competencies, and the impacts on participants (CSWE, 1994). This is not to say that it should not be challenging and demanding, rather the first year generalist field instructional experience should provide a healthy start and broad community spectrum to a social work career. The more specialized second year field instructional experience should build on and enhance the generalist skills and academic knowledge gained in course work and the first year field practicum. Kissman and Tran (1990) highlighted the importance of quality field training, where they postulated that the importance of field placements in social work education could hardly be overemphasized.

Since social work is an "applied discipline, much emphasis is placed on socializing students into the profession by providing hands-on experience in the field". Tolson and Kopp (1988) indicated that many traditional placements are in an agency setting with some combination of experiential and academic components (the articulated model), where "the level of learning has not been evaluated consistently... the most important influence on social work practice is the practicum". Rodgers and Williams (1977) suggested that because a social work student may spend half of their educational experience in a practice setting, field instruction should be considered a most valuable aspect of the training process. It is therefore important to include multiple options for field experience along with coursework offerings that enhance the particular type of placement. This concept applies well to the next area of discussion, which will focus on field placements and community practice.

FIELD INSTRUCTION AND COMMUNITY PRACTICE

The importance of teaching group as well as community practice skills and theory in social work and related disciplines cannot be stated strongly enough. Brzuzy and Segal (1996) suggested that "teaching students to understand, appreciate, and use research based in the community" is desperately needed in social work education. Many schools of social work have no community development courses available and group courses are limited, many times to one advanced course in group theory. The tasks that most social workers perform in their daily jobs are entrenched in community ideology. In order to perform these tasks adequately some expertise in community practice is necessary. For example, Birnbam and Auerbach (1994) found "graduate social work education has practically eliminated group work as a specialized area of study, and students in foundation courses learn little about group work theory and have limited or no group field work experience in which to develop practice skills". According to Kurland and Salmon, (1989), "requirements for concentrations offer a unique opportunity to add depth and sophistication to the teaching of group work and to better prepare students for the demands of contemporary professional practice, which requires a great amount of substantive expertise".

This expertise can be applied to micro, mezzo, and macro practice in the larger community as well as the agency setting. The current paradigms evolving from CSWE seem to be changing direction toward more generalist foci in social work education, which is supportive of the broader scope that group and community practices offer. Elliott (1993) indicated that social work interventions are predominantly delivered through a residual service delivery model. Elliot indicated that in social work today, a large degree of privatization and the logical positivist research model is prevalent alongside a medical model of intervention, both of which address individual pathology. "This combination does not fully represent the social work tradition that along with individual change has always aimed to also encompass social action, social change, and community development".

Training students in the theory and methodology of community practice through placements in the community and focused directly on the community is one way of accomplishing this goal, which is also a timely focus for social work researchers. Coulton (1995) stated that "compared to our knowledge of individuals and families, research attention to the functioning of communities has been scant". Because social work has a long-standing relationship with varied community based practices, sociological theories, and principles of group dynamics as they apply to individual functioning in the context of community, the opportunities for research through studying social work students in community placements are vast. There is little doubt that with the current globalized economic conditions and changing roles for social workers, alternative training options need to be considered; where changes from for profit, nonprofit, and governmental agencies are resulting in social crises at all levels of service provision. Providing services in the community, in the home, etc. may become more the norm than the exception.

The nonprofit and government sectors, in which most social workers practice, will face great challenges in dealing with local social problems and needs. Social work practitioners, managers, students, and faculty must be prepared to recognize and seize the opportunities in these crises and to use knowledge, research, and practice skills to develop and strengthen community-based practice and service models. They will also need to build policy and research agendas that are grounded in community and family development.

The way to achieve this is through field training experiences, grounded in community practices, coordinated by well-established community curricula for the classroom experience, and includes greater balance between prevention, development, and remediation. Universities need to consider being "partners in promoting" community involvement and interdisciplinary social work.

True generalist practitioners need to possess a holistic approach that emphasizes the environment as well as the person. There is a need for an expanded community-oriented focus in social work education and field instruction. To achieve connections between social work education, the practice community, and the larger cultural community students could be placed in a neighborhood network rather than in a single agency, where they can experience the "context" of services as well as perform a variety of social work roles. Such placements might offer enough variety to be used for more than one year. This practice in "neighborhoods and communities" needs to be based on solid social work perspectives with focus on "changing the culture of what is seen as valued, possible, and appropriate in these communities, which in turn will modify the opportunity systems for children and families".

COMMUNITY BASED FIELD PLACEMENTS

Models and techniques for community practice have been with us for some time and social work history is rich with community oriented practices, and providing alternative field placement opportunities along with the more traditional individual agency-based field placements, is a responsible way to reflect this domain of practice. Community development programs are on the cutting edge of social work practice, and it is encouraging to see innovative schools of social work developing field-training experiences that include alternative models. The community oriented model that is the focus of the following study exposes students to a wide array of challenges that result in them being better prepared as social work practitioners, policy makers, administrators, educators and researches, within the spectrum of community practice. This paper is the result of this two-year study in which the writer completed dissertation research requirements. This involved the writer in an intermittent-active role as will be discussed later.

The Winslow Project

The project took place in the small Northern Arizona desert community of Winslow, with a 12,325 population, located on historic U. S. Route 66. This multi-phase project provided a cross-cultural and interstate generalist community development practicum, for Ohio State University social work master's students. It was conducted on-site and was funded through a partnership between business constituencies with interests in Winslow, civic and community organizations on-site, private donors, and the students involved in the project. The student interns were able to pursue increasing levels of involvement in overlapping spheres of intervention. These spheres include:

- Creation and maintenance of a civic association (La Familia), community micro-enterprise confederation in the underdeveloped, principally Hispanic neighborhoods of Coopertown and Southside, which included community-based, needs assessment longitudinal research.
- Development and provision of ongoing violence prevention and citizenship enhancement programs for elementary and high school students.
- Coordination and improvement of citywide social service, church, civic, and business collaborative networking to create a national model for community-building for the 21st century, and
- Traditional placements in various social service agencies in and around Winslow, with emphasis on networking, and collaborative interrelated wrap-around service provision.

The Center for Peace Studies and Community Development in Columbus, Ohio administered this project in conjunction with its role as a Field Internship Agency for Ohio State's College of Social Work and relative to its various community development activities.

The executive director for The Center for Peace Studies and Community Development, William D. Eldridge, Ph.D., was the project director and is a full time faculty member in the College of social work. Conjoint on site weekly classes in community development were required of all student participants as they are a requirement for all field placements. Residence and activity offices were located at Madre de Dios Catholic Church in Coopertown, a sub community in Winslow. All operations for the Winslow project began at the Madre de

Dios church and many of the community functions took place there as well.

The field placement involved students completing their first year (MSW I) generalist field experience as required by The Ohio State University Masters of Social Work program. This first year fieldwork design was a block placement, conducted between June and August of the summer following the students' first year of academic course work. The Winslow project integrated student cohort team building, Hispanic American and Native American cultural learning, personal experience, and comprehensive community services into a consolidated eight-week period. The students assumed their professional roles approximately six days per week, ten hours per day, through the eight-week project. This constitutes a total community service commitment of approximately 480 contact service hours. The students actually exceeded the typical non-block first year placement of 320 hours. The extra hours was considered volunteer time, which the students had contractually agreed to when, accepting the field placement.

Sample

Twenty-one students took part in the Winslow Project. Of the seven students who participated during the summer of 1997, there were six females and one male. The mean age for the females was 27.8 years, while the male students' age was 57 years. All of the students had social work employment history and three were volunteers who had already completed their field placements before this project.

Among the 14 students participating during the second summer of 1998, there were 12 females and 2 males. The mean age for the females was 27.4 with the youngest being 20 years and the oldest 34. The mean age for the males was 23.5 aged 23 and 24 respectively. One of the female students was an upper level social work undergraduate and not in an official field placement. The students that participated in this experience assumed a good deal of the cost including their airfare and some food costs. The Winslow experience involved these students living together as a group in dormitory housing.

Project Activities

The students were involved in a variety of different, but related, service delivery functions. Personal learning consultations, team evaluation, and cohort feedback procedures were parts of their generalized first year learning experience. The students also met together for training throughout the nine months before their experience in Winslow; which focused on preparing them to work and relate effectively and compassionately within the cultures and environment they discovered in Arizona. During these training sessions, they also worked on group cohesiveness, which would prove beneficial to them later.

While in Winslow, they were engaged in learning about community-based practice while actually residing together as a small group microcosm (a student community), while at the same time spending eight weeks working with community leaders, adults, families, and children in and around Winslow. The needs of the community and the agency involvement added to the experiential foundation of the Winslow project.

The project also involved specific task objectives as follows:

- Develop and support a neighborhood residents (civic) association.
- Develop a leadership coalition in the Hispanic neighborhoods of Coopertown and Southside.
- Work with children on literacy and anti-violence programs.
- Assist in various social service activities on the Hopi and Navajo Reservations.
- Assist adults and teenagers with career planning activities.
- Conduct individual and family counseling sessions.
- Facilitate small group meetings related to community projects.
- Network and conduct community cooperation planning functions among human service organizations.

- Create plans and needs assessments for micro-enterprise development, and provide physical labor to help build parks, repair homes, etc.

Each student worked and learned as a member of smaller teams with other students, community members, and professionals; and had an opportunity to be involved in a range of differing activities from which their experiences and newly acquired skills and knowledge were shared with other teams and within the whole student community.

As described, the students all resided, ate, slept, and worked together. They slept in bunk beds with three to four persons per bedroom. In this context, one of the most significant aspects of this internship was the opportunity for them to become a community in the process of learning and caring for each other, while also engaging the exterior community neighborhoods. The project provided the opportunity for these two communities to develop simultaneously.

Winslow provided a rich and extraordinary opportunity to learn about and work with members of the Southwestern Hispanic community.

The social work students were able to work extensively with the Hopi and Navajo Native American Tribes living in Winslow, and on adjacent reservations just north of the city. The students attended cultural orientation lectures and group training seminars. The focus of these workshops was to formally learn about Hispanic, Native American, and Southwestern cultures.

Their experiences provided many learning opportunities. Some of the learning challenges included solving conflicts within their own group and with one another, living in a new environment, being away from family and friendship supports in Ohio, and "becoming a group."

These contexts of the experience created a symbiotic developmental process as the students, the community members and, the two communities conjoined and separated many times during the processes of community development.

MAJOR RESEARCH QUESTIONS

The writer and the project director developed research questions focused on the experiences and knowledge gained by internship participants, as follows

- Are there changes in feelings/attitudes related to community practice for the students that chose to take part in this field placement experience?
- Is there any perceived personal or professional growth for these students through this experience?
- What is the Program Director's evaluation of the student's progress and the project?

The study included a longitudinal/multi-baseline, ABA (pre-test-interim-posttest) research design, focusing on the students and their perceived and observed experiential growth and learning processes, as well as the perceptions of the program director related to these dynamics. These variables were extracted and analyzed through narrative analysis of written self-report and observation during the experience.

DATA COLLECTION

Data collection included:

1. an initial questionnaire session one month prior to each group of students leaving for Winslow,
2. an on-site mid-term questionnaire and observation session at week five in Winslow and,
3. a follow-up questionnaire session one month following each group's return from Winslow.

The same interviewer administered the questionnaire at the three data collection sessions by the. The mid-term and follow-up sessions included the original interview questions slightly altered to elicit information about how students had applied their learning to their present situations. The questions contained a significant focus on community, community-based practice, and identity as social workers, social work field experience, and the student's feelings about these topics. The researcher acquired the observation data through the two-on-site visits and the follow-up interview with the project director. The data is narrative in nature and therefore, evaluated through this analysis method. The outcome variables relate to the concept that students can benefit from an experience like the Winslow Project.

Presentation of the Questionnaire Data

The questionnaire contained multi-layered items focusing on community, community-based practice, field experience, and the students' feelings about the experience. The questionnaire also assessed student's goals of the project and relationship dynamics within the student groups, beginning with questions regarding the student's expectations of the experience, to elicit their projections of what the Winslow experience could provide related to their field instruction, personal, and professional growth. The follow-up questionnaire included questions that asked if the experience had met expectations.

As evidenced by the data, all 21 students believed that they were meeting their expectations at mid-point and 19 reported that they had met or exceeded their expectations at follow-up. Among the expectations reported as met by the students, are the following. Twelve students reported better communication skills, ten improved assertiveness skills, twenty increased cultural awareness, twenty-one achieved better relationship skills, nineteen gained in social work practice skills, twenty-one added community development experience, fifteen increased their sense of self-awareness, seventeen reported gains in spiritual growth, fifteen felt they grew emotionally, and ten described better general well being.

An interesting phenomenon observed during this experience was that the students began to see their group as a community early on, with 19 out of the 21 students describing their group as a community with all of the characteristics and roles that would be expected. It was during this process that the concept of the student group as a community began to develop and expand. The cohesiveness of the group was also significant in this data set in that, all of the students reported that they felt bonded with their fellow group members at mid-point. The purpose of question one was to elicit this information. The purpose of question 2 was to elicit each student's concept of community and then to apply that concept to the student group, to measure growth relative to knowledge of community. The initial definitions related to what constitutes a community were consistent as applied to groups of people in similar situations. All 21 students agreed that community involves some form of mutual focus and working together. Twenty reported their student groups were able to meet this criterion and thus develop as communities while working in the larger community of Winslow.

The students described their groups as typical communities, with the relationships and conflicts consistent with the dynamics of community. There was a definite change in the way the students viewed community throughout the experience as evidenced by 19 students remaining consistent with their responses throughout the process. These students first described community as groups of people who all have one characteristic in common, live in a shared area, have shared interests, etc. At mid-point 16 students expanded the definition to groups of people whom live near one another and interconnect in their development and prosperity. Finally, at follow-up, 18 students described community as independent personalities that work together for a common cause, have shared strengths and goals, are mutually committed to the whole, etc. When asked to apply these concepts to the groups, the students again showed their cohesion and community growth. The members of the cohorts spoke fondly of one another and related that the group members became very close, although there was some resentment stated by six students related to a few members who did not perform as expected by the majority, though there was much resistance by these students to label them. When asked to talk about the problems in the group, these six students responses included the following

- The group works well together overall.
- It was nice to have such a group of people with such diverse personalities and styles.
- The group got along better than expected.

For the most part, we worked well together although at time there was a bit of strain due to so many independent personalities. It is interesting that one can view the process for these students in terms of their changing perspective of community. The idea of bonding with others in a way that connects the larger whole or that community has a dynamic of family or people who are connected suggests the cohesiveness of the students as groups.

Question 3 follows the same concepts as question number two. The difference here is that the students were to define community development related to social work practice. The hypothesis here is that the Winslow experience will enhance the definition of social work practice and community development for these students. The purpose of question one was to elicit this information. The simple definition at the beginning changed at mid-point and follow-up. The cohorts started with a standard textbook definition of social work in the community, moved to an appreciation of community building as a long-term process, and finally to working at community building from within the community. The students redefined their concept of social work in the community throughout the experience, constituting a transition from individual change agent to active participant in a larger collaborative, contextual, and interdependent process.

The students appear to have realized the complexity of communities. Their willingness to allow for and respect differences increased through trial and error during this experience. Their realization was that social workers do not bring people together for community practice as much as they "practice life" with and among people through active problem solving and planning. The data indicates that the students conceptualize community building as not something that you do to a community but rather, it is an experiential process that involves people and their collective evolvement.

Each student shared their feelings about personal relationships and the importance of these in their lives. The focus was on family and friendships on the initial questionnaire, and on the group members and community on the mid-term and follow-up questionnaires. The results showed growth in relation to group cohesiveness over the experience and, the level of commitment between group members to one another and to the group as a whole.

It was interesting to see the struggle that these students took part in as they attempted to redefine their concept of community. The idea of their group as a community or family was foreign to their prior beliefs about what community was. By the end of this experience, the students reported achievement and growth as the result of the relationships formed and, that constant contact with others was an essential element to the group development. The concept of family, advocacy, social action and interdependency all became themes for these students, and concepts of location, common goals, group as a community, and the ability to be tolerant of others were reported as positive outcomes of this experience.

In the next data set, the object was to elicit students' feelings and thoughts about how they performed in their field placement and in their student community. It sought to get the students to self-assess their roles in these teams, as well as, the larger community of Winslow. One student described the role of caretaker in the beginning, which seemed to continue as time progressed. Another described roles in terms of task orientation, which remained consistent throughout the experience, which is an outcome that might be expected. Another group of students were able to define their task roles well initially, but by the end of the process, they described a combination of task and group roles. From family roles to group roles was the transition for these students. Some stated the roles were not clear and indicated that they would have preferred more structure, while others thrived on the challenges of the unknown. There were several self-proclaimed leaders in the groups and though these are characteristics most often described by the other students as problematic, they can be very positive in the practice of community development. The main result presented as a feeling of achievement and, even though the students may have seen their roles as static and not changing much, they related that the roles they assumed were more beneficial due to the experience. The goal of self-assessment continued as students began to look inward for the answers and discover what it was about them that enhanced this experience. The data showed evidence of a difference in thinking related to the concept of responsibility as applied to self, other individuals, and communities. The process of learning as evidenced by self-report showed an eagerness to learn and grow as a student community.

They recognized and confronted some of their own behaviors and applied the needed changes. The nature of the Winslow experience allowed for this self-evaluation to take place through the challenges faced outside the comfort zone of home, time spent in contemplation in the desert, and in personal meetings with Dr. Eldridge. The reported values remained consistent throughout the experience and the student's were able to apply these to the experience without much conflict. There was reported insight into recognizing their limitations and utilizing the strengths of others as a way of maintaining balance. Other characteristics were the ability to be flexible and remain strength based, openness, seeing humour and caring about others, putting strengths into action, utilizing self as a tool, and acceptance of the opinion of others.

When stated their goals and evaluated them, the data indicated patterned wishes to be more active and social, and less withdrawn, along with goals related to an inner sense of peace and self-nurturing. The opportunity to challenge self in such a way as to take some new risks, learning to live with and get along with the group, and interacting with people from Hispanic and Native American cultures were goals that were achieved. Some students had seen the initial goals as being different somehow then the outcomes, but the transition process suggests the outcomes and goals were not different at all. The ability to learn about ones' self and apply this knowledge was a positive outcome of this field experience; and the experience provided a means for self-assessment and change and, in the process, challenged assumptions and concepts that interns brought into the experience. The work related to "just getting along" with others in the group environment was challenging in itself while the students reported that the greatest challenges were dealing with their own agendas. The Winslow experience provided a catalyst for solidifying the blend of students and the cultures that they were involved in, and the process of identifying their roles and goals helped them identify insights gained and the changes made.

The final question allowed students to add any final comments to the experience. Closure and the ability to gain a synopsis of the student's feelings was the desire. Some of the feelings shared focused on relationships among group members. The most positive note was that the students were able to recognize their own potential and the importance of the learning experience as a whole. Many of them described the experience as rewarding, challenging, fulfilling and, had met their expectations. One student related satisfaction with the experience and rated it as the greatest of their life. They agreed that they were able to learn more about self in the process of dealing with others in the group, and these relationships were their greatest challenges at times. There was an expressed need for more prior training, which might have enhanced the preparation for this experience, including prior coursework on the local culture and customs, theory and method of community development, and race and ethnicity coursework that includes more focus on Hispanic American and Native American information. The strength of the group experience and the process of applying personal growth and experiential learning to personal and professional settings were follow-up goals for some of the students. The students as a whole reported that their coursework in this area was limited to race with little focus on cultures.

PROJECT DIRECTORS' NARRATIVE

The Project Director, William D. Eldridge, Ph.D. was asked by the researcher to narratively address four content areas in a review of the two-year Winslow Project, including the impact on the community of Winslow and the future of social work in terms of such projects. The four content areas were knowledge of community, knowledge of community development, cohort development among the students, and community outcomes.

The response to this topic area indicated there is no better way to "learn very quickly about a community other than actually living in the community." This data suggests that the knowledge of community continues far beyond the Winslow experience and many of the students supported this in their responses to the questionnaires. One point made in the interview was that if the project continued it would include "story telling" about the community as an introduction to Winslow. This situation would include ten or fifteen people invited to come together and tell the Winslow story; the students and possibly other people in the community could be the audience.

As they relate their story through pictures, videos, audiotapes, narrative, or anecdotal discussions the knowledge of community enhances. Knowledge about community and community involvement are synonymous terms when viewed from a pragmatic perspective, as are social work and community ideologies. Another salient point is the need for concentrations in community development at schools of social work. Because the students "really don't have any knowledge of community development," it was necessary to teach a concurrent course while they were on-site, although they need far better preparation in terms of the theory and methodology of community practice.

The ideal would be to move community development and community theory academic courses to the first-year and then have second year students involved in Winslow type field placements. There is agreement that if this would most likely contradict CSWE requirements that the first year placement be generic, while the second year placement is specific. However, it was concluded, "a community development placement is very clearly an example of generalist practice."

The ideal would be to have generalist practice orientation be part of the second year scenario, which provides students the opportunity to complete courses in community development and community practice in the first year. Finally, "the greatest advantage of community practice outcomes is start up activities, followed in subsequent years by more comprehensive work putting icing on the various components of the cake that are built in previous sessions." It is important to finish what we start and this requires follow-up. The follow-up could utilize telephone interviews, e-mail, the Internet, or other means of contact. Follow-up community evaluation, "particularly when you have a neighborhood association that is built (like LaFamilia in Winslow) comes through a local indigenous organization that remains after the students depart." The continuation of the projects and activities initiated by the students while in Winslow are evidence of positive outcomes as well.

Promoting community-based experiences in social work education is important and exemplified within the primary service interventions for the Winslow project. All the information presented points to the fact that these students benefited from the Winslow experience in many ways. Learning to work as team members and challenging themselves in a new environment was an important element of their learning. This study investigated the concepts of community, community development, and social work in communities. In the processes of analyzing the experiences of the twenty-one students, the research questions acted as filters for the information. The following includes a summary of each research question and student responses.

First, are there any differences in feelings/attitudes for the students taking part in this field placement experience? The narrative responses of the students support this outcome and suggest that students gained knowledge during their experience. Secondly, many reported that they would practice social work differently because of the impact of this experience, and many reported they would repeat this experience again if given the chance. This is a testimonial to this experience repeated many times during the interview process with both cohorts. Third, what is the Program Director's evaluation of the student's progress and the project?

As was presented in the Program Director's narrative there are many benefits to this type of placement, including service delivery to communities along with personal & cohort development among interns. The need for more support and community focus at schools of social work was also postulated.

The impact of this type of training is supported in the data presented.

IMPLICATIONS

Because the profession of social work has a longstanding relationship with community-based practices, community development and strengthening the bonds that support families and communities; students of social work could benefit from training within the community-based environment, as with the training received in the Winslow Project.

Attitudes and Feelings

The narrative analysis of the questionnaire data sustained the reported differences in student feelings about themselves, the members of their group, and about the people and community of Winslow, where students believed that they were not only meeting their initial expectations but also exceeding them by the end of their experience. Both groups of students indicated better communication skills, assertiveness skills, cultural awareness, relationship skills, social work practice skills, community development experience, self-awareness, spiritual growth, emotional growth, and general well being. As these are all related to self-growth, awareness, and social functioning they fit very nicely with the research question related to personal and professional growth.

Social Work Knowledge

Students saw their group as a community early on and presented this with all of the characteristics and roles that one might expect in a community. It was during this process that the concept of the student groups as a community began to develop and expand for both cohorts, suggesting the validity of the common Winslow internship experience. The student's concepts of community expanded, and developed through the Winslow experience, including, growing cohesiveness of the groups, and struggles with their concepts of what community should be. They reported achievement and growth as the result of the relationships they formed, whereby constant contact with their group members was an essential element to the community identity and each person's identity as a member of that community. The concept of family, advocacy, social action, interdependency, location, common goals, the group as a community, and the ability to be tolerant of others were positive outcomes of this experience. Their insight into the dynamics of community practice increased through the various experiences that were taking place.

The concept of measuring how students feel about their field placements is not new. The importance here is that as these students were involved in many field placements in and around the Winslow community, though they were all related to one actual community placement. In reviewing the data it appears that the ability to learn about ones' self and apply this knowledge is a positive outcome of the Winslow experience. The students suggested they "had been forever changed" through this experience and, that they would practice social work differently as a result. The students in both cohorts suggested that this experience provided a means for self-assessment and change and, their involvement was rewarding, challenging, and fulfilling and as having met and exceeded their expectations. The community development course that was part of their field instruction was highly rated, though all agreed that coursework integrated into their first year curriculum would have enhanced this curriculum.

Project Director's Evaluation

The final area for review here is the project directors' thoughts related to the experience of the students. It is important to note that this data closely mirrors the reported experiences of the students. The "group-block" field placement experience is a positive experiential method for training future community-oriented social work practitioners, and the profession of social work must be responsible for encouraging this opportunity. It was postulated that because social work includes theoretical frameworks from various disciplines and paradigms including but not limited to, sociology, psychology, anthropology, and political science that this phenomenon helps define social work as a profession.

The Winslow project was a generalist approach with a community involvement commitment. It is from this focus on social action, social change, and community development that the study is presented. The conclusion is that social work as a profession has linkages to community practice and the practice of community development. The results of this study provide the following

- There are perceived differences related to how these students perceive community because of this experience.
- There are differences reported in insight and/or knowledge base in reference to social work in community on the part of the students involved.
- The social work students were provided with a well-defined concept of group and community practice.

They were indoctrinated in the theories involved with group and community contexts and this was clearly established in the training and educational component they received during their experience.

- Their training in community practice through working as a community in the community appears to have influenced their self-reported enhancement as practicing social workers.
- The students reported that they are better able to connect theory, practice, and research because of their field training activities.
- Community oriented field placements is an important method for this training.
- The block-group field experience method is a positive alternative to other more traditional training agency based models.
- These alternative training opportunities need to be available as community practice and demand for trained social workers grows.
- These options can be excellent training activities for students and outcomes from these can have far reaching positive influences on the profession of social work.

Providing social work intervention practices in the community is paramount to the further development of social work as a profession. It will also provide support and encouragement for communities to provide these supportive services within the community context. Social work history is rich with the type of models necessary for this to occur.

Final Thoughts

The study has provided information that can guide and suggest changes in curriculum for schools of social work. The development and provision of community practice programs or concentrations is timely for the social work profession. The struggle related to forces within the profession that requires one to choose between focusing on individual change or working as an advocate for social change must be resolved. Schools of social work need to place greater emphasis on social work practice in communities. This community orientation is needed in today's complicated practice environment. There are some salient points made here and they are as follows

- Schools of social work should provide quality-learning experiences, which incorporate community into the social work educational process, the classroom instruction, and into field placements.
- Schools of social work might need to consider setting up their own field units (agency) rather than relying on outside agencies for placement opportunities.
- Schools of social work should promote community development on the part of their students.

The focus on community will help students to prepare for professional roles.

These points are supported through the study and are congruent with the research hypothesis which indicates that community based training is important to social work education and to the profession of social work.

There is a need for development of an expanded community-oriented focus in social work education and more specifically in field instruction. The field placement experience is and has been the cornerstone of the graduate level social work preparation as has been implied and supported. The process of developing new social workers within this conceptual context lies in community-based field experiences. The community-based training experience should be a priority for schools of social work. Development of alternative learning experiences will provide greater opportunities for social work students in their preparation and entry into the professional roles as social workers. Traditionally schools of social work have relied on external agencies for placing students for field experience. This results in a detachment of the school from the community in which they exist. The suggestion that schools of social work become their own agencies would allow schools to become more directly involved in their local communities. Community development programs are on the cutting edge of social work practice and that it is encouraging to see innovative schools of social work developing field-training experiences that include alternative models. The body of knowledge in social work includes solid theoretical foundations in community practice. In fact, much of the foundation coursework for BSW and MSW programs according to the CSWE adhere to these theoretical roots.

4

Social Work Practice in Community Development

Social workers in the field of community development can be found in many areas of practice and a variety of settings. The work is often not situated within legislated programs, and workers may or may not be required to be registered with the provincial regulatory body. Community practice can involve community economic development such as improving local economies in rural areas experiencing out-migration, or it can include working with citizens, groups, and organizations to interface with large systems, institutions, and the political process. The identity of "community" varies widely and changes depending on the context of the specific issue or social problem. Social workers who practise from a community development or community organizing perspective attempt to address the systemic issues that create social problems. In many cases, they may also be engaged in the kinds of individual problem-solving practices embodied in many social work positions.

Community social work involves understanding the power dynamics and social relations that govern the relationships between various structures and diverse communities and working to achieve social justice through structural change. If the issue is poverty, for example, a social worker practising from a community perspective may focus on the political economy that creates these conditions. This may include trying to address the policies that perpetuate poverty or organizing groups around the issue to lobby decisionmakers for change. The main approach to this work is a belief that people acting together have a great capacity to improve their own circumstances, as they have first-hand knowledge of the situation and what needs to happen to change things for the better. In fact, this reflects the fundamental values of the social work profession generally. Some of the tools utilized by community social workers are developing community awareness, leadership identification and development, creating strategic alliances, adult education, fostering collaboration, and building community capacity. The community social worker can be involved in various large-scale social movements and broad issues such as homelessness, or in the development of programs or projects and research.

To achieve a better understanding of conditions from social, economic, and political perspectives, social workers practising at the community level concern themselves with matters of public policy and often engage with others in policy analysis. The analysis assists in developing strategies towards achieving some form of sustainable change. In any situation, the communities of focus must play a leading role in defining the issues and developing the solutions. Community social workers spend much time working with leaders and allies to identify common goals among community members. The social worker becomes a leading organizer to generate a strategic direction in the context of goals identified and defined by the group and that the group works toward. The social worker shares any and all information related to the presenting problem or issue so that stakeholders are better able to participate in formulating solutions.

Social workers who practise as community organizers or developers are guided by the ethics and standards of the profession and by principles of sustainable community development. Research approaches most commonly used in this area of practice are qualitative, such as participatory action or ethnographic research. From a community perspective, the social work role is to conduct assessments and share information with the identified community of interest. Research knowledge is often used to formulate the steps needed in developing a strategy. In turn, the social worker learns from the people in their communities, enhancing collaboration and partnerships that lead to achieving real social change.

COMMUNITY

In biological terms, a community is a group of interacting organisms sharing a populated environment. In human communities, intent, belief, resources, preferences, needs, risks, and a number of other conditions may be present and common, affecting the identity of the participants and their degree of cohesiveness.

In sociology, the concept of community has led to significant debate, and sociologists are yet to reach agreement on a definition of the term. There were ninety-four discrete definitions of the term by the mid-1950s. Traditionally a "community" has been defined as a group of interacting people living in a common location. The word is often used to refer to a group that is organized around common values and is attributed with social cohesion within a shared geographical location, generally in social units larger than a household. The word can also refer to the national community or global community.

The word "community" is derived from the Old French *communité* which is derived from the Latin *communitas* (*cum*, "with/together" + *munus*, "gift"), a broad term for fellowship or organized society.

Since the advent of the Internet, the concept of community no longer has geographical limitations, as people can now virtually gather in an online community and share common interests regardless of physical location.

PERSPECTIVES FROM VARIOUS DISCIPLINES

German sociologist Ferdinand Tönnies distinguished between two types of human association: *Gemeinschaft* (usually translated as "community") and *Gesellschaft* ("society" or "association"). In his 1887 work, *Gemeinschaft and Gesellschaft*, Tönnies argued that *Gemeinschaft* is perceived to be a tighter and more cohesive social entity, due to the presence of a "unity of will." He added that family and kinship were the perfect expressions of *Gemeinschaft*, but that other shared characteristics, such as place or belief, could also result in *Gemeinschaft*. This paradigm of communal networks and shared social understanding has been applied to multiple cultures in many places throughout history. *Gesellschaft*, on the other hand, is a group in which the individuals who make up that group are motivated to take part in the group purely by self-interest. He also proposed that in the real world, no group was either pure *Gemeinschaft* or pure *Gesellschaft,* but, rather, a mixture of the two.

Social Capital

If community exists, both freedom and security may exist as well. The community then takes on a life of its own, as people become free enough to share and secure enough to get along. The sense of connectedness and formation of social networks comprise what has become known as social capital.

Social capital is defined by Robert D. Putnam as "the collective value of all social networks and species (who people know) and the inclinations that arise from these networks to do things for each other (norms of reciprocity)." Social capital in action can be seen in all sorts of groups, including neighbors keeping an eye on each others' homes. However, as Putnam notes in *Bowling Alone: The Collapse and Revival of American Community* (2000), social capital has been falling in the United States. Putnam found that over the past 25 years, attendance at club meetings has fallen 58 percent, family dinners are down 33 percent, and having friends visit has fallen 45 percent.

The same patterns are also evident in many other western countries. Western cultures are thus said to be losing the spirit of community that once were found in institutions including churches and community centers. Sociologist Ray Oldenburg states in *The Great Good Place* that people need three places: 1) the home, 2) the office, and, 3) the community hangout or gathering place. With this philosophy in mind, many grassroots efforts such as The Project for Public Spaces are being started to create this "Third Place" in communities. They are taking form in independent bookstores, coffeehouses, local pubs, and through many innovative means to create the social capital needed to foster the sense and spirit of community.

Sense of Community

In a seminal 1986 study, McMillan and Chavis identify four elements of "sense of community": 1) membership, 2) influence, 3) integration and fulfillment of needs, and 4) shared emotional connection. They give the following example of the interplay between these factors:

Someone puts an announcement on the dormitory bulletin board about the formation of an intramural dormitory basketball team. People attend the organizational meeting as strangers out of their individual needs (integration and fulfillment of needs). The team is bound by place of residence (membership boundaries are set) and spends time together in practice (the contact hypothesis). They play a game and win (successful shared valent event). While playing, members exert energy on behalf of the team (personal investment in the group). As the team continues to win, team members become recognized and congratulated (gaining honor and status for being members), Influencing new members to join and continue to do the same. Someone suggests that they all buy matching shirts and shoes (common symbols) and they do so (influence).

A *Sense of Community Index* (SCI) has been developed by Chavis and colleagues and revised and adapted by others. Although originally designed to assess sense of community in neighborhoods, the index has been adapted for use in schools, the workplace, and a variety of types of communities.

Studies conducted by the APPA show substantial evidence that young adults who feel a sense of belonging in a community, particularly small communities, develop fewer psychiatric and depressive disorders than those who do not have the feeling of love and belonging.

Anthropolog Cultural (or social) anthropology has traditionally looked at community through the lens of ethnographic fieldwork and ethnography continues to be an important methodology for study of modern communities. Other anthropological approaches that deal with various aspects of community include cross-cultural studies and the anthropology of religion. Cultures in modern society are also studied in the fields of urban anthropology, ethnic studies, ecological anthropology, and psychological anthropology. Since the 1990s, internet communities have increasingly been the subject of research in the emerging field of cyber anthropology.

Archaeology

Archaeological studies of social communities. The term "community" is used in two ways in archaeology, paralleling usage in other areas. The first is an informal definition of community as a place where people used to live. In this sense it is synonymous with the concept of an ancient settlement, whether a hamlet, village, town, or city. The second meaning is similar to the usage of the term in other social sciences: a community is a group of people living near one another who interact socially. Social interaction on a small scale can be difficult to identify with archaeological data. Most reconstructions of social communities by archaeologists rely on the principle that social interaction is conditioned by physical distance. Therefore a small village settlement likely constituted a social community, and spatial subdivisions of cities and other large settlements may have formed communities. Archaeologists typically use similarities in material culture—from house types to styles of pottery—to reconstruct communities in the past. This is based on the assumption that people or households will share more similarities in the types and styles of their material goods with other members of a social community than they will with outsiders.

SOCIAL PHILOSOPHY AND COMMUNITARIANISM

Communitarianism as a group of related but distinct philosophies (or ideologies) began in the late 20th century, opposing classical liberalism and capitalism while advocating phenomena such as civil society. Not necessarily hostile to social liberalism, communitarianism rather has a different emphasis, shifting the focus of interest toward communities and societies and away from the individual. The question of priority, whether for the individual or community, must be determined in dealing with pressing ethical questions about a variety of social issues, such as health care, abortion, multiculturalism, and hate speech. Gad Barzilai has critically examined both liberalism and communitarianism and has developed the theory of critical communitarianism. Barzilai has explicated how non-ruling communities are constructing legal cultures while interacting with various facets of political power. Being venues of identity construction justifies collective protections of communities in law, while the boundaries with other communities, states, and global forces should be sensitive to preservation of various cultures. Gad Barzilai has accordingly offered how to protect human rights, individual rights, and multiculturalism in inter-communal context that allows to generating cultural relativism.

BUSINESS AND COMMUNICATIONS

Effective communication practices in group and organizational settings are very important to the formation and maintenance of communities. The ways that ideas and values are communicated within communities are important to the induction of new members, the formulation of agendas, the selection of leaders and many other aspects. Organizational communication is the study of how people communicate within an organizational context and the influences and interactions within organizational structures. Group members depend on the flow of communication to establish their own identity within these structures and learn to function in the group setting. Although organizational communication, as a field of study, is usually geared toward companies and business groups, these may also be seen as communities. The principles of organizational communication can also be applied to other types of communities.

Ecology

In ecology, a community is an assemblage of populations of different species, interacting with one another. Community ecology is the branch of ecology that studies interactions between and among species. It considers how such interactions, along with interactions between species and the abiotic environment, affect community structure and species richness, diversity and patterns of abundance. Species interact in three ways: competition, predation and mutualism. Competition typically results in a double negative—that is both species lose in the interaction. Predation is a win/lose situation with one species winning. Mutualism, on the other hand, involves both species cooperating in some way, with both winning.

INTERDISCIPLINARY PERSPECTIVES

The process of learning to adopt the behavior patterns of the community is called socialization. The most fertile time of socialization is usually the early stages of life, during which individuals develop the skills and knowledge and learn the roles necessary to function within their culture and social environment. For some psychologists, especially those in the psychodynamic tradition, the most important period of socialization is between the ages of one and ten. But socialization also includes adults moving into a significantly different environment, where they must learn a new set of behaviors.

Socialization is influenced primarily by the family, through which children first learn community norms. Other important influences include school, peer groups, people, schools, mass media, the workplace, and government. The degree to which the norms of a particular society or community are adopted determines one's willingness to engage with others. The norms of tolerance, reciprocity, and trust are important "habits of the heart," as de Tocqueville put it, in an individual's involvement in community.

Community Development

Community development, often linked with Community Work or Community Planning, is often formally conducted by non-government organisations (NGOs), universities or government agencies to progress the social well-being of local, regional and, sometimes, national communities. Less formal efforts, called community building or community organizing, seek to empower individuals and groups of people by providing them with the skills they need to effect change in their own communities. These skills often assist in building political power through the formation of large social groups working for a common agenda. Community development practitioners must understand both how to work with individuals and how to affect communities' positions within the context of larger social institutions.

Formal programs conducted by universities are often used to build a knowledge base to drive curricula in sociology and community studies. The General Social Survey from the National Opinion Research Center at the University of Chicago and the Saguaro Seminar at the John F. Kennedy School of Government at Harvard University are examples of national community development in the United States. In The United Kingdom, Oxford University has led in providing extensive research in the field through its *Community Development Journal,* used worldwide by sociologists and community development practitioners.

At the intersection between community *development* and community *building* are a number of programs and organizations with community development tools. One example of this is the program of the Asset Based Community Development Institute of Northwestern University. The institute makes available downloadable tools to assess community assets and make connections between non-profit groups and other organizations that can help in community building. The Institute focuses on helping communities develop by "mobilizing neighborhood assets" — building from the inside out rather than the outside in.

Community Building and Organizing

In *The Different Drum: Community-Making and Peace,* Scott Peck argues that the almost accidental sense of community that exists at times of crisis can be consciously built. Peck believes that conscious community building is a process of deliberate design based on the knowledge and application of certain rules. He states that this process goes through four stages:

1. Pseudo-community: Where participants are "nice with each other", playing-safe, and presenting what they feel is the most favourable sides of their personalities.
2. Chaos: When people move beyond the inauthenticity of pseudo-community and feel safe enough to present their "shadow" selves. This stage places great demands upon the facilitator for greater leadership and organization, but Peck believes that "organizations are not communities", and this pressure should be resisted.
3. Emptiness: This stage moves beyond the attempts to fix, heal and convert of the chaos stage, when all people become capable of acknowledging their own woundedness and brokenness, common to us all as human beings. Out of this emptiness comes
4. True community: the process of deep respect and true listening for the needs of the other people in this community. This stage Peck believes can only be described as "glory" and reflects a deep yearning in every human soul for compassionate understanding from one's fellows.

More recently Peck remarked that building a sense of community is easy but maintaining this sense of community is difficult in the modern world. Community building can use a wide variety of practices, ranging from simple events such as potlucks and small book clubs to larger--scale efforts such as mass festivals and construction projects that involve local participants rather than outside contractors.

Community building that is geared toward citizen action is usually termed "community organizing." In these cases, organized community groups seek accountability from elected officials and increased direct representation within decision-making bodies. Where good-faith negotiations fail, these constituency-led organizations seek to pressure the decision-makers through a variety of means, including picketing, boycotting, sit-ins, petitioning, and electoral politics. The ARISE Detroit! coalition and the Toronto Public Space Committee are examples of activist networks committed to shielding local communities from government and corporate domination and inordinate influence.

Community organizing is sometimes focused on more than just resolving specific issues. Organizing often means building a widely accessible power structure, often with the end goal of distributing power equally throughout the community. Community organizers generally seek to build groups that are open and democratic in governance. Such groups facilitate and encourage consensus decision-making with a focus on the general health of the community rather than a specific interest group. The three basic types of community organizing are grassroots organizing, coalition building, and "institution-based community organizing," (also called "broad-based community organizing," an example of which is faith-based community organizing, or "congregation-based community organizing").

Community Currencies

Some communities have developed their own "Local Exchange Trading Systems" (LETS) and local currencies, such as the Ithaca Hours system, to encourage economic growth and an enhanced sense of community. Community Currencies have recently proven valuable in meeting the needs of people living in various South American nations, particularly Argentina, that recently suffered as a result of the collapse of the Argentinian national currency.

COMMUNITY SERVICE

Community service is usually performed in connection with a nonprofit organization, but it may also be undertaken under the auspices of government, one or more businesses, or by individuals. It is typically unpaid and voluntary. However, it can be part of alternative sentencing approaches in a justice system and it can be required by educational institutions.

TYPES OF COMMUNITY

A number of ways to categorize types of community have been proposed; one such breakdown is:

1. Geographic communities: range from the local

neighbourhood, suburb, village, town or city, region, nation or even the planet as a whole. These refer to communities of *location*.

2. Communities of culture: range from the local clique, sub-culture, ethnic group, religious, multicultural or pluralistic civilisation, or the global community cultures of today. They may be included as *communities of need* or *identity*, such as disabled persons, or frail aged people.
3. Community organizations: range from informal family or kinship networks, to more formal incorporated associations, political decision making structures, economic enterprises, or professional associations at a small, national or international scale.

Communities are nested; one community can contain another—for example a geographic community may contain a number of ethnic communities.

Location

Possibly the most common usage of the word *"community"* indicates a large group living in close proximity. Examples of local community include:

- A municipality is an administrative local area generally composed of a clearly defined territory and commonly referring to a town or village.

Although large cities are also municipalities, they are often thought of as a collection of communities, due to their diversity.

- A neighborhood is a geographically localized community, often within a larger city or suburb.
- A planned community is one that was designed from scratch and grew up more or less following the plan. Several of the world's capital cities are planned cities, notably Washington, D.C., in the United States, Canberra in Australia, and Brasília in Brazil. It was also common during the European colonization of the Americas to build according to a plan either on fresh ground or on the ruins of earlier Amerindian cities.

Identity

In some contexts, *"community"* indicates a group of people with a common identity other than location. Members often interact regularly.

Common examples in everyday usage include:

- A "professional community" is a group of people with the same or related occupations. Some of those members may join a professional society, making a more defined and formalized group. These are also sometimes known as communities of practice.
- A virtual community is a group of people primarily or initially communicating or interacting with each other by means of information technologies, typically over the Internet, rather than in person. These may be either communities of interest, practice or communion. Research interest is evolving in the motivations for contributing to online communities.

Overlaps

Some communities share both location and other attributes. Members choose to live near each other because of one or more common interests.

- A retirement community is designated and at least usually designed for retirees and seniors—often restricted to those over a certain age, such as 56. It differs from a retirement home, which is a single building or small complex, by having a number of autonomous households.
- An intentional community is a deliberate residential community with a much higher degree of social communication than other communities. The members of an intentional community typically hold a common social, political or spiritual vision and share responsibilities and resources. Intentional communities include Amish villages, ashrams, cohousing, communes, ecovillages, housing cooperatives, kibbutzim, and land trusts.

Internet communities

To a growing part of people the meaning of the word *"community"* indicates a smaller or larger group of internet users signing up to become members of a community page/ system on internet. Examples of internet communities include:

- A business community is often an administrative community with possibilities to add CV's and other business-related information.
- An interest community is a based on specialized areas such as art, golf or bird watching.
- A general community is wider in its range-opening for its users to create areas, pages and groups.

SPECIAL NATURE OF HUMAN COMMUNITY

Definitions of community as "organisms inhabiting a common environment and interacting with one another," while scientifically accurate, do not convey the richness, diversity and complexity of human communities. Their classification, likewise is almost never precise. Untidy as it may be, community is vital for humans. M. Scott Peck expresses this in the following way: "There can be no vulnerability without risk; there can be no community without vulnerability; there can be no peace, and ultimately no life, without community."

The term *community service* refers to any act that is performed for the benefit of the community at large. Community service acts can range from a one-time effort to collect canned goods for the local food pantry to a weekly commitment to serve meals to the homeless. People do not receive financial compensation for their community service, although a number of award programs exist to recognize the contributions of volunteers.

In many cases, community service is performed as part of a person's membership in a social organization. Young Boy Scouts or Girl Scouts may volunteer to read to the elderly residents at a local nursing home or collect toys to distribute to needy children in the community. Members of a church fellowship may take a weekend trip to help build houses for

Habitat for Humanity. A professional association for accountants may organize an effort to provide low-income people with tax preparation assistance.

A person does not have to be a member of a specific organization to participate in community service activities, however. Many people choose to volunteer as a way to meet other people with similar interests, much like how one might socialize at a nightclub or a sporting event. Volunteering can be a great way for retirees to remain active in their community. Stay at home parents often use volunteer work to keep their professional skills sharp during their break from the workforce.

Community service, while ideally a voluntary act, is sometimes required by schools as a condition for high school graduation. In addition to enhancing a student's college application, studies have shown that teenagers who perform community service typically show improved academic performance. Under mandatory community service arrangements, teenagers must complete a specified number of hours of supervised community service per semester. However, they are usually allowed to choose activities that best fit their own personal interests, such as singing in the church choir or helping to organize library books.

Community service may also be ordered as punishment for a crime. In the case of nonviolent offenders, such as people convicted of drunk driving, community service may be ordered instead of jail time. For incarcerated inmates, community service is sometimes required as part of the prison's rehabilitation program. Cleaning up trash, removing graffiti, planting trees, or building community playground equipment while under the supervision of prison guards are common tasks performed under this type of arrangement.

TYPES OF RURAL COMMUNITIES

Sociologists have identified a number of different types of rural communities, which have arisen as a result of changing economic trends within rural regions of industrial nations. The basic trend seems to be one in which communities are required to become entrepreneurial. Those that lack the sort of characteristics mentioned below, are forced to either seek out their niche or accept eventual economic defeat. These towns focus on marketing and public relations whilst bidding for business and government operations; such as, off-site data processing or, perhaps, a factory.

For instance; International Falls, Minnesota markets itself as a site for sub-zero temperature experiments; Ottawa, Illinois managed to attract three Japanese firms; Freeport, Maine has become a center for mail-order companies such as L. L. Bean; and Mobile, Arizona has become the home of a number of solid-waste landfills.

Academic Communities

Academic communities are those in which the primary employers are boarding schools, colleges, universities, research laboratories, and corporate training facilities. These communities bring people away from other regions and thus bring new capital into the area. Academic institutions, in rural areas, are very much like a factory in that the economic success of the community depends upon the success of the institution. Unlike factories, academic institutions tend to primarily offer jobs in the medium-skilled to professional range.

Area Trade-Centers

The automobile allows rural residents to travel farther, in less time, for goods and services. This reduces the importance of the rural store, along with decreasing rural population. As business relocate from impoverished communities, one town will become the trade center for its region, sometimes doing so by constructing a shopping mall. Generally, business in a trade-center town, except for those in competition with the mall, will benefit from the mall's presence as shoppers spill over. These trade centers will knock out businesses in, and thus impoverish, nearby towns as shoppers converge on the town with the greatest variety of stores.

Government Centers

Rural regions are undergoing increasing government consolidation. This results in a small number of towns becoming centers of government activity, while the rest are devoid of government infrastructure. These centers include state and local capitals, and areas with prisons or military bases. Centralized public administration focuses public-sector employment on a single community, assisting it over its neighbors. Benefits, for the government center, include improved public services, increased efficiency, and economic savings.

Recreation Communities

Recreation communities (tourist towns) define some local feature, usually a historic site or scenic vista, as a "natural resource" and market this to tourists. Travelers will then spend money on food, hotels, and the like, which brings capital into the town.

Retirement Communities

Retirement communities tend to house large numbers of elderly people. These retirees, bring pensions, Social Security, and savings which infuse the area with capital. Rural hospitals are increasingly unable to bring enough patients to support their operational budget, and retirement communities have developed, in some areas, as a means to solve this problem.

Elderly residents, who migrate from the cities, tend to have above average wealth, thus creating an income disparity between the migrant retirees and the local elderly.

COMMUNITY BASED SOCIO-ECONOMIC DEVELOPMENT

India is the second largest populated country in the world with nearly 1.1 billion people. Out of this around 26.1 percent are poor, living with less than a dollar a day (ADB 2004; UNDP 2003). The country is thus home to more than one-fourth of the world's poor. Further the degree of poverty varies from state to state. The poverty estimate in percent of population below poverty line is as high as 47.15 percent for Orissa and 42.6 percent for Bihar to lower values 3.5 percent for Jammu and Kashmir and 4.4 percent for Goa during 1999-2000 as reported in National Human Development Report 2001 of Govt. of India (Planning Commission, 2002).

Poverty alleviation is the most important objective of Indian planning through creation of employment opportunities, income generation activities and growth promotion. However, underdeveloped infrastructure, such as power, transport, irrigation, water supply, sewerage, and lack of accessibility to health facilities, have impaired economic growth and the poverty eradication drive. At the same time, environmental problems are also worsening in India, while the forest area is shrinking day by day and at the same time urbanization is increasingly causing river water contamination and air pollution.

In the 10th Five Year Plan (April 2002-March 2007), the Government of India called for equitable and sustainable growth, and to achieve this goal, it has designated the following as the priority development issues: not only eradication of the existing poverty but long-term poverty reduction through economic growth and environmental conservation to make these efforts sustainable.

Water resources management and development are central to sustainable agricultural growth and poverty reduction. Currently, integrated water resources management is highly emphasized for enhancing food security, poverty eradication, economic growth and rural upliftment in the developing countries including India. Further, most of the developing countries have insufficient hydraulic infrastructure and hence, the governments, international funding agencies need to assist these countries in developing and maintaining adequat number of well-performing hydraulic structures and in mobilizing public and private financing, while meeting environmental and social standards. Moreover, the below-optimal performance of the existing irrigation systems is of serious concern to farmers who depend on them for their crops and livelihoods and to governments as well as funding agencies that have made massive investment in their development.

The most severe problems encountered by irrigation systems in the developing countries are the increasing costs of new schemes, the huge backlog of incomplete schemes, and the increasing neglect of existing systems. Large-scale canal irrigation systems, in particular, are in poor condition: they are not properly maintained, operations are inadequate, water supplies do not reach the end of systems, and the timing of water supply is unreliable. The wide gap between actual and desirable performance threatens the sustainability of irrigated agriculture. This state of affairs warrants proper investment strategies with institutional reforms and comprehensive plans for implementation starting from Micro-level.

It is established that in democratic and developing countries like India, genuinely participatory governance of a common property resource like irrigation at the micro level can yield benefits in terms of both efficiency and equity, by giving the water users a sense of ownership, by allocating resources according to people's demand and need and by utilising their skills and knowledge. The reform or decentralisation of governance of irrigation infrastructure or Irrigation Management Transfer to Farmers' Organisations is now widely accepted and used as an effective tool for improving management efficiency, accountability, agricultural and economic productivity and cost recovery and finally sustainable irrigated agriculture. As a result, it is now observed that an increasing number of governments around the world are adopting programmes to devolve responsibility for irrigation management to farmers' organisations or to Water Users Associations (WUAs) in their reform process, which is known as Participatory Irrigation Management (PIM) and is found place in their national policies.

Indian irrigation sector in recent years is also in the same PIM trail where attempts are being made to increase farmers' direct participation in decision-making and investment. Further, conventionally Indian agriculture is largely based on rural villages, as it draws most of its inputs from farms and village industries. Consequently, it establishes the fact that transforming agriculture to effective enterprise or industrialization of agriculture has potential to provide the rural poor with on-farm and off-farm employment, induce economic growth and promote food security. On the other hand, studies of De Boer et. al. (1997), Simons and Supri (1999), White (1999) and Grossmann and Poston (2003) reveal that India's agriculture extension system has missing links to secondary or primary education and is not reaching effectively to the women and the rural poor including the lower castes.

Though India is one of the potential producers of large number of agricultural researchers and scientists but it lacks in providing basic skills required to improve farming methods or job opportunities in the rural off-farm sector. Now high priority should be given to equip the rural poor with appropriate skills by improving the currently inadequate agriculture extension system. The situation altogether warrants a comprehensive micro plan with reforms in irrigation governance.

THE ROLE OF INDIVIDUAL ENTERPRISE

The Indian economy provides a revealing contrast between how individuals react under a government-controlled environment and how they respond to a market-based environment. Evidence suggests that recent market reforms that encouraged individual enterprise have ledto higher economic growth in that country. India can generate additional economic growth by fostering entrepreneurial activity within its borders. To pursue further the entrepreneurial approach to economic growth, India must now provide opportunities for (1) education directed specifically at entrepreneurial skills, (2) financing of entrepreneurial efforts, and (3) networking among potential entrepreneurs and their experienced counterparts. Further, although the Indian government should establish policies supportive of entrepreneurial efforts, its role overall should be minimized so that the influence of the free market and individual self-interest can be fully realized.

Economic development, achieved largely through productivity growth, is very important to both developed and developing nations. However, even though we know that higher productivity leads to improved economic outcomes (for example, higher income, more choices to the consumers, better quality products, etc.), there has been no consensus among researchers about either the desired path of development or the role of state in economic development. Concerning the path of development, Lall (2001) says that the appropriate strategy for any country depends not only on its objective economic situation but also on its government policies and national views regarding the appropriate role of the state.

Regarding the appropriate role of the state, it seems that for every argument in favour of a smaller government role one can find a counter argument in favour of a more active government role. The role of the state in economic development began to change dramatically with the advent of the Industrial Revolution. In the West, the resulting industrialization and economic development were based on the establishment of individual property rights that encouraged the growth of private capital. Competition and individual enterprise thrive in this environment because individuals pursue their self-interest of survival and wealth accumulation. The instinct to survive under competitive pressures yields innovation and productivity increases, which eventually lead to both increased profits for business and lower prices to consumers.

However, the rise and spread of capitalism led a number of thinkers to examine the consequences of the market-based approach to development. Socialists argued that capitalism (or private ownership of capital) can lead to greater inequalities of income and wealth, while developmental economists argued that private decisions may not always lead to socially desirable outcomes (particularly in the case of market imperfections). Indeed, many policy makers at the time saw market failures as quite common and therefore assumed that only appropriate government interventions could guide an economy to a path of sustained economic development.

In the early 20th century, the former Soviet Union attempted a bold experiment of improving individual well-being without sacrificing the objective of greater equality of income and wealth through total ownership of capital by the government. Initially, the Soviet Government was able to raise productivity through directed industrialization and, within a span of 25 years, emerged as a superpower. It was around this time that a substantial number of colonized nations were gaining their independence (for example, India, Pakistanand Burma). Unfortunately, during their time as colonies to the Western nations, these countries, for the most part, had been deprived of the industrialization that had engulfed those same Western nations. Based on the successful experience of the former Soviet Union, many economists and policy makers concluded that, particularly in a poor country, planning was essential for the efficient allocation of an economy's resources.

The governments in these newly independent nations assumed a significant role in economic development. They sought to quickly and substantially raise the standard of living through directed and controlled economic development. Apart from everything else, these developing countries invested heavily in education to promote literacy and to ensure an adequate supply of technical manpower to meet their growing needs. Further, these previously colonized nations did not want to subject their poor and weak economies to international economic fluctuations and thus sought to industrialize through import substituting industrialization, where imports were expected to be increasingly replaced by domestic production.

In this paper we examine economic development in India, a former British colony that became one of the most closed economies in the world, to contrast the roles of government intervention and individual enterprise in that country's economic growth. In particular, we demonstrate that, given recent economic reforms in India, along with the evidence for the role that individual enterprise can play in a country's economic growth, the Indian government should devise policies that rely more on individual enterprise, with its emphasis upon individual initiative and self-interest, to spur economic development. Further, we describe the special role that can be played in the economic development of India by a greater emphasis upon entrepreneurship.

The plan of the paper is as follows. Section I summarizes the strategy of economic development and the overall economic environment that has prevailed in India since its independence from the United Kingdom. Section II analyses the consequences of regulated economic development in India, with particular emphasis on the implications of the micro-economic aspects of India's approach to its economic environment. Section III assesses the results of India's economic reforms since the country's economic crisis of 1990, and highlights the role that individual enterprise has played and can continue to play in that country's economic fortunes. Section IV describes the special role that entrepreneurship can play in India's efforts at economic growth. Finally, section V summarizes the main findings and concludes the paper.

INDIA'S STRATEGY OF ECONOMIC DEVELOPMENT

India's economic development strategy immediately after Independence was based primarily on the Mahalanobis model, which gave preference to the investment goods industries sector, with secondary importance accorded to the services and household goods sector (Nayar, 2001). For example, the Mahalanobis model placed strong emphasis on mining and manufacturing (for the production of capital goods) and infrastructural development (including electricity generation and transportation).

The model down played the role of the factory goods sector because it was more capital intensive and therefore would not address the problem of high unemployment in India. Any increase in planned investments in India required higher level of savings than existed in the country. Because of the low average incomes in India, the needed higher levels of savings had to be generated mainly by restrictions on the growth of consumption expenditures. Therefore, the Indian government implemented a progressive tax system not only to generate the higher levels of savings but also to restrict increases in income and wealth inequalities.

Among other things, this strategy involved canalization of resources into their most productive uses. Investments were carried out both by the government and the private sector, with the government investing in strategic sectors (such as national defence) and also those sectors in which private capital would not be forthcoming because of lags or the size of investment required (such as infrastructure). The private sector was required to contribute to India's economic growth in ways envisaged by the government planners. Not only did the government determine where businesses could invest in terms of location, but it also identified what businesses could produce, what they could sell, and what prices they could charge.

Thus the strategy of economic development in India meant (1) direct participation of the government in economic activities such as production and selling and (2) regulation of private sector economic activities through a complex system of controls. In addition, the Indian economy was sheltered from foreign competition through use of both the "infant industry argument" and a binding foreign exchange constraint. Imports were limited to goods considered essential either to the development of the economy (such as raw materials and machines) or to the maintenance of minimal living standards (such as crude oil and food items). It was further decided that exports should play a limited role in economic development, thereby minimizing the need to compete in the global market place. As a result, India became a relatively closed economy, permitting only limited economic transactions with other countries. Domestic producers were sheltered from foreign competition not only from abroad but also from within India itself.

Over time, India created a large number of government institutions to meet the objective of growth with equity. The size of the government grew substantially as it played an increasingly larger role in the economy in such areas as investment, production, retailing, and regulation of the private sector. For example, in the late 1950s and 1960s, the government established public sector enterprises in such areas as production and distribution of electricity, petroleum products, steel, coal, and engineering goods. In the late 1960s, it nationalized the banking and insurance sectors. To alleviate the shortages of food and other agricultural outputs, it provided modern agricultural inputs (for example farm machinery, irrigation, high yielding varieties of seeds, chemical fertilizers) to farmers at highly subsidized prices.

In 1970, to increase foreign exchange earnings, it designated exports as a priority sector for active government help and established, among other things, a duty drawback system, programmes of assistance for market development, and 100 percent export-oriented entities to help producers export.

Finally, from the late 1970s through the mid-1980s, India liberalized imports such that those not subject to licensing as a proportion to total imports grew from five percent in 1980-1981 to about 30 percent in 1987-1988. However, this partial removal of quantitative restrictions was accompanied by a steep rise in tariff rates.

This active and dominant participation by the government in economic activities resulted in the creation of a protected, highly-regulated, public sector-dominated economic environment. Along with this government domination of the economy, India soon faced not only some major problems in its overall approach to development, particularly in the area of industrialization (Ahluwalia, 1985), but also a dramatic increase in corruption in its economy. Finally, like any other growing economy, the Indian economy faced a number of serious sectoral imbalances, with shortages in some sectors and surpluses in others.

CONSEQUENCES OF INDIA'S REGULATED ECONOMIC DEVELOPMENT

India's environment of regulated economic development led to the formulation of policies that were concerned with both macroeconomic and micro-economic aspects. Whereas much attention in the literature has been devoted to the macroeconomic issues, we focus primarily on the micro-economic aspects of Indian economic policies. In particular, we examine how individuals guided by their self-interests of survival and wealth accumulation will act in a regulated environment, which in fact discourages the pursuit of those self-interests. To do so, we describe the consequences of India's use of price ceilings, in which prices are set below their equilibrium level to make products and services affordable to relatively poorer sections of the society. In contrast to the supply side options just considered, if the government had decided instead to limit demand, it could have done so by increasing taxes or by regulating the level of demand itself, usually by restricting how much an individual or a family could consume. To ensure the availability of the scarce products and services to Indian consumers, albeit at less than desired levels, the Indian government in fact resorted to large-scale rationing. This rationing was undertaken by government agencies themselves or by licensed private retailers. As might be expected, the rationing regulations required those licensed private retailers to follow government stipulations in their sale of the scarce products and services. The policy of price ceilings, along with the quantitative restrictions on production and consumption, led to an economic environment ripe for corruption. Specifically, because of the general scarcity of products and services, individuals competed to receive the privilege of economic rights to produce or consume. The implementing authority responsible for allocating these economic rights – politicians, government officials and businesses – enjoyed monopoly power in this situation and, as might be expected, were susceptible to bribes and other illegal favours.

The result was an informal and illegal market in which the desired economic rights could be traded. Also, the lure of higher profits led producers and sellers (1) to have little concern for quality such that many deliberately produced and sold inferior quality products, and (2) to resort to the creation of artificial shortages by not releasing to the market all of the products that were available for selling. Bardhan (1997) defines corruption as the use of public office for private gain, in which an official entrusted with the responsibility for certain public duties engages in malfeasance for personal enrichment that is not easy to monitor.

He says that corruption has multiple effects on economic development. For example, it diminishes the efficiency of economic transactions, because corrupt officials will delay or otherwise obstruct those transactions until they receive their expected favours. Also, the payment of a bribe to receive an investment license tends to reduce the incentive to in vest. Honest investors will see the futility of competing with dishonest investors who are guaranteed, through their bribes, to receive the privilege of investment rights.

To fully understand the widespread nature of the corruption that existed in India at this time, it is necessary to consider the roles played by the many participants. For example, business people bribed government officials not only for the right to enter a particular line of business, but also to prevent others from entering that same line of business. Government officials made pay-offs to politicians to receive the premium government positions that would allow them to easily contact businesses to seek illegal income and wealth. Indeed, as Wade (1985) indicates, those officials could earn far more through bribes and other corrupt behaviour than they could earn in salary. Consumers bribed government officials, politicians, and business people to receive a particular amount of a scarce good or a higher quality version of the good. Even individuals and organizations outside India took part in the corruption. Some bribed both officials and politicians, particularly those connected with the revenue and police departments, to smuggle scarce goods into India at a high profit.

The complex system of government controls, including price ceilings, along with the resultant corruption, meant that decision making was arbitrary and the transactions non-transparent. The result was an increase in transaction costs. For example, businesses had to spend more to "stay connected' with appropriate government officials and politicians. And consumers, in addition to waiting in line to purchase needed products and services, also made illegal payments for what they should have received at a reasonable price in the first place. It has already been explained how India's government grew in size as it played an increasing role in controlling the economy. It grew even further in trying to be appropriately vigilant in dealing with the increased corruption among government officials, businesses, and other participants.

Price controls were only one example of the regulated economic environment. Another example of a harmful policy was the control of ownership of private capital (both income and wealth) by Indian nationals in India and also by foreign nationals doing business in India. Such policies, coupled with high individual and corporate income tax rates and high customs and excise duties, led to outcomes similar to those resulting from price ceilings namely, increased corruption and higher transaction costs.

In conclusion, this section has shown how individuals guided by their self-interests, will act in a regulated environment. Government controls based on arbitrary and ad hoc administrative decisions lead not only to greater concealed income and wealth but also to diminished productivity, particularly due to the resulting higher transaction costs.

THE MIXED RESULTS FOR INDIA

Due to government intervention, particularly the high levels of government subsidies, it was clear by 1990 that India was living beyond its means. The result was a severe payments crisis in which, for the first time, the government physically transported gold overseas to prevent defaulting on foreign commitments.

To meet its immediate balance of payments crisis, India also entered into a structural loan adjustment agreement with the International Monetary Fund (IMF). However, one condition of this loan required India to undertake economic reforms to move from a centrally-planned development strategy to one based on market-based resource allocations. As a result, the government of India undertook a package of economic reforms between 1991 and 1993, with the intent of placing the market in place of government controls as the prime mover in the economic development process.

As one might expect, macroeconomic policy played a major role in India's economic progress in the 1990s. For example, Acharya (2001) concludes that India's devaluation of the rupee and its decision to increase the level of allowable foreign investment helped it to make considerable economic progress. Joshi (2001) and Karunaratne (2001) both say that India's policy of selective capital account liberalization helped it to achieve important economic objectives (and still avoided the crises faced by the East Asian countries). Gupta (1999) highlights the important role played by India's prudent management of exchange rate policy and its tight monetary policy. Bhalla (2000) notes both the privatization of the public sector enterprises and the gradual dismantling of the government planning process in favour of market forces.

Overall, there can be no doubt that the reforms implemented since 1991 have led to considerable economic progress in India. For example, from 1992-1993 through 2000-2001, economic growth averaged an unprecedented 6.3 percent per year (Acharya, 2001). Further, as Bhalla (2000) indicates, the rate of inflation and the fiscal deficit have both decreased substantially. He also says that India's improved exchange rate management has restored the confidence of foreign investors, which in turn has led to improved financing of the current account deficit and higher levels of foreign exchange reserves.

However, even though India has made substantial economic progress in recent years, it still has several areas in need of major market-based reforms. Below, we identify three examples from India's economy that reveal a restriction of the pursuit of individual self-interest and a diversion of resources away from their most efficient use. The first example concerns the obstacle still presented by the Indian tax system, the second highlights the inefficiencies of the Indian civil service, and the third describes the need for further land reform in India.

1. In spite of recent tax reforms in India, the present tax system still works against the individual self-interest to survive and accumulate wealth and, as a result, still leads to the hiding of income, wealth and expenditures. Indeed, whereas in the United States and the Republic of Korea, the highest tax rate applies to an income level of $250,000 and $66,000, respectively, in India that same tax rate applies to an income of only $3,400. Simply reforming its tax system to bring it in line with comparable nations should yield several substantial benefits to the Indian economy.
2. The Indian civil service provides attractive career choices for young job seekers due mainly to the excellent job security, non-monetary compensation, and opportunities for influence available in those careers. For example, despite minimal salaries for individuals holding top-tier positions in such areas as administration, police, revenue and railways, these civil servants are entitled to high job security and heavily subsidized housing, transport,

medical services, telephone privileges, and at times domestic help. We believe that the policies underlying compensation to government employees should be reformed such that they are based primarily on market principles. The advantages of doing so include eliminating departments known for corrupt practices, making explicit the true cost of a government employee's performance, and giving government employees a good sense of their market worth.

3. Finally, considerable reform is needed in the Indian real estate sector. A large proportion of the land is owned by the government, and any land made available for private use is governed by archaic ownership, zoning, tenancy, and rent laws. Further, this government control of land has reduced the amount of land available for trading purposes. The result is that Indian land prices are the highest among all Asian nations relative to average income (Lewis, 2001).

Further, the officially assessed values of real estate are low, while the true market price is very high. This situation leads, among other things, to higher levels of corruption as individuals use real estate as a major hiding place for investments of illegally acquired income (DiLodovico, Lewis, Palmade and Sankhe, 2001). Examples such as these indicate that there are still a large number of areas where the individual self-interests of survival and wealth accumulation are not respected. In the next section, we examine how one fairly new approach to micro-economic policy – the encouragement of entrepreneurship – can help India to continue its recent economic growth.

INDIA'S FUTURE ECONOMIC DEVELOPMENT

The progress of Indian economic development from 1947 to the present provides further evidence that individuals do respond to incentives in their pursuit of self-survival and accumulation of wealth. Further, the nature of this response depends on the economic climate, particularly the role of the government. India's economy struggled as long as it was based in a system of government regulation with little interaction with economic forces outside the country. The economic reforms of the early 1990s set the stage for substantial improvements in the Indian economy.

As was stated earlier, India's economy grew at an average of 6.3 percent from 1992-1993 to 2000-2001 (Acharya, 2001). Further, its rate of inflation and fiscal deficit both decreased substantially (Bhalla, 2000). Improved exchange rate management led to improved financing of the current account deficit and higher foreign exchange reserves. Finally, India's GDP and per capita income both increased substantially from 1990-1991 to 1998-1999.

India can do more, however, to further advance its economic development. Indeed, one of the more recent micro-economic approaches to economic growth is the promotion of entrepreneurial activities.

Entrepreneurial efforts have been found to generate a wide range of economic benefits, including new businesses, new jobs, innovative products and services, and increased wealth for future community investment (Kayne, 1999). The following narrative explains in considerable depth how entrepreneurial activities have succeeded in several countries and how it can now be used to further India's economic development.

Following an extensive study of entrepreneurship in 21 countries, Reynolds, Hay, Bygrave, Camp and Autio (2000) concluded that successful entrepreneurial activity is strongly associated with economic growth. Their research was subsumed under the "Global Entrepreneurship Monitor" (GEM), a joint research initiative conducted by Babson College and London Business School and supported by the Kauffman Centre for Entrepreneurial Leadership.

Their findings, based on surveys of the adult population of each country, in-depth interviews of experts on entrepreneurship in each country, and the use of standardized national data, supported their conceptual model depicting the role of the entrepreneurial process in a country's economic development.

The GEM Conceptual Model

The GEM Conceptual Model suggests that the social-cultural-political context within a country must foster certain "General National Framework Conditions," which can generate not only the opportunities for entrepreneurship but also the capacity for entrepreneurship – in particular, the skills and motivation necessary to succeed. Together, the entrepreneurship opportunities, on the one hand, and the skills and motivation, on the other, lead to business dynamics that yield creative destruction, a process in which new firms are created and older, less efficient firms are destroyed. The overall result for a country is economic growth.

Given India's economic progress in recent years, the country may now be ready for the implementation of micro-economic policies that will foster entrepreneurial activities. Fortunately, in addition to the macroeconomic reforms mentioned earlier, India has taken other steps to lay the foundation for the type of economic growth that can be fostered only by entrepreneurial activities and appropriate economic policies that reflect individual rights and responsibilities. For example, in recent years India has made several important structural changes, including the construction of telecommunications networks and the implementation of a nationwide road-construction programme (Solomon, 2003). Further, several thousand "new economy" businesses – the types of businesses especially suited for entrepreneurship efforts-were started in 2000 alone.

However, more than just opportunities should lead India to consider entrepreneurial activities as a way to economic growth. At least one major threat, a growing population, also should motivate it to consider entrepreneurial effort as an economic policy. Specifically, the country's population is expected to increase by 110 to 130 million people over the next 10 years, with approximately 80 to 100 million of those new citizens seeking jobs that do not currently exist (Gupta, 2001).

5

Aspects of Community Organizing Groups

Community organizing is a process where people who live in proximity to each other come together into an organization that acts in their shared self-interest. Unlike those who promote more-consensual "community building," community organizers generally assume that social change necessarily involves conflict and social struggle in order to generate collective power for the powerless. A core goal of community organizing is to generate *durable* power for an organization representing the community, allowing it to influence key decision-makers on a range of issues over time. In the ideal, for example, this can get community organizing groups a place at the table *before* important decisions are made. Community organizers work with and develop new local leaders, facilitating coalitions and assisting in the development of campaigns.

COMMON ASPECTS OF COMMUNITY ORGANIZING GROUPS

Organized community groups attempt to influence government, corporations and institutions, seek to increase direct representation within decision-making bodies, and foster social reform more generally. Where negotiations fail, these organizations seek to inform others outside of the organization of the issues being addressed and expose or pressure the decision-makers through a variety of means, including picketing, boycotting, sit-ins, petitioning, and electoral politics. Organizing groups often seek out issues they know will generate controversy and conflict. This allows them to draw in and educate participants, build commitment, and establish a reputation for winning. Thus, community organizing is usually focused on more than just resolving specific issues. In fact, specific issues are often vehicles for other organizational goals as much as they are ends in themselves. Community organizers generally seek to build groups that are democratic in governance, open and accessible to community members, and concerned with the general health of the community rather than a specific interest group.

Organizing seeks to broadly empower community members, with the end goal of distributing power more equally throughout the community. The three basic types of community organizing are grassroots or "door-knocking" organizing, faith-based community organizing (FBCO), and coalition building. Political campaigns often claim that their door-to-door operations are in fact an effort to organize the community, though often these operations are focused exclusively on voter identification and turnout. FBCOs and many grassroots organizing models are built on the work of Saul Alinsky, discussed below, from the 1930s into the 1970s.

Grassroots and "Door-Knocking" Groups

Grassroots organizing builds community groups from scratch, developing new leadership where none existed and organizing the unorganized. It is a values based process where people are brought together to act in the interest of their communities and the common good. Networks of community organizations that employ this method and support local organizing groups include National People's Action and ACORN.

"Door knocking" grassroots organizations like ACORN organize poor and working-class members recruiting members one by one in the community. Because they go door-to-door, they are able to reach beyond established organizations and the "churched" to bring together a wide range of less privileged people. ACORN tended to stress the importance of constant action in order to maintain the commitment of a less rooted group of participants. ACORN had a reputation of being more forceful than faith-based (FBCO) groups, and there are indications that their local groups were more staff (organizer) directed than leader (local volunteer) directed. (However, the same can be said for many forms of organizing, including FBCOs.) The "door-knocking" approach is more time-intensive than the "organization of organizations" approach of FBCOs and requires more organizers who, partly as a result, can be lower paid with more turnover.

Unlike existing FBCO national "umbrella" and other grassroots organizations, ACORN maintained a centralized national agenda, and exerted some centralized control over local organizations. Because ACORN was a 501(c)4 organization under the tax code, it was able to participate directly in election activities, but contributions to it were not tax exempt.

Faith-Based Community Organizing (FBCO)

Faith-based community organizing (FBCO), also known as Congregation-based Community Organizing, is a methodology for developing power and relationships throughout a community of institutions: today mostly congregations, but these can also include unions, neighborhood associations, and other groups. Progressive and centrist FBCO organizations join together around basic values derived from common aspects of their faith instead of around strict dogmas. There are now at least 180 FBCOs in the US as well as in South Africa, England, Germany, and other nations. Local FBCO organizations are often linked through organizing networks such as the Industrial Areas Foundation, Gamaliel Foundation, PICO National Network, and Direct Action and Research Training Center (DART). In the United States starting in 2001, the Bush Administration launched a department to promote community organizing that included faith-based organizing as well other community groups.

FBCOs tend to have mostly middle-class participants because the congregations involved are generally mainline Protestant and Catholic (although "middle-class" can mean different things in white communities and communities of color, which can lead to class tensions within these organizations).

Holiness, Pentecostal, and other related denominations (often "storefront") churches with mostly poor and working-class members tend not to join FBCOs because of their focus on "faith" over "works," among other issues. FBCOs have increasingly expanded outside impoverished areas into churches where middle-class professionals predominate in an effort to expand their power to contest inequality.

Because of their "organization of organizations" approach, FBCOs can organize large numbers of members with a relatively small number of organizers that generally are better paid and more professionalized than those in "door-knocking" groups like ACORN.

FBCOs focus on the long-term development of a culture and common language of organizing and on the development of relational ties between members. They are more stable during fallow periods than grassroots groups because of the continuing existence of member churches.

FBCOs are 501(c)3 organizations. Contributions to them are tax exempt. As a result, while they can conduct campaigns over "issues" they cannot promote the election of specific individuals.

Power vs. Protest

While community organizing groups often engage in protest actions designed to force powerful groups to respond to their demands, protest is only one aspect of the activity of organizing groups. To the extent that groups' actions generate a sense in the larger community that they have "power," they are often able to engage with and influence powerful groups through dialogue, backed up by a history of successful protest-based campaigns. Similar to the way unions gain recognition as the representatives of workers for a particular business, community organizing groups can gain recognition as key representatives of particular communities. In this way, representatives of community organizing groups are often able to bring key government officials or corporate leaders to the table without engaging in "actions" because of their reputation. As Alinsky said, "the first rule of power tactics" is that "power is not only what you have but what the enemy thinks you have." The development of durable "power" and influence is a key aim of community organizing.

"Rights-based" community organizing, in which municipal governments are used to exercise community power, was first experimented with by the Community Environmental Legal Defence Fund (CELDF.org) in Pennsylvania, beginning in 2002. Community groups are organized to influence municipal governments to enact local ordinances. These ordinances challenge preemptive state and federal laws that forbid local governments from prohibiting corporate activities deemed harmful by community residents.

The ordinances are drafted specifically to assert the rights of "human and natural communities," and include provisions that deny the legal concepts of "corporate personhood," and "corporate rights." Since 2006 they have been drafted to include the recognition of legally enforceable rights for "natural communities and ecosystems."

Although this type of community organizing focuses on the adoption of local laws, the intent is to demonstrate the use of governing authority to protect community rights and expose the misuse of governing authority to benefit corporations. As such, the adoption of rights-based municipal ordinances is not a legal strategy, but an organizing strategy. Courts predictably deny the legal authority of municipalities to legislate in defiance of state and federal law. Corporations and government agencies that initiate legal actions to overturn these ordinances have been forced to argue in opposition to the community's right to make governing decisions on issues with harmful and direct local impact.

The first rights-based municipal laws prohibited corporations from monopolizing agriculture (factory farming), and banned corporate waste dumping within municipal jurisdictions. More recent rights-based organizing, in Pennsylvania, New Hampshire, Maine, Virginia and California has prohibited corporate mining, large-scale water withdrawals and chemical trespass.

Political Orientations

Community organizing is not solely the domain of progressive politics, as dozens of fundamentalist organizations are in operation, such as the Christian Coalition. However, the term "community organizing" generally refers to more centrist or progressive organizations, as evidenced, for example, by the reaction against community organizing in the 2008 US presidential election by Republicans and conservatives on the web and elsewhere.

Fundraising

Organizing groups often struggle to find resources. They rarely receive funding from government since their activities often seek to contest government policies. Foundations and others who usually fund service activities generally don't understand what organizing groups do or how they do it, or shy away from their contentious approaches. The constituency of progressive and centrist organizing groups is largely low-or middle-income, so they are generally unable to support themselves through dues. In search of resources, some organizing groups have accepted funding for direct service activities in the past. As noted below, this has frequently led these groups to drop their conflictual organizing activities, in part because these threatened funding for their "service" arms. Recent studies have shown, however, that funding for community organizing can produce large returns on investment ($512 in community benefits to $1 of Needmor funding, according to the Needmor Fund Study, $157 to 1 in New Mexico and $89 to 1 in North Carolina according to National Committee for Responsive Philanthropy studies) through legislation and agreements with corporations, among other sources, not including non-fiscal accomplishments.

HISTORY OF COMMUNITY ORGANIZING IN THE UNITED STATES

Robert Fisher and Peter Romanofsky have grouped the history of "community organizing" (also known as "social agitation") in the United States into four rough periods:

1880 to 1900

People sought to meet the pressures of rapid immigration and industrialization by organizing immigrant neighborhoods in urban centers. Since the emphasis of the reformers was mostly on building community through settlement houses and other service mechanisms, the dominant approach was what Fisher calls social work. During this period The Newsboys Strike provided an early model of youth-led organizing.

1900 to 1940

Community organizing was established distinct from social work, with much energy coming from those critical of capitalist doctrines. Studs Terkel documented community organizing in the depression era, perhaps most notably that of Dorothy Day. Most organizations had a national orientation because the economic problems the nation faced did not seem possible to change at the neighborhood levels.

1940 to 1960

Saul Alinsky, based in Chicago, is credited with originating the term *community organizer* during this time period. Alinsky wrote *Reveille for Radicals*, published in 1946, and *Rules for Radicals*, published in 1971. With these books, Alinsky was the first person in America to codify key strategies and aims of community organizing. He also founded the first national community organizing training network, the Industrial Areas Foundation, now led by one of his former lieutenants, Edward Chambers.

The following quotations from Alinsky's 1946 "Reveille for Radicals" give a good sense of his perspective on organizing and of his public style of engagement:

- *A People's Organization is a conflict group, [and] this must be openly and fully recognized. Its sole reason in coming into being is to wage war against all evils which cause suffering and unhappiness. A People's Organization is the banding together of large numbers of men and women to fight for those rights which insure a decent way of life....*

- *A People's Organization is dedicated to an eternal war. It is a war against poverty, misery, delinquency, disease, injustice, hopelessness, despair, and unhappiness. They are basically the same issues for which nations have gone to war in almost every generation.... War is not an intellectual debate, and in the war against social evils there are no rules of fair play....*
- *A People's Organization lives in a world of hard reality. It lives in the midst of smashing forces, dashing struggles, sweeping cross-currents, ripping passions, conflict, confusion, seeming chaos, the hot and the cold, the squalor and the drama, which people prosaically refer to as life and students describe as "society.*

1960 to present

The American Civil Rights Movement, the anti-war movements, the Chicano movement, the feminist movement, and the gay rights movement all influenced and were influenced by ideas of neighborhood organizing. Experience with federal anti-poverty programs and the upheavals in the cities produced a thoughtful response among activists and theorists in the early 1970s that has informed activities, organizations, strategies and movements through the end of the century. Less dramatically, civic associations and neighborhood block clubs were formed all across the country to foster community spirit and civic duty, as well as provide a social outlet.

Urban Community and Its Effect on Organizing

During these decades, the emergence of an ongoing process of white flight, the ability of middle-class African Americans to move out of majority Black areas, and the professionalization of community organizations into 501(c)3 nonprofits, among other issues, increasingly dissolved the tight ethnic and racial communities that had been so prevalent in urban areas during the first part of the century. As a result, community organizers began to move away from efforts to mobilize existing communities and towards efforts to *create* community, fostering relationships between community members. While community organizers like Alinsky had long worked with churches, these trends led to an increasing focus on congregational organizing during the 1980s, as organizing groups rooted themselves in one of the few remaining broad-based community institutions. This shift also led to an increased focus on relationships among religion, faith, and social struggle.

Emergence of National Organizing Support Organizations

A collection of training and support organizations for national coalitions of mostly locally governed and mostly FBCO community organizing groups were founded in the Alinsky tradition. The Industrial Areas Foundation was the first, created by Alinsky himself in 1940. The other key organizations include ACORN, PICO National Network, Direct Action and Research Training Center, and the Gamaliel Foundation. The role of the organizer in these organizations was "professionalized" to some extent and resources were sought so that being an organizer could be more of a long term career than a relatively brief, mostly unfunded interlude. The training provided by these national "umbrella" organizations helps local volunteer leaders learn a common "language" about organizing while seeking to expand the skills of organizers. The Midwest Academy, based in Chicago, provides week-long training in organizing nationally to organizers and leaders who are not part of these established national organizations. The Center for Third World Organizing provides training focused on "change efforts in communities of color."

The distinction between an "organizer" who staffs a community organization and "leaders" who make decisions and provide the public face of their groups was increasingly standardized over these years, even in many organizations not linked to "umbrella" training groups as the Alinsky tradition became increasingly influential.

Examples of Community Organizers

Many of the most notable leaders in community organizing today emerged from the National Welfare Rights Organization. John Calkins of DART, Ernesto Cortes of the Industrial Areas Foundation, Wade Rathke of ACORN, John Dodds of

Philadelphia Unemployment Project and Mark Splain of the AFL-CIO, among others.

There are many other notable community organizers: Heather Booth, César Chávez, Lois Gibbs, Ella Baker, Huey P. Newton, Mary Harris "Mother" Jones, Martin Luther King, Jr., Ralph Nader, Barack Obama, and Paul Wellstone.

Youth Organizing

More recently has come the emergence of youth organizing groups around the country. These groups use neo-Alinsky strategies while also usually providing social and sometimes material support to less-privileged youth. Most of these groups are created by and directed by youth or former youth organizers.

Barack Obama and the 2008 Presidential Election

Prior to his entry into politics, President Barack Obama worked as an organizer for a Gamaliel Foundation FBCO organization in Chicago. Marshall Ganz, former lieutenant of César Chávez, adapted techniques from community organizing for Obama's 2008 presidential election. At the 2008 Republican National Convention, former New York City mayor Rudolph Giuliani sarcastically mocked Obama's role as a community organizer, asking the crowd "What does a community organizer actually do?", and was answered with resounding applause. This was seconded by the Vice Presidential nominee, Alaska governor Sarah Palin, who stated that her experience as the mayor of Wasilla, Alaska was "sort of like being a community organizer, except that you have actual responsibilities." In response, some progressives, such as Congressman Steve Cohen (D-TN) and liberal pundit Donna Brazile, started saying that "Jesus was a community organizer, Pontius Pilate was a governor", a phrase produced on bumper stickers and elsewhere. Pontius Pilate was the Roman Prefect who ordered the execution of Jesus.

Since Obama's election, the campaign website, formerly part of "Obama for America," has been renamed "Organizing for America," and has been placed under the auspices of the Democratic National Committee (DNC). This rebranded organization promotes the president's legislative agenda items, such as health care reform, which was a key focus of the new "OFA" during 2009, but as an arm of the DNC engages in little that resembles independent "community organizing."

HISTORY OF COMMUNITY ORGANIZING IN THE UNITED KINGDOM

Attempts were made to establish a number of Broad Based Organizations in the UK in the 1990s under the sponsorship of the Citizen Organising Foundation. The first organization to be launched was in Bristol and subsequently organizations were launched in a number of places including The Black Country, Sheffield, Liverpool, and North Wales. Together Creating Communities/Trefnu Cymunedol Cymru in North Wales is the longest established BBO in the UK. The organisations in Sheffield, Liverpool, Bristol and the Black Country did not survive but Manchester Changemakers was formed in 2007. The London based organisation, London Citizens, now encompasses over 160 schools, churches, mosques, trade unions, synagogues and voluntary organisations. It has won over £35 million pounds with the working poor through its Living Wage campaign and successfully ended child detention in the UK for immigration reasons via the Sanctuary pledge campaign.

History of Community Organizing in Australia

Since 2000, active discussion about community organizing had begun in Sydney. A community organizing schools was held in 2005 in Currawong, involving unions, community organizations and religious organizations. In 2007, Amanda Tattersall, a union and community organizer, approached Unions NSW to sponsor the initial stages of a new community organizing coalition called the Sydney Alliance. She had learned about community organizing from interest in coalitions between unions and community organizations, reading Saul Alinsky and spending time with a variety of community organizations in the US and UK.

By November 2007, thirteen organizations had agreed to sponsor the building of an Alliance in Sydney, including the

Uniting Church Synod, the Jewish Board of Deputies and six unions. By November 2008, twenty two organizations had joined, including the Archdiocese of the Catholic Church. But mid-2010 it was 28 organizations. The Sydney Alliance is set to launch in September 2011 and is supporting the establishment of other community organizing coalitions across the country.

What Community Organizing is Not

Understanding what community organizing *is* can be aided by understanding what it *is not* from the perspective of community organizers.

- Activism: Community Organization may or may not include activism.
- Mobilizing: When people "mobilize" they get together to effect a specific social change, but have no long term plan. When the particular campaign that mobilized them is over, these groups dissolve and durable power is not built
- Advocacy: Advocates speak for others instead of trying to get those affected to speak for themselves.
- Social Movements: A broad Social movement often encompasses diverse collections of individual activists, local and national organizations, advocacy groups, multiple and often conflicting spokespersons, and more, held together by relatively common aims but not a common organizational structure. A community organizing group might be *part* of a "movement." Movements generally dissolve when the motivating issue(s) are addressed, although organizations created during movements can continue and shift their focuses.
- Legal Action: Lawyers are often quite important to those engaged in social action. The problem comes when a social action strategy is designed primarily around a lawsuit. When lawyers take the center stage, it can push grassroots struggle into the background, short circuiting the development of collective power and capacity. There are examples where community

organizing groups and legal strategies have worked together well, however, including the Williams v. California lawsuit over inequality in k-12 education.

- Direct Service: Americans today often equate civic engagement with direct service. Organizing groups usually avoid actually providing services, today, however, because history indicates that when they do, organizing for collective power is often left behind. Powerful groups often threaten the "service" wings of organizing groups in an effort to prevent collective action. In the nonprofit world there are many organizations that used to do community organizing but lost this focus in the shift to service.
- Community Development : Consensual community development efforts to improve communities through a range of strategies, usually directed by educated professionals working in government, policy, non-profit, or business organizations, is not community organizing. Community development projects increasingly include a community participation component, and often seek to empower residents of impoverished areas with skills for collaboration and job training, among others. However, community development generally assumes that groups and individuals can work together collaboratively without significant conflict or struggles over power to solve community challenges. One currently popular form is Asset Based Community Development that seeks out existing community strengths.
- Nonpartisan Dialogues About Community Problems: A range of efforts create opportunities for people to meet together and engage in dialogue about community problems. Like community organizing, the effort in contexts like these is generally to be open to a diverse range of opinions, out of which some consensus may be reached. A Study circle is a good example of this. However, beyond the dialogue that also happens inside organizing groups, the focus is on generating a collective and singular "voice" in order to gain power and resources

for the organization's members as well as constituents in the broader community.

Power gained and exerted in community organizing is also not the coercion applied by legal, illegal, physical, or economic means, such as those be applied by banks, syndicates, corporations, governments, or other institutions. Rather, organizing makes use of the voluntary efforts of a community's members acting jointly to achieve an economic or other benefit. As opposed to commercial ventures, gains that result from community organizing automatically accrue to persons in similar circumstances who are not necessarily members, e.g. residents in a geographic area or in a similar socioeconomic status, or persons having conditions or circumstances in common who benefit from gains won by the organizing effort. This may include workers who benefit from a campaign affecting their industry, for example, or persons with disabilities who benefit from gains made in their legal or economic eligibility or status.

6

Minorities Community

MINORITY INFLUENCE

Minority influence is a form of social influence, which takes place when a majority is being influenced to accept the beliefs or behaviour of a minority. Unlike other forms of influence this usually involves a personal shift in private opinion. This personal shift in opinion is called conversion. This type of influence is most likely to take place if the minority is consistent, flexible, and appealing to the majority. Minority influence is a central component of identity politics.

Studies on Minority Influence

Nearly all-early research on minority influence concentrated on the way in which the majority influenced the minority. This was due to the assumption of many psychologists that it would be very hard for the minority to have any influence on the majority.

Moscovici was different, as he believed that it was possible for a minority influence to overcome majority influence. Therefore he conducted his own study on minority influence in 1969. The study was important because it was one of the first studies to show that a minority is able to change the opinions of the majority. It also showed the great importance of consistency within the minority – if influence on the majority is to be achieved. The research of Moscovici and his colleges opened the door to more research on the subject.

FACTORS THAT AFFECT MINORITY INFLUENCE

Moscovici and Nemeth (1974) both argue that a minority of one is more influential than a minority of more than one, as one person is more likely to be consistent over long periods of time and will not divide the majority's attention. On the other hand two people are more likely to be more influential than one as they are less likely to be seen as strange or eccentric. More recent research has supported the latter due to the belief that a minority with two or more, if consistent, has more credibility and is therefore more likely to influence the majority. However large and growing minorities are influential. If the size of the minority doesn't grow, there is a possibility of lone dissenter to change his position. This would affect his consistency and credibility.

Size of Majority

The social impact model (Latané and Wolf. 1981) predicts that as the size of the majority grows the influence of the minority decreases, both in public and in private. Clark and Maass (1990) looked at the interaction between minority influence and majorities of varying sizes. The minority for the study was set at 2 confederates who would be consistent as in Moscovici's study. The majority in Moscovici's study was 4 to a minority of 2. This time the majority was increased to 8 and 12 to the same size minority. The results showed that if in Moscovici's study the majority had gone above 4 there wouldn't have been any evidence of minority influence.

Behavioural Style

Serge Moscovici and Nemeth (1974) argued that minority influence is effective as it is consistent over time and there is agreement among the members of the minority. If this consistency were lost then the minority would lose its credibility. This can become the case if a member of the minority deserts and joins the majority, as this damages the consistency and unity of the minority. After this has taken place members of the majority are less likely to shift their position to that of the minority.

Situational Factors

Some studies have shown that a person's position may affect the level of minority influence they exert. For example someone positioned close to another is more likely to influence the opinion and/or behaviour of that person. Furthermore those positioned at the head of a table will have more influence than another in a less 'important' position.

Non-situational Factors

Moscovici suggested that consistency was the key characteristic of successful minority influence, while Nemeth pointed out that unreasonable consistency has a negative effect on influence. Unreasonable confidence and lack of flexibility have also been pointed out as another factor that has been picked out as a constraint on minority influence.

Group Identification

Maass & Clark (1984) arranged for a group of heterosexual participants to hear a debate on gay rights. The results showed that the majority heterosexual group debating were easier for the heterosexual participants to relate to. Therefore the minority homosexual group had less of an influence. Influence is more likely to occur if the minority (or majority) is part of our 'in-group' as we are more likely to be influenced by those who are like us. This research contradicts with Moscovici's view that deviant minorities (or out-groups) are essential for minority influence to occur. In-group minorities are more likely to be successful, as they are seen as part of the group and therefore their ideas are seen as more acceptable. Out-groups on the other hand are more likely to be discriminated against, as they are not seen as part of the group and therefore they are likely to be seen as strange.

Social Cryptoamnesia

In a group after a number of members have shifted opinion to agree with the minority, that minority becomes a majority. This was named the snowball effect by Van Avermaet (1996), as it is the gradual build up of support that gains momentum. However, minority is a change in personal opinion, while majority influence is only a change of opinion in public – so how can this still be minority influence? This may be due to social cryptoamnesia. It has been observed that major attitude changes take place when the zeitgeist has changed. In history minorities have changed the attitude of society, and the attitude of society changes the personal opinion of the majority in that society. Perez et al. (1995) called this social cryptoamnesia and is due to the innovation of a minority.

Further Research

There is evidence that suggests that it is possible for minority influence and majority influence to work together. A study by Clark (1994) uses a jury setting from the film *12 Angry Men* to investigate social influence. Some of the participants were asked to just read the arguments from one of the characters (who acted as the minority), while the other group were also told how he changed the opinion of the rest of the jury. Social influence was present in both groups, but was stronger in the group that was exposed to both the arguments (minority influence) and the knowledge that the jury conformed (majority influence).

MINORITY GROUP

A minority is a sociological group that does not make up a politically dominant voting majority of the total population of a given society. A sociological minority is not necessarily a numerical minority — it may include any group that is subnormal with respect to a dominant group in terms of social status, education, employment, wealth and political power. To avoid confusion, some writers prefer the terms "subordinate group" and "dominant group" rather than "minority" and "majority", respectively. In socioeconomics, the term "minority" typically refers to a socially subordinate ethnic group (understood in terms of language, nationality, religion and/or culture). Other minority groups include people with disabilities, "economic minorities" (working poor or unemployed), "age minorities" (who are younger or older than a typical working age) and sexual minorities. The term "minority group" often occurs alongside a discourse of civil rights and collective rights which gained prominence in the 20th century. Members of minority groups are prone to different treatment in the countries and societies in which they live. This discrimination may be directly based on an individual's perceived membership of a minority group, without consideration of that individual's personal achievement. It may also occur indirectly, due to social structures that are not equally accessible to all. Activists campaigning on a range of issues may use the language of minority rights, including student rights, consumer rights and animal rights. In recent years, some members of social groups traditionally perceived as dominant have attempted to present themselves as an oppressed minority, such as white, middle-class heterosexual males.

Controversial Issues

Refers to members of minority groups. The term is used to address the controversy with the use of the word minority. Cultural diversity definitions can be as controversial as diversity projects and initiatives. The word minority is an example; it has an academic and colloquial usage. Academics refer to power differences among groups, rather than differences in population size among groups. Barzilai (2003) Feagin (1984) states that a minority group has five characteristics: (1) suffering discrimination and subordination, (2) physical and/or cultural traits that set them apart, and which are disapproved by the dominant group, (3) a shared sense of collective identity and common burdens, (4) socially shared rules about who belongs and who does not determine minority status, and (5) tendency to marry within the group. In South Africa under apartheid, Caucasian-South Africans were a majority even though there were many more black South Africans.

In the United States, the term majority refers to a group that is larger in population size and controls economic, political, and social resources. Given the shift of people of color growing in size that trends indicate will make them a majority, some argue that Caucasian-Americans should no longer be considered the majority. Historically excluded groups (HEGs) is a term that points out the differences among different groups based on the degree of experiencing oppression and domination. The

Feagin defining features are maintained while overcoming the complication with using demographics.

SOCIOLOGY OF MINORITY GROUPS

Sociologist Louis Wirth defined a minority group as "a group of people who, because of their physical or cultural characteristics, are singled out from the others in the society in which they live for differential and unequal treatment, and who therefore regard themselves as objects of collective discrimination." This definition includes both objective and subjective criteria: membership of a minority group is objectively ascribed by society, based on an individual's physical or behavioral characteristics; it is also subjectively applied by its members, who may use their status as the basis of group identity or solidarity. In any case, minority group status is categorical in nature: an individual who exhibits the physical or behavioral characteristics of a given minority group will be accorded the status of that group and be subject to the same treatment as other members of that group.

Racial or Ethnic Minorities

Every large society contains ethnic minorities. Their style of life, language, culture and origin can differ from the majority. The minority status is conditioned not only by a clearly numerical relations but also by questions of political power. In some places, subordinate ethnic groups may constitute a numerical majority, such as e.g. Blacks in South Africa under apartheid. In addition to the "traditional" (long time resident) minorities they may be migrant, indigenous or landless nomadic communities. There is no legal definition of national (ethnic) minorities in international law. Only in Europe is this exact definition (probably) provided by the European Charter for Regional or Minority Languages and by the Recommendation 1201 (1993) of the Parliamentary Assembly of the Council of Europe. However, national minority can be theoretically (not legally) defined as a group of people within a given national state:

1. which is numerically smaller than the rest of population of the state or a part of the state

2. which is not in a dominant position
3. which has culture, language, religion, race etc. distinct from that of the rest of the population
4. whose members have a will to preserve their specificity
5. whose members are citizens of the state where they have the status of a minority.
6. which have a long-term presence on the territory where it has lived.

International criminal law can protect the rights of racial or ethnic minorities in a number of ways. The right to self-determination is a key issue. The formal level of protection of national (ethnic) minorities is highest in European countries.

Gender and Sexuality Minorities

An understanding of lesbian, gay, bisexual and transgender people as a minority group or groups has gained prominence in the Western world since the 19th century. The abbreviation LGBT is currently used to group these identities together. The term queer is sometimes understood as an umbrella term for all non-normative sexualities and gender expressions, but does not always seek to be understood as a minority; rather, as with many Gay Liberationists of the 1960s and '70s, it sometimes represents an attempt to uncover and embrace the sexual diversity in everyone.

While in most societies, numbers of men and women are roughly equal, the status of women as a "subordinate" group has led some (i.e. the feminist and Women's Rights movements) to equate them with minorities. In addition, various gender variant people can be seen as constituting a minority group or groups, such as intersexuals, transsexuals, and gender nonconformists (i.e. metrosexuals) — especially when such phenomena are understood as intrinsic characteristics of an identifiable group.

Religious Minorities

Persons belonging to religious minorities have a faith which is different from that held by the majority. Most countries of the world have religious minorities. It is now widely accepted in the west that people should have the freedom to choose their own religion, including not having any religion (atheism or agnosticism), and including the right to convert from one religion to another. However in many countries this freedom is constricted. For example in Egypt, a new system of identity cards requires all citizens to state their religion-and the only choices are Islam, Christianity or Judaism.

A 2006 study suggests that atheists constitute a religious minority in the United States, with researchers concluding: "Americans rate atheists below Muslims, recent immigrants, gays and lesbians and other minority groups in 'sharing their vision of American society.' Atheists are also the minority group most Americans are least willing to allow their children to marry."

Age Minorities

The elderly, while traditionally influential or even (in a gerontocracy) dominant in the past, have in the modern age usually been reduced to the minority role of economically 'non-active' groups. Children can also be understood as a minority group in these terms, and the discrimination faced by the young is known as adultism. Discrimination against the elderly is known as ageism.

Various local and international statutes are in place to mitigate the exploitation of children, such as the Convention on the Rights of the Child, as well as a number of organizations that make up the children's rights movement. The youth rights movement campaigns for social empowerment for young people, and against the legal and social restrictions placed on legal minors. Groups that advocate the interests of senior citizens range from the charitable (Help the Aged) to grass-roots activism (Gray Panthers), and often overlap with disability rights issues.

Disabled Minorities

The Disability rights movement has contributed to an understanding of disabled people as a minority or a coalition of minorities who are disadvantaged by society, not just as people who are disadvantaged by their impairments. Advocates of disability rights emphasise difference in physical or psychological functioning, rather than inferiority — for example, some people with autism argue for acceptance of neurodiversity, much as opponents of racism argue for acceptance of ethnic diversity. The Deaf community is often regarded as a linguistic and cultural minority rather than a disabled group, and many Deaf people do not see themselves as disabled at all. Rather, they are disadvantaged by technologies and social institutions that are designed to cater for the dominant group.

MINORITIES IN LAW AND GOVERNMENT

In the politics of some countries, a minority is an ethnic group that is recognized as such by respective laws of its country and therefore has some rights that other groups lack. Speakers of a legally-recognized minority language, for instance, might have the right to education or communication with the government in their mother tongue. Countries that have special provisions for minorities include Canada, China, Ethiopia, Germany, India, the Netherlands, Poland, Romania, Russia, the United Kingdom. Differing minority groups often are not given identical treatment.

Some groups are too small or too indistinct compared to the majority, that they either identify as part of the same nation as the members of the majority, or they identify as a separate nation but are ignored by the majority because of the costs or some other aspect of providing preferences. For example, a member of a particularly small ethnic group might be forced to check "Other" on a checklist of different backgrounds, and consequently might receive fewer privileges than a member of a more defined group. Many contemporary governments prefer to assume the people they rule all belong to the same nationality rather than separate ones based on ethnicity.

The United States asks for race and ethnicity on its official census forms, which thus breaks up and organizes its population into different sub-groups, but primarily on racial origin rather than national one. Spain does not divide its nationals by ethnic group, although it does maintain an official notion of minority languages. Some minorities are so relatively large or historically or otherwise important that the system is set up in a way to guarantee them comprehensive protection and political representation.

As an example, the former Yugoslav republic of Bosnia and Herzegovina recognizes the three main nations, none of which constitute a numerical majority, as constitutive nations, see nations of Bosnia and Herzegovina. However, other minorities such as Roma and Jews, are officially labelled as "others" and are excluded from many of these protections-for example they may not be elected to a range of high political positions including the presidency. The issue of establishing minority groups, and determining the extent of privileges they might derive from their status, is controversial.

There are some who argue that minorities are owed special recognition and rights, while others feel that minorities are unjustified in demanding special rights, as this amounts to preferential discrimination and could hamper the ability of the minority to integrate itself into mainstream society-perhaps to the point at which the minority follows a path to separatism or supremacism. In Canada, some feel that the failure of the dominant English-speaking majority to integrate French Canadians has given rise to Quebec separatism.

Affirmative Action

One particularly controversial issue is affirmative action. This can be, for example, a government program to provide immigrant or minority groups who primarily speak a marginalized language with extra teaching in the majority language, so that they are better able to compete for places at university or for jobs.

These may be considered necessary because the minority group in question is socially disadvantaged. Another form of affirmative action is quotas, where a percentage of places at university, or in employment in public services, are set aside for minority groups because a court has found that there has been a history of exclusion as it pertains to certain groups in certain sectors of society.

Views on Minorities from Objectivists

Adherents of Ayn Rand's laissez-faire philosophy of Objectivism regard people — every person — as an independent, sovereign entity who possesses an inalienable right to his/her own life, a right derived from his/her nature as a rational being. Objectivism holds that a civilized society, or any form of association, cooperation or peaceful coexistence among people, can be achieved only on the basis of the recognition of individual rights — and that a group, as such, has no rights other than the individual rights of its members. The principle of individual rights is the only moral base of all groups or associations. Since only an individual person can possess rights, the expression "individual rights" is a redundancy (which one has to use for purposes of clarification in today's intellectual chaos), but the expression "collective rights" is a contradiction in terms. Individual rights are not subject to a public vote; a majority has no right to vote away the rights of a minority; the political function of rights is precisely to protect minorities from oppression by majorities (and the smallest minority on earth is the individual).

MINORITY RELIGION

A minority religion is a religion held by a minority of the population of a country, state, or region. Minority religions may be subject to stigma or discrimination. An example of a stigma is using the term cult with its extremely negative connotations for certain new religious movements. People who belong to a minority religion may be subject to discrimination and prejudice, especially when the religious differences correlate with ethnic differences. Laws are made in some countries to protect the rights of religious minorities, such as protecting the minorities' culture and to promote harmony with the majority.

MINORITY RIGHTS

The term Minority Rights embodies two separate concepts: first, normal individual rights as applied to members of racial, ethnic, class, religious, linguistic or sexual minorities, and second, collective rights accorded to minority groups. The term may also apply simply to individual rights of anyone who is not part of a majority decision. Civil rights movements often seek to ensure that individual rights are not denied on the basis of membership in a minority group. There are many political bodies which also feature minority group rights. This might be seen in affirmative action quotas, or in guaranteed minority representation in a consociational state.

MINORITY RIGHTS IN NATIONAL AND INTERNATIONAL LAW

The first minority rights were created by revolutionary Parliament of Hungary in 1849. Minority rights, as applying to ethnic, religious or linguistic minorities and indigenous peoples, are an integral part of international human rights law. Like children's rights, women's rights and refugee rights, minority rights are a legal framework designed to ensure that a specific group which is in a vulnerable, disadvantaged or marginalised position in society, is able to achieve equality and is protected from persecution. The first post-war international treaty to protect minorities, designed to protect them from the greatest threat to their existence, was the U.N. Convention on the Prevention and Punishment of the Crime of Genocide.

Subsequent human rights standards that codify minority rights include the International Covenant on Civil and Political Rights (Article 27), the United Nations Declaration on the Rights of Persons Belonging to National or Ethnic, Religious and Linguistic Minorities, two Council of Europe treaties (the Framework Convention for the Protection of National Minorities and the European Charter for Regional or Minority Languages, and the OSCE Copenhagen Document of 1990.

Minority rights cover protection of existence, protection from discrimination and persecution, protection and promotion of identity, and participation in political life. For the rights of LGBT, The Yogyakarta Principles have been approved by the United Nations Human Rights Council and for the rights of persons with disabilities, the Convention on the Rights of Persons with Disabilities was adopted by United Nations General Assembly. To protect minority rights, many countries have specific laws and/or commissions or ombudsman institutions (for example the Hungarian Parliamentary Commissioner for National and Ethnic Minorities Rights).

While initially, the United Nations treated indigenous peoples as a sub-category of minorities, there is an expanding body of international law specifically devoted to them, in particular Convention 169 of the International Labour Organization and the UN Declaration on the Rights of Indigenous Peoples (adopted 14 September 2007). Attempts to codify the rights of sexual minorities in international human rights law have met with strong opposition from a number of member states of the United Nations.

National Minorities in the Law of the EC/EU

The direct role of the European Union (and also the Law of the EU/EC) in the area of protection of national minorities is still very limited (likewise the general protection of human rights). The EU has relied on general international law and a European regional system of international law (based on the Council of Europe, OSCE etc.). and in a case of necessity accepted their norms. But the "de-economisation of European integration", which started in 1990s is changing this situation. The political relevance of national minorities´ protection is very high. Now (2009) although a protection of the national minorities has not become a generally accepted legally binding principle of the EU, in several legal acts issues of national minorities are mentioned. In external relations protection of national minorities became one of the main criteria for cooperation with the EU or accession.

THE INDIVIDUAL: THE SMALLEST MINORITY ON EARTH

Ayn Rand, philosopher of Objectivism asserted that a group, as such, has no rights. A man can neither acquire new rights by joining a group nor lose the rights which he does possess. The principle of individual rights is the only moral base of all groups or associations. She maintained that since only an individual man can possess rights, the expression "individual rights" is a redundancy, but the expression "collective rights" is a contradiction in terms. Individual rights are not subject to a public vote; a majority has no right to vote away the rights of a minority; the political function of rights is precisely to protect minorities from oppression by majorities (and the smallest minority on earth is the individual).

MINORITY STATUS AND THE INDIVIDUAL

The term *minority group* and its opposite, *majority group,* have been widely used both among social scientists and the general public in recent decades. In social scientific (and often popular) use of these terms, they do not usually refer per se to a numerical minority or majority. Rather, the social-scientific meaning of a minority group is a group that is assigned an inferior status in society, one that enjoys less than its proportionate share of scarce resources. Frequently, minority group members are discriminated against, and in some cases they are severely and systematically exploited for economic gain by the majority group, as illustrated in U.S. history by enslavement of African-Americans and by the taking of land from American Indians and from Mexicans who settled in what became the U.S. Southwest.

Usually, a minority group is defined on the basis of a relatively permanent and unchanging status and on the basis of being different—often visibly—from the majority group. This definition includes minorities based on ascribed statuses such as race, ethnicity, and gender and other statuses that are difficult or impossible to change, such as sexual orientation and disability. It also includes groups with common identities that are deeply held and relatively unlikely to change, most commonly religious or linguistic groups. When minority status is assigned on the basis of race or ethnicity, it often involves groups that have been conquered or colonized in the past, as is the case, in the United States, of African-Americans, Mexican-Americans and Puerto Ricans, and American Indians. In these instances, the degree of subordination experienced by the groups tends to be particularly intense. It is notable, for example, that the present and historic status of the four aforementioned groups is significantly more disadvantaged than that of most immigrant groups in the United States. For all types of minority groups, it is typically true that (1) the group is different in some way that is regarded as socially significant from those who hold the dominant influence in society, and (2) on the basis of that difference the group is assigned to a subordinate or disadvantaged status.

A CRITICAL ANALYSIS

It would be proper at the outset, to pose a question as to who are the inheritors or scions of right under Article 301 of the Indian Constitution. It is a sad commentary on our constitution that it nowhere defines minority nor does it prescribe sufficient guidelines to determine a group as minority. Perhaps the founding fathers of our constitution and member of Constituent Assembly presumably left it to the wisdom of the cauldron of Courts of Law to supply the omission. It was believed that, in the claptrap of the democracy, if we don't solve a problem it will go away. Indeed it has been the practice to ignore the problem if we do not solve it. The next step is to create division so as to sow the confusion and hope that the problem will be forgotten. If the problem remains and the majority refuses to sell their dreams for peaces of silver or get lost in the maze, then the negotiations start and a trade-off is set up. Why it cannot be done in the first, the answer lies in the escapism that we all feel is a valid exercise.

That expression 'minority' needs to be discussed in details in order to pierce the miasma of confusion and misunderstanding. The expression "minority" has been derived from the Latin word "minor" and the suffix 'ity', which means "small in number". According to Encyclopedia Britannica minorities means "group held together by ties of common descent, language or religious faith and feeling different in these respects from the inhabitants of a given political entity". J.A Laponce in his book "the protection to minority" describes "minority" as a group of persons having different race, language, or religion from that of majority of inhabitants. In the Year Book of Human Rights (U.N Publication 1950 edition) minority has been described as nondominant group having different religious or linguistic traditions than the majority population2. The U.N Sub commission on Prevention of discrimination of minorities has defined minority as under:

The term 'minority' includes only those non-documents group of the population which possess and wish to preserve stable ethnic, religious or linguistic traditions or characteristics markedly different from those of the rest of the population;

Such minorities should properly include the number of persons sufficient by themselves to preserve such traditions or characteristics; and Such minorities should be loyal to the state of which they nationals Before making further attempt at giving answers to the questions, it is desirable to delineate article 29 & 30 of the Constitution of India, which are relevant subject matter for the purpose of this paper. The purpose of creating minorities stems from Article 29 and 30 which guarantees minorities the following privileges.

Article 29:

(1) any section of the citizen residing in the territory of India or any part thereof having a distinct language, script or culture of his own shall have right to conserve the same.

(2) No citizen shall be denied admission into any educational institution maintained by the state or receiving aid out of state funds on grounds any of religion, race, caste, language or any of them.

Article 30:

(1) All minorities whether based on religion or language shall have the right to establish and administer educational institution of their choice. 1(a) in making any law providing for the compulsory acquisition of any property of an educational institution established and administered by a minority. Referred to in clause (1), the state shall insure that the amount fixed by or determined under such law for the acquisition of such property is such as would not restrict or abrogate the right guaranteed under that is under the management of a minority whether based on religion or language. From the thorough perusal of the Constitution of India it was found that the expression "minorities" has been employed only at four places in the constitution of India. Head note of Article 29 uses the word minorities.. Then again the expression minorities or minority has been employed in head note of article 30 and Sub-

clauses (1) & (2) of article 30. At this stage it may be noted that the expression" minorities" has been used in Article 30 in two senses-one based on religion and other on the basis of language.

But the question arises regarding what is the test to determine minority status base4d on religion or language of a group of persons residing in state or union territory. The question on definition of minorities arose for the first time in the case of Kerala Education Bill case 1959 SCR at page 995 held " the existence of a minority community should in all circumstances and for purposes of all law of that state be determined on the basis of the population of the whole state or whether it should be determined on the state basis only when the validity of law extending to whole state is in question or it should be determined on the basis of the population of a particular locality, for the bill in practice before us extends to the whole of state of Kerala and consequently the minority must be determined by reference to the entire state. By this test Christians, Muslims and Anglo-Indians will certainly be minorities in the state of Kerala." In addition to the Kerala Education Bill (supra) it has been settled by catena of decisions of the Hon'ble Supreme Court in Rev Sidhajbhai& Others vs. State of Bombay & Others [(1963) (3) SCR 837], the ahmedabad St Xavier's college society and others vs. state of Gujarat [1975(1) scr 1973] and st Stephens college [1992(1) scc 558]; that a minority means a non dominant group. It is a relative term and is referred to, to represent the smaller of the two numbers; section or group called majority. In that sense there may be political minority, religious minority or linguistic minority.

CATEGORIES OF MINORITIES ·

In India minorities can be broadly classified as:

Religious Minorities

According to the Central government there are 5 noted religious minorities viz Muslims, Christians, Sikhs, Buddhists and Zoroastrians (Parsis). 10 These 5 communities constitute 17%3 of the country's population. At this juncture it's imperative to question the basis of this division. Just because our

Constitution making were of the opinion that Hindus are in majority therefore other religions should be labelled as minorities or it was the policy of appeasing the Muslims who were left in India after the creation of Pakistan, and because other communities would not have kept silent so this pacification process started.

This lack of proper base has extended its arms in today's scenario that also can be glanced with the statement of MR.A.R.Antulay, Minister for minority affairs that Jains should also be given status of minority. But in Jain community though opinion is quite divided among various sects4, but by a large community leaders think that the centre is acting in haste and they call it a political ploy. "We are a separate as believers of a religion but as a community we are Hindus only. This is a ploy to divide hi8ndus and jains and nothing else". Others give the argument as "Hindus are not in minority and thus there is no question of jains accepting the minority status" History always repeats itself, the player's change but the essence remains the same. Way back in 1952, it was the policy of pacification and establishment of congress party as the dominant one that triggered the debate and today it is the policy of vote bank initiated by a newly created ministry that is trying hard to include Jainism also as one of the minority community.

Linguistic Minority

According to the 38th report of National Commission of linguistic Minority (NCLM) "In each state there is a language which is spoken by the majority of the residents of that state. All others who do not speak that language belong to linguistic minority." According to Kerela education Case referred earlier minority has to be defined on the basis of state. Considering this fact Bengali, Punjabi, Malayalam, Sindhi, Tamil, Telgu and Marathi are linguistic minority in the union territory of Delhi. 5 There is anachronism in the definition of linguistic minority also. To put it simply, if five Maharastrians get together and start a Marathi medium school in Mumbai it will not be treated as a minority institution. But if five gujratis get together and start a Marathi medium school in Mumbai it will be treated as a minority school!

CONSTITUTIONAL SAFEGUARDS

In addition to Constitutional safeguards of Article 29 and 30 mentioned earlier, following the reorganization of the states on the linguistic basis, there emerged some safeguards on consensual basis for linguistic minorities. These were called consensual safe guards and were as listed under:

1) Translation and publication of important rules, regulations, notes etc into all languages, which are spoken by at least 15% of the total population at district or sub district level.
2) Declaration of minority languages as second official language in district where persons speaking such languages constitute at least 60% of the population.
3) Receipt of and reply to, representations in minority languages.
4) Institution through mother tongue of minority languages at the primary age of education;
5) Institution through secondary languages the secondary stage of education.
6) Linguistic minority pupils, and inter-school adjustments.
7) Provision for textbooks and teachers in minority languages.
8) Implementation of three languages formula.
9) No insistence upon knowledge of state's official language at the time of recruitment.
10) Issue of pamphlets in minority languages detailing safeguards available to linguistic minorities.
11) Setting up of proper machinery at the state and district levels.

A more meticulous perusal of Article 30 makes it clear that it is the progeny of pseudo secularists and a deliberately designed legal contraption to appease the minority, underneath, which flows vicious current of divisive politics of vote bank. A more pertinent question is what prevents the minority from establishing their educational institutions. The Constitution is unambiguous about it. The futility of Article 30 becomes obvious when we take into consideration article 14, 15, 16 and Article 19. It says the state shall not deny equality before the laws or the equal protection of laws within the territory of India. Article 15 explains this fundamental guarantee.

It lays the state shall not discriminate against on groups only on religion, race, class, sex, place of birth or any of them." Article 16 further adds "There is opportunity for all citizens in matter relating to employment or appointment, to any office under the state and there will be no discrimination in this respect. Article 19 gives a fundamental right to establish educational institutions and unions. Are not minorities included in "all"? Do they not form association of educational institutions? Where is the obstacle? Where is the hindrance? Where is the constraint? In short Article 30 in our Constitution is unnecessary because ample guarantees are given to all in different articles of our Constitution.

MINORITY EDUCATIONAL INSTITUTIONS

Minority educational institution means an institution established and administered by a minority having the right to do so under clause of article 30 of the constitution. Following conditions are laid down for grant of recognition to minority educational institutions: Following conditions are laid down for grant of recognition to minority educational institution:

i. The aims and objectives of the educational agency incorporated in its bylaws should be clearly specified that it is meant to primarily serve the interests of the minority community to which it belongs.

ii. The minority educational institution shall not compel any of its religious activities.

iii. The minority educational institution shall observe general laws of the land relating to educational institutions.

iv. The minority educational institution will not use its privilege as minority institution for any pecuniary benefit.

v. The minority educational institution shall charge the fees as prescribed by competent authority.

vi. The minority educational institution shall appoint teachers as per qualifications laid down by the authority concerned but it will be advisable for them to select teachers and other employees through emplayment exchange or open advertisement.

vii. In all academic, administrative and financial matters rules and regulations laid down by respective statutory authorities from time to time shall be wholly applicable to these institutions.

viii. The minority educational institution shall do nothing, which may come in the way of communal and social harmony.

ix. Fifty percent of seats permitted to be filled up from minority communities shall be equally distributed between free and payment seats.

There are separate rules for recognition of linguistic minority institutions the criteria being:

1) Institutes conducting definable and verifiable activity for promotion of minorities

2) Minority language is taught as a language subject of study

3) Minority language is the medium of instruction.

It would be pertinent to define terminologies used here for understanding the clear meaning of the following terms:

Recognized – means an institution recognized by an appropriate authority where 'appropriate authority' can be defined as administrator or any other officer authorized by central or state government.

Aid – means any aid granted to a recognized school by the central government, administrator, a local authority or any other authority designated by the central government or administrator of a local authority.

Aided schools or colleges – means a recognized school or

college which is receiving aid in the form of maintenance grant from the central government, administrator or local authority or any other authority designated by the central government, administrator or a local authority.

Unaided schools or colleges – means a recognized school or college, which does not receive any aid. In terms of government regulations also, there is difference between aided and unaided institutions:

1) State can't impose its reservation policy on minority and non-minority on unaided private colleges including professional colleges.
2) Up to the level of undergraduate education, the minority unaided educational institution enjoys total freedom.
3) However, different considerations would apply for graduate and postgraduate level of education as also for technical and professional educational institution i.e. such education cannot be imparted by any institution unless recognized or affiliated by any competent authority created by law such as university, board, central or state government or alike.

Regulatory Bodies Involved

National Commission for Minority Educational Institution. An ordinance was promulgated on 11 November 2004, to enable setting up of a National Commission for minority educational institutions to advise the central government or any state government on any question regarding the regarding the education of minorities, to look into the complaints regarding violation of the rights of the minorities, to establish and administer educational institution of their choice.

Functions of the Commission

(a) Advised the Central Government or any State Government on any question relating to the education of minorities that may be referred to it;
(b) Look into specific complaints regarding deprivation or violation of rights of minorities to establish and administer educational institutions of their choice and

any dispute relating affiliation to a Scheduled University and report its findings to the Central Government for its implementation; and

(c) To do such other acts and things as may be necessary, incidental or conducive to the attainment of all or any of the objects of the Commission.

This commission also decides on all questions relating to the status of any institution as a minority educational institution.

PROCEDURE FOR ESTABLISHING A MINORITY EDUCATIONAL INSTITUTION

To establish and educational institution by minorities first a society needs to be formed under Societies Registration Act, 1860 comprising minimum of 3 members, designating within themselves posts of Chairman, Director, Treasurer etc. They contribute their own funds or funds through 'chanda' process to establish an educational institution after which comes process of recognition.

Talking about schools, through the application form attached the school applies to the Directorate of Education of the particular state.

Conditions for recognition—No private school shall be recognized, or continue to be recognized, by the appropriate authority unless the school fulfils the following conditions:

1) The school is run by a society registered under the Societies Registration Act, 1860 (21 of 1860), or a public trust constituted under any law for the time being force and is managed in accordance with a scheme of management made under these rules;
2) Subject to the provisions of clause (1) of article 30 of the Constitution of India, the schools serves a real need of the locality and is not likely to affect adversely the enrolment in a nearby school which has already been recognized by the appropriate authority;
3) The school follows approved courses of instruction as provided elsewhere in these rules;

4) The school is not run for profit to any individual, group of association of individual or any other person;
5) Admission to the school is open to all without any discrimination based on religion, caste, race, place of birth or any of them;
6) The managing committee observes the provisions of the Act and the rules made there under;

Grant in-aid

Institutions can choose to be self financed and those who want aid can fill up a form. Aid is given after inspection by the inspector for authorized infrastructure and satisfactory report about infrastructure, buildings, and libraries of these schools. Aid generally comprise of 95% of the teaching staff's salary. The conditions for grant in-aid are following:

1) A permanent income, whether from endowments or other sources (excluding fees and the Pupils Funds) which, when supplemented by grant in aid, shall be adequate to discharge it's obligations under the act and enable it to carry on it's work efficiently;
2) A reserve fund of an amount which shall not be less than the amount indicating or the amount specified by rules and regulations of the Affiliating Board, which ever is higher: Provided that the amount specified shall be subject to review, every five years, by the Advisory Board;
3) The reserve fund shall be the property of the school, shall be maintained in its name and shall be kept deposited in a scheduled bank or a nationalized bank or a post office and such account shall ordinarily be operated jointly by the Director or any officer authorized by him in this behalf and the manager of the school; Provided that where it is urgently necessary to draw any money from the reserve fund to meet any emergent expenditure or to meet the salary and allowance of the employees of the school in the event of the omission or failure of the managing committee to discharge the

obligations imposed upon it by sub-section (2) of section 10, the account may be operated by the Director alone.

Up to this, procedure is same for both the minority as well as the non-minority institution. In order to get minority status, government in Southern States Kerela, Karnataka etc. issue an application form related to minority status also. After filling up of this form and inspection by the govt., the state govt. issues certificate of recognition as minority institution. This process may happen simultaneously with the process of recognition. But in Delhi this process does not exist. According to ADE Delhi miss. Abha Joshi "govt. does not recognize any institution as minority institution" but she failed to provide information that in other states it does exist, giving one the impression as if minority institutions are nowhere certified as minority institution in India. Certificate of minority institute needs to be issued within 30 days of making an application, otherwise reason for non-compliance have to be cited.

Regulations

It is necessary to analyse the Supreme Court pronouncements on regulations on reservation and admissions in educational institutions In view of the 42nd amendment to the constitution, the subject of education was transferred to the concurrent list from the state list under the 7th schedule of the constitution, the question of who would be regarded as minority was required to be considered. It was urgent because the earlier case law related to the pre amendment period, when education was in the state list. The latest exercise is the judgment of 11-member bench of Supreme Court on October 31st in the T.M.A PAI Foundation vs. State of Karnataka [2002 SCC (8) 481], which inter alia laid down that:

1) Religious and linguistic minorities under article 30 have to be considered state wise
2) Article 30 (1) include the right to establish and administer even professional educational institutions
3) There would be minimal regulatory measures to ensure educational standards and to maintain excellence of minority educational institutions

4) That the procedure and method of admissions as well as selection of students must be fair and transparent.
5) That minority educational institution should be able o raise reasonable surplus to meet the cost of expansion and augmentation of facilities without resorting to capitation fee or profiteering.
6) And that al citizens have the right to establish and administer educational under article 19(1) g and 26, but the right is subject to the provisions of article 19 (6) and 26 a whereas the right of minority educational institution stems from article 30(1)

The effect of the judgment by the 11-member bench is that a centralized counseling and single window system will no longer do admissions, and the government for all types of colleges would fix the fee structure. As government puts it, the following shall be applicable for admissions to minority educational institutions

Following guidelines shall be applicable for admission to minority educational institutions:

i. Admissions shall be made by merit on the basis of Common Entrance Test to be conducted by competent authority.
ii. Fifty percent of the total sanctioned seats in a course shall be filled from the candidates of other communities.
iii. The remaining 50% seats shall be filled from candidates belonging to minority community by merit on the basis of Common Entrance Test.
iv. Fifty percent seats earmarked for minority community and other communities shall be distributed equally in free seats and payment seats and will be filled by merit.
v. All reservations of seats as prescribed by competent authority shall also be applicable to free seats available to minority communities.
vi. Any seat remaining unfilled in the minority quota shall be filled from candidates of other communities.

vii. All admissions shall be made on the basis of merit as per the Common Entrance Test held by competent authority. No admission outside the merit list shall be allowed until and unless competent authority allows doing so.

Minority Educational Institutions

Privileges to minority institutions also stems from the judgment delivered from the Supreme Court:

1) A minority educational institution would continue to be so whether the government declared it as such or not (n.ammad vs. manager, emjay high school and others)
2) Minority educational institutions do not have to reserve seats for SCs, ST's or OBCs, as required to be done by other educational institutions.
3) Minority educational institutions can reserve up to 50% of the seats for students of their own community.
4) In term of control over employees, minority educational institutions have much greater powers than other institutions. For instance, in the selection of teachers and principles the minority educational institution can have a selection committee, which does not include the university representative. Similarly, while in ordinary schools the headmasters normally have to be appointed on the basis of seniority; minority managements can select a headmaster of their choice.
5) NCMEI amendment bill provides for the right to establish a minority educational institution and also provides that wherever 'no objection certificate' for establishing a minority educational institution is either not granted within a period of 60 days or where a decision in this regard is not communicated within such a period, the MEI would proceed with the establishment of the institution as if the 'no objection certificate' has been granted to it.
6) MEI can seek affiliation to any of six universities listed in the schedule.

Financial Assistance: As mentioned earlier a minority institution can be self-financed as well as government aided. There are other organizations also which provide financial assistance to minority institution.

National Minorities Development Finance Corporation (NMDFC) was set up by the Government of India to provide a "special focus to economic development of minorities". The people belonging to five communities i.e. Muslims, Christians, Sikhs, Buddhists & Parsis have been notified as minorities under the National Commission for Minorities Act, 1992. The prime mandate of NMDFC has been to provide concessional finance to the minorities living below double the poverty line for self-employment. NMDFC functions under the administrative control of the Ministry of Social Justice & Empowerment, Government of India. The authorized share capital of NMDFC is Rs. 500 crores. The paid up share capital (till 31/03/2003) was Rs. 318.21 crores, of which Rs. 258.42 crores has been contributed by the Government of India and Rs. 59.79 crores by various state governments as well as union territory administrations.

MAULANA AZAD EDUCATION FOUNDATION

Maulana Azad Education Foundation is a voluntary, non-political, non-profit making organisation established to promote education amongst the educationally backward minorities. The Maulana Azad Education Foundation was established in July, 1989 as a society under the Societies Registration Act, 1960 and it is fully funded by the Ministry of Social Justice & Empowerment, Government of India. Presently the Foundation has a Corpus Fund of Rs.70.01 crore. The Hon'ble Minister for Social Justice & Empowerment is ex-officio President of the Foundation. The aim of the Foundation is to formulate and implement educational schemes and plans for the benefit of the educationally backward minorities in particular and weaker sections in general. The Foundation is providing financial assistance to NGOs for various educational activities. At present, the Maulana Azad Education Foundation is providing grant-in-aid to NGOs under following Schemes:-

i. Financial assistance for establishment/expansion of schools/residential schools/colleges,

ii. Financial assistance for purchase of lab equipments and furniture etc.

iii. Financial assistance for setting-up/strengthening of Vocational/Technical Training Centres/Institutes,

iv. Financial assistance for construction of hostel buildings,

v. Financial assistance for Remedial Coaching,

Achievements: Up to 31st March 2003, the Foundation has assisted 474 NGOs with a grant of Rs.64.68 crore, since inception. Apart from this, the Foundation arranges training programme for teachers of the Institutions assisted by the Foundation. The Foundation has provided free training to more than 3000 girls, till now, at the Vocational Training Centres run by the Foundation in collaboration with South Delhi Polytechnic at Ajmeri Gate, Delhi in the following trades: Cutting & Tailoring, Textile Designing, Beauty Culture, Arts & Crafts & Computers.

Wakf Board

The grant-in-aid received by the Central Wakf Council is forwarded to the loanee Wakf in the form of interest free loans for the Development of Urban Wakf Properties while the Council bears the entire expenditure on the staff working in the Scheme as well as other expenses on paper, postage etc. Against this service rendered by the Council, it puts two conditions on the loanee Wakf institutions i.e.

(i) they would pay 6% donation on the outstanding loan to the Education Fund for the Educational Scheme of the Council meant for educational upliftment of the poor Muslims;

(ii) after the repayment of the loan, they would spend 40% of their enhanced income on the education of the Muslims particularly on the technical educations.

The 6% donation received from loanee Wakfs on the outstanding, as well as the interest accrued on the Bank deposits of the Revolving Fund form the Education Fund of the Council.

This Fund is utilized for implementing the following programmes:

i) Scholarship to the poor student pursuing Technical/ Professional Degree Courses @ Rs. 8,000/-per annum, during the course period.

ii) Adhoc grant to poor and needy students of General degree courses @ Rs. 3,500/-

iii) Matching Grant to the State Wakf Boards for providing scholarship in their respective States to the School students, Madrasa students and to the students doing Technical/Professional Diploma Courses.

iv) Grant for the establishment of I.T.Is. in the Muslim concentrated areas.

v) Financial assistance to Voluntary Organizations for Vocational Training Centres.

vi) Financial assistance to Libraries for developing Book Bank.

Up to Jan 31, 2006, the Council has issued a total of 10,802 scholarships to the students of Technical Degree courses like MBBS, BUMS, BAMS, B.Tech and B.Sc. (Ag) etc. Similarly in 3766 cases "Ad-hoc" grant have been given under the scheme of Ad-hoc Grant to Poor and Needy Students. 600 Voluntary Organizations/Technical Institutes have been assisted for technical training/vocational training. Under the scheme for setting of I.T.Is., up to Jan 31, 2006 the Central Wakf Council has approved eleven I.T.Is. in the Muslim concentrated areas.

EXCEPTION TO MINORITY INSTITUTIONS

Aligarh Muslim University

The case of Aligarh Muslim University is a very good example of an exception to the common rule applied to minority institutions. The AMU was set up through an act of the legislature. It is primarily because of this fact that there is such a big controversy regarding the status of AMU though it was already settled by the Hon'ble Supreme Court in the case of Azeez Basha vs Union of India (AIR 1986 S.C. 663)17 that as the university was set up by a Central legislation and hence it could not be said to be established by the minority community and hence on this core it was not declared and given minority status. But the controversial decision of the Aligarh Muslim University (AMU) authorities in ministry of human resource and development (MHRD) to reserve 50% of the seats in post graduate courses in the university for Muslims, resulted in the filing of the Writ petition in the Hon'ble High Court of Allahabad and later special leave petition in the Hon'ble Supreme Court.

The AMU authorities in their honest or dishonest belief applied the decisions given in the T.M.A PAI Foundation Case judgment that allowed for reservation of seats for minorities in minority institutions. In fact that verdict referred only to schools, colleges and professional institutions owned by religious minorities. Now, where did it refer to reservations in universities. It is for the first time since 1920 that reservation on the basis of religion is being given or at least tried to be given by the AMU. Even after the 1981 amendment to the AMU Act that harped on promoting "especially the educational and cultural advancement of the Muslims of India". No reservation based on religion was ever made during the last 25 years.

That it is unfortunate to say that the Central Government succumbed to the pressure of all affluent minorities within the minority communities. The Minority Education Commission Act, passed by the Central Government is an instance in this regard. The provisions of the act are such that they benefit minorities by legalizing the commercial interest of managements. There has been a spectacular increase in the number of institutions seeking minority status in the resent past. In all of 2005, the National Commission for minority educational institution received just 380 applications from institutions seeking minority status. This year with the government decision to reserve an additional 27% of the seats for OBCs in all centrally funded educational institutions, the number of applications received by the Commission is already more than 2,000. As Mahajan said "It is time to recognize that steady increase in reservation quotas is likely to trigger a process of desecularisation along with the consideration of majority community identity which will have serious implication for the future of secular India."

MUSLIMS/MINORITY AND MADRASA

In the archival records of the British colonial state, the indigenous school of North India is referred to by the generic term 'Madrasa'. There is no exclusive implication of this institution as Islamic. This is close to the literal meaning of 'Madrasa' that is the Place of 'dars', dars being teaching institutions a lesson or lecture. Today the terms 'madrasa' stands for Islam. It does so, moreover, not in a neutral state like 'masjid'. Still means place of congregation, but rather in a heavily loaded sense of a place of biased and distorted learning. The madrasas in India are heterogeneous in their character-Madrasas belong to a certain sect each, such as Barelwi, Deobandis or Ahl-e-hadis. For some including among the madrasa administrators, the differences between the sects is of utmost importance for others it is trivia verging on inconsequential. Any one who walks around to observe classes in say, madrasa Hamidia, Madrasa Dar-ul-islam are madrasa Umahul-ul-uloom each of a different sect cannot distinguishes how the sectarian, differences play themselves out. By definition, the equitable education is open to all. Where there is the necessity of opening separate schools for Muslim children? It is no argument to say that madrasas are meant to inculcate the true spirit of Islam in the minds of Muslim children. One can understand a handful of schools strictly intended to train young Muslims to become mullahs and to conduct religious rites. We have Christians Seminaries and even Sanskrit 'Pathshalas' that are meant to keep society well supplied with priests. But to set up madrasas to teach children right from childhood how to be Muslims, is to keep them deliberately out of mainstream.

According to 'The economic and political weekly' "The Hamdard Education Society has tried to do a survey of madrasa's but has not succeeded. That is indeed remarkable, one estimate is that there are around 60,000 madrasas in the country. A small number is affiliated to the madrasas boards are State

Boards of Education. The exact figures are not indicated. As a part of primary research, it was found that area comprising of Jama Masjid, Chandini Chowk, Balli Maran have a variety of madrasas in Delhi. As there is no registration required for starting of madrasas, there is no authentic and convert recorded number of madrasas. It can be started in a masjid or nearby or just in one room building. Those by one rough estimate there are as many as 1,00020 or more than that madrasas in Delhi, which are not registered under any authority and majority also, function from local mosque.

While doing a primary research to find out the number of madrasas in Delhi and the method of teaching and the curricula, I visited a madrasa called Nasuritul-Islam. People there were quite co-operative and patiently satisfied my inquisitive enquiries. Due to parental pressures a large number of madrasas have been converted into school whose curricula are similar to other schools, which impart lessons in Mathematics, English, Science.

Nasurutal-Islam is one of them, which has been converted into a primary school where all courses related to mainstream as well as Quran and Urdu are taught till class 5th. Madrasa receive financial aid from Wakf board, NGOs, Masjids and through voluntary organization. The state government in Delhi has also decided to regulate the functioning of over 1,000 madrasas through the State Board. Now National Policy on Education has adopted the concept of National System of Education, which implies that up to a certain level all students irrespective of caste, creed, location or sex have access to education of comparable quality. From the tenth five year plan the scheme has been renamed with the title "Area Intensive and madrasa modernization programme by clubbing two competent in it. In the revised scheme there will be two components:

1) Financial assistance for modernization of madrasa organizations requesting for financial assistance will apply on the prescribed application form.
2) Area intensive programme for education of backward minorities.

The application will be addressed to the Education Secretary in the state/UT, who will be the Chairperson of Grant-in-aid committee in the state. In Delhi, no financial assistance under this scheme has been given to madrasa. According to official many madrasa are NGOs run who need not want meager government find as assistance.

GROWTH OF MINORITY INSTITUTION

To track down the growth of minority institutions it was pertinent to give details regarding the number of minority institutions presently running in Delhi as well as to know the number in the past.

7

Marginalized Groups

In many countries young people, the disabled, ethnic and religious minorities and indigenous peoples have been excluded from the political process. As more countries join the growing number of democracies, these groups are demanding and gaining a greater say in their governments and communities.

YOUTH

In Cambodia, IRI helped to establish a nonpartisan youth organization, the Youth Council of Cambodia (YCC) that trains young people in how to become civic activists. A basic civics class teaches 14-17 year olds about how their government works and citizens' role in effective democratic governance. A more advanced course for 18-24 year olds teaches effective activism by engaging government officials at public meetings, conducting petition drives, fundraising campaigns and grassroots advocacy. Graduates have access to additional training in topics like debate, public speaking, information technology as well as access to YCC's libraries, matching funds for community service projects, and networking opportunities with other youth activists around the country. IRI spreads the concepts taught by YCC through two additional channels – provincial Youth Democracy Festivals and the Youth Leadership Challenge reality-TV show. The formats reach millions of young people throughout the country empowering Cambodian youth to become more active in their communities and more interested and engaged in the political process. A network of future political and civil society leaders, the Europe and Eurasia Young Political Leaders (EEYPL) Seminar provides a space, both through periodic seminars and online forums, for up-and-coming young leaders to share experiences and ideas. One of the most prominent features of EEYPL has been the Democratic Youth Network website, which allows participants to engage in a dialogue on social and political issues. In addition to its online community, EEYPL has gathered more than 150 young political and civic leaders at conferences in Macedonia, Moldova, Serbia and Turkey. Organized by IRI and its partners the National Democratic Institute and the American Council for Young Political Leaders, these conferences have focused on leadership attributes, communication skills, political and community organization, and the use of technology and social media.

The Disabled

In Albania, IRI provides support and advocacy training for a coalition of civil society organizations working to secure greater rights and participation for the disabled. IRI began its efforts to strengthen and unify disability organizations into a coalition in 2005, training them on how to develop an agenda and lobby elected officials and government institutions for its implementation. Eleven organizations joined together to draft the National Platform for the Disabled, highlighting needs in areas such as education, employment, transportation and social services. The coalition lobbied candidates, launched a media campaign, organized debates and received the support of five of Albania's major parties, including the two largest. The disability organizations have also focused their efforts on political participation, and with IRI's support, observed the 2007 local elections. The observation mission revealed that only two percent of registered and eligible disabled voters took part in the elections. Election commissions had little knowledge or training on how to accommodate the disabled, many were not included in the electoral registers, and more than half of the polling places visited lacked ramps or elevators to enable access. In 2007 and 2008, IRI's disability partners lobbied parliament on the adoption of the new electoral code. Based on the recommendations of the disability coalition, the new election law included a number of provisions to accommodate disabled voters. For the first time, the election law requires polling places to be accessible and mandates Braille ballots for the blind. These reforms are an important step forward for Albania's disabled citizens.

Ethnic and Religious Minorities

Iraq is a country richly diverse in ancient ethnic and religious minorities. To ensure their voices are heard in the country's newly developing democracy, IRI works in partnership with the Civic Coalition for Minorities (CCM), which counts among its members Chaldean Christians, Assyrians, Turkmen and Sabean communities. Among the primary advocacy activities of CCM is the Unified Iraqi ID campaign, which seeks to remove divisive markers of ethnic or religious affiliation from official forms of personal identification. IRI supports CCM as it lobbies elected members of parliament and seeks to educate their fellow Iraqis through the media on the campaign' goals and objectives. One highly visible accomplishment of CCM's campaign occurred when the members of the Iraqi national soccer team, winner of the 2007 Asia Cup, agreed to star in an advocacy television commercial which promoted Iraqi national unity and identity. CCM also works to educate and turnout minority communities in Iraqi elections.

Indigenous Peoples

In Guatemala, IRI works with municipal governments in the *altiplano* region, providing public opinion research to highlight local needs, subsequently providing training and capacity building to help mayors respond to citizen needs. For example, public opinion research conducted in the local indigenous language of K'iche in the municipality of Cantel, revealed that citizens do not feel that they have full access to municipal services because public servants do not speak the Maya K'iche language. As a result, IRI worked with the mayor and town council to pass a law requiring that all new public servants must be bilingual to be considered for the position. Many of the current town council members decided to take refresher courses in K'iche to be able to serve the population better. Additionally, in response to strong citizen demand, IRI worked with municipal governments to create opportunities for local economic development in indigenous municipalities by organizing cultural festivals to celebrate local indigenous culture and promote commerce and tourism. IRI also works with local governments to involve indigenous peoples in local decision-making through the development of more inclusive participatory processes.

MARGINALIZED GROUPS AND THE COMMON MINIMUM PROGRAM

In recognition of the unique problems of the Dalits, Adiwasis and other religious minorities like the Muslims, the Indian government has developed policies for their economic, social and political empowerment. Dalits and Adiwasis are the two largest groups, constituting about 250 million in 2001 (about 167 million and 86 million respectively). Additionally, Muslims account for about 12% the population. The deprivation of such a vast mass of population is closely associated with the process of exclusion and discrimination based on group identity. The government has used a two-fold strategy for the empowerment of the SC/ST (Scheduled Caste/Scheduled Tribe) communities, which includes (a) Anti-discrimination legal and protective measures, and (b) Developmental or empowering measures. Anti-discrimination measures include the enactment of the Anti-Untouchability Act of 1955, and the Schedule Caste/Tribe Prevention of Atrocities Act,1989. Reservations in government services and political bodies also fall under the purview of protective measures. The reservation policy is confined to the public sector; and the private sector wherein more than 90% of the SC/ST workers are engaged remains unprotected. The focus of the government's 'general programmes' therefore has been on the educational, social and economic empowerment of the SC/STs and on improving the private ownership of fixed capital assets (land and non-land), human resources, and on improving access to basic services like housing, health, drinking water, electricity etc.

The goal of the government's interventionist policy has thus been focusing on the improvement of levels of human indicators of the SC/ST and on bringing them at par with other non-scheduled groups. The pertinent question therefore is where do the marginalized groups stand today? Though there has been some improvement in certain spheres and despite some positive changes, the standard of living for the marginalized communities has not improved. In 2000, close to 40% of the SC and 48% of ST were poor as compared with 20% among others in rural areas. About 36% of SC/ST remained poor in urban areas as against 20% for others. The poverty level of wage labour among the SC/ST was also particularly high, varying between 46% and 60% in the rural and urban areas respectively. In urban areas, the ratio of poor among casual labourers was also high, 58% for SC, 64% for ST and 45% for non-scheduled population. Among the Muslims, the percentage of poor was about 30% compared to 21% for other religions groups. Similarly, the incidence of poverty in urban areas was higher among the Muslims (36.66% compared to 23% all India average).

What (Minimum) Needs to be Done?

The reasons for the high incidences of poverty and deprivation among the marginalized social groups are to be found in their continuing lack of access to income-earning capital assets, (agricultural land and non-land assets), heavy dependence on wage employment, high unemployment, low education and other factors.

Therefore, there is a need to focus on policies to improve the ownership of income-earning capital assets (agriculture land, and non-land assets), employment, human resource & health situation, and prevention of discrimination to ensure fair participation of the marginalized community in the private and the pubic sectors.

ACTIVE ROLE OF THE STATE IN PLANNING

It is necessary to recognize that for the vast majority of the discriminated groups, State intervention is crucial and necessary. Similarly, the use of economic and social planning as an instrument of planned development is equally necessary. Economic discrimination, in general and market discrimination in particular, is a serious market failure. Thus, planned State intervention to ensure fair access and participation in social and economic development in the country is necessary.

Improved Access to Agricultural Land

The problem of landlessness is more serious among the SC as compared to the ST and the Muslims, as 70% of the SC rural households are landless and near landless (owning less than 1 acre). Government record on land redistribution has been quite disappointing. So far, only 2% of the total cultivable land has been distributed under the ceiling to landless and the share goes up marginally to 10% if we include government land. Only 18 lakh acres of land have been distributed so far to 18.5 lakh SC beneficiaries with 0.977 acre per beneficiary. Therefore, it is a cause for concern that a large section of SC households remain without viable land even today.

Therefore, the CMP should include serious land reform measures to distribute minimum land to landless households. For this purpose, the Government should clear the cultivable wasteland and other lands, including land under ceiling and develop these large tracts of land through employment programs and thus, create a 'Common pool of State land' free from litigation by private parties and redistribute it to the Scheduled Castes and others. As the present system failed to give possession of even legally distributed land to the SCs and STs due to their extremely powerless position in village societies, a special organization at the Centre and in the States should be set up for the purpose of acquiring, developing and distribution of government land and land under ceiling. For example, there are large tracts of customary lands whose rights were given to SCs, but which were encroached by the high caste landlords. These lands include Mahar Vatan land in Maharashtra, Panchami land in Tamilnadu, and Depressed Caste land in A.P. The government through the new organization should release these lands from the encroachers and hand them to their legitimate owners.

IMPROVED ACCESS TO CAPITAL

The poverty level among the SC and ST cultivators is 30% and 40% respectively, which is much higher compared with non-scheduled cultivators (18%). Similarly, the poverty incidences of those in business is very high 33% for SC and 41% for ST compared with only 21% among non-scheduled businesses. The viability and productivity of self-employed households need to be improved by providing adequate capital, information, technology and access to markets. It is a pity that though the STs do own some land, they lack the relevant technological inputs to improve the productivity of their agriculture. The capital at the disposable of SC/ST Finance Corporation at the Centre and in the States, therefore, needs to be increased so as to meet the capital requirements of these groups. Under the impact of liberalization regime, even the priority lending of 10% by commercial banks to the weaker sections has been reduced to 6%. This trend too needs to be reversed.

IMPROVED EMPLOYMENT IN PUBLIC AND PRIVATE SECTORS

Public Employment

In 2000, about 61% of rural and urban SC households and about half of ST households were wage labourers, and poverty levels among them were about 46% for SC and 61% for ST households respectively. The poverty levels among casual labourers' households were as high as 58% and 64% in urban areas for SC and ST respectively. The unemployment rates were also high among these two groups as compared with non-scheduled groups. There is a need to review and strengthen employment guarantee schemes both in rural and urban areas, particularly in drought-prone and poverty-ridden areas. Rural infrastructure and other productive capital assets can be generated through large-scale employment programmes. This will serve the duel purpose of reducing poverty and ensuring economic growth through improvement in the stock of capital assets and infrastructure.

Private Sector Employment

Due to privatization, the subsequent withdrawal of the State and the decline in government and public employment, the employment of SC/ST under reservation has declined quite significantly. Therefore, reservation should continue in the undertakings that have been privatized during the 1990s under the policy of privatization.

Reservation in the Private Sector

The CMP has promised to undertake necessary steps to incorporate reservation in the private sector. Given the prevalence of significant discrimination in employment in the private sector, the formulation of a reservation policy is necessary to ensure fair access to the discriminated groups. For this purpose, a Committee at the Central Government level should be set up to formulate the policy of reservation in the private sector.

Firstly, the government should enact the 'Equal Opportunity Act' of which 'Equal Employment Opportunity Act' should be a part, so that legal provisions are in place.

Secondly, legislation should be passed by the Central government for reservation both for private and public sector, to ensure fair access to the discriminated groups like SC and ST in private employment.

Thirdly, the 'Equal Opportunity Act' and reservation measures should be applicable not only to employment in private sector but be extended to other areas or markets like private capital market, product and consumer market etc.

Fourthly, 'Equal Opportunity Act and Reservation should be applicable to private education. 'Equal Opportunity Act' is also necessary for private housing sector to prevent discrimination in the housing markets.

Fifthly, reservation should be applicable in government contracts given to private contractors for construction and a number of other dealings and also in purchase of goods by the State. Certain quotas should be fixed for SC/ST contractors as they face discrimination in the sale of some consumer goods due to notions of purity and pollution.

Lastly, an 'Affirmative Action Policy' of some sort should be envisaged for multinational companies in the framework of

UN provisions. Some countries have taken initiative in this respect under the provisions of the Global Compact and other UN Equal Employment Opportunity provisions.

Education and Human Resource Development

Firstly, lower literacy/level of education and the continual discrimination of SC/STs in educational institutions pose a major problem. The government should take a second look at the Education Policy and develop major programmes for strengthening the public education system in villages and cities on a much larger scale than today. There is a necessity to reallocate government resources for education and vocational training.

For millions of poor students located in rural areas, the loan schemes do not work. We should develop an affordable, uniform and better quality public educational system up to the university level. Public education system is our strength and needs to be further strengthened.

Promotion of such private education systems that creates inequality and hierarchy should be discouraged. In this regard, we may draw some lessons from Sweden, where only 3% of educational institutions are privately managed, but their syllabus, tuition structure and infrastructure facilities are similar to that of public education institutions. The gradation and hierarchy that we are introducing in the private sector at rapid rate should be discouraged and public education system should be strengthened in terms of infrastructure, quality of teacher and other facilities.

Vocational training should be made part of the normal education system. In this respect, the system of vocational education developed by Germany could be tried in India.

Secondly, there is hardly any financial support to SC/ST students at higher levels of education and research. The University Grants Commission should institute a special fellowship scheme for these groups. The UGC had earlier introduced a special fellowship for SC/ST Ph.D. students from which many students had benefited. This scheme too should be reviewed.

Public Health System

The public health system in rural areas has also been by and large neglected. Therefore, the primary health system for rural areas and public health system in urban areas must be revived and more funds should be allocated for the same.

Food Security Programs

The public distribution system should also be revived and strengthened. In distributing Fair Price Shops in villages, priority should be given to the SC/ST female and male groups, as a number of studies have pointed out that they are discriminated upon in the Public Distribution System and in Mid-day Meal schemes.

Untouchability and Discrimination

The practice of untouchability and the large number of atrocities inflicted on Dalits continue even today mainly because of hidden prejudices and neglect on the part of officials responsible for the implementation of Special Legislations; i.e. the Protection of Civil Rights Act (PCRA) and the Prevention of Atrocities Act (POA). The Government should make a meaningful intervention in this regard so as to mitigate the sufferings of Dalits due to practice of untouchability and atrocities inflicted upon them and should also treat this matter on a priority basis to ensure that the officials and the civil society at large are sensitized on this issue.

The government should also establish a special department to continue the social reform process and to educate the masses on the evils of untouchability and caste discrimination on the pattern of Tamil Nadu government. The law by itself often does not help to remove the practice of untouchability, unless there is change in the attitude and behaviour of high castes. So there is a need to have a program of social and moral education of high caste individuals in the society.

MARGINALIZED GROUPS BLENDING THE OLD AND THE NEW

International development goals now place high priority on

addressing the needs of the poorest of the poor, and with the advent of the Information Age, communication is increasingly recognized as essential to achieving these goals. However, information, communication and knowledge are essential but not sufficient elements to address poverty. Marginal communities do not exist in isolation from wider contexts of social, political and economic forces and unequal power structures. These constraints need to be taken into account, and it must be recognized that information and communication cannot substitute for structural changes.

There have been many changes since the discipline of communication for development began some 50 years ago. Business as usual is no longer possible. There is need for new directions to respond to a changing environment, the effects of globalization, new social actors and the opportunities offered by new information and communication technologies. At the same time, there is a wealth of lessons learned from years of experience working with disadvantaged groups, and a variety of participatory approaches developed in the past are still valid. The paper suggests that there is need to blend the old with the new.

Although there are no-one size fits all – rules, based on what has worked in the past, the paper describes some principles which are still valid as guidelines on how participatory communication can best be used to work with isolated and marginalized groups. The paper also analyses different media and approaches, which are suitable for working at community level. It analyses the potential and limitations of new information and communication technologies for working with the poor and identifies areas for improving local access and appropriation by marginal groups. It concludes that communication practitioners must learn to adapt to the new information age, and select the most appropriate communication channels, making use of all the tools in their toolbox. An essential element for successful and sustainable efforts with the disadvantaged will continue to be dialogue, ownership on the part of communities and integration with existing indigenous communication systems. As a basis for discussion, the paper asks: Why is it that after so many years of experience there are still few participatory communication processes in programs to alleviate poverty and improve the livelihoods of vulnerable groups? A number of constraints and possible reasons are suggested.

The paper also proposes ideas for action, which could help to overcome some of the constraints and improve the effectiveness of communication with isolated and marginalized groups. These include:

For Governments:

- To establish regulatory frameworks and an enabling policy environment for communication with the poor, involving all stakeholders.
- To respect the identities, languages, cultural diversity and traditions of minorities.

For Donors and Development Agencies:

- To plan for strategic communication in poverty alleviation programs, with adequate timeframes and resources.
- To establish units with professional staff in communication for development.
- To provide time and personnel in projects for participatory research, monitoring and evaluation.
- To establish partnerships to promote local access to ICTs for the poor, and ensure meaningful use and social appropriation.

For Communication Practitioners:

- To train communication professionals at all levels, with a focus on participatory approaches for social change.
- To advocate with decision makers for the inclusion of communication in poverty alleviation programs.
- To identify new instruments and indicators for monitoring and evaluation of participatory communication processes with disadvantaged groups.
- To address the issue of sustainability.

- To share more information and experiences of successful participatory communication approaches with marginalized people.

CHALLENGES AND OPPORTUNITIES

We are living in an era of radical transformation, which presents new challenges as well as opportunities for communication for development practitioners. The images of the attack on the New York Trade towers on 11 September 2001, and the aftermath of the Madrid train bombings on 11 March 2004 reached the remotest corners of the globe in real time. The constant flow of information and images of the War on Terror are there to remind us of the power and potential of the new information age. But how much of this potential is directed towards improving the quality of lives of the poorest? How is the global information society affecting communication for isolated and marginalized groups ?

New Scenarios

Governments and traditional institutions have withdrawn from certain functions that are now being taken over by civil society and the private sector. Globalisation is shaping the world economy, and privatisation of public services, free markets and international trade agreements have created new scenarios for development with serious effects on governments, local communities and marginalized groups. In addition, globalisation without social justice has created new and dramatic tensions. Political, social, cultural and economic disparities are the root cause of current international problems such as poverty, ethnic conflicts, wars, terrorism, religious fundamentalism, migrations, and Diasporas.

The Communication Age

New information and communication technologies (ICTs) have created the so-called information and knowledge society. Communication technologies are becoming more appropriate for developing countries, and experiments with ICTs are demonstrating that the benefits of the information revolution can have positive repercussions for economic and social development. But infrastructure, access and use are still limited for vulnerable groups in the rural areas of developing countries. They are on the wrong side of the digital divide, and risk further marginalization. At the same time, processes of democratisation, decentralisation and pluralism have paved the way for community-based ownership of various communication media such as newspapers, radio, and video and in some cases even the Internet. Thus, horizontal people to people processes are emerging alongside dominant structures and vertical lines of communication. But global media markets are now dominated by a mere handful of multinationals, and the globalisation of communication is threatening cultural diversity and the traditional values of minorities.

Human Development

There has been a shift in development thinking from top down approaches based on economic growth and transfer of technology to people centred development, at least on paper. The participation of rural and urban communities in decision-making about their own lives, gender analysis, equity, social factors, holistic approaches and respect for indigenous knowledge are becoming elements of many development programs. There is more emphasis on the cultural and local dimensions of development. It is also more widely accepted that human development requires dialogue, interaction and sharing of ideas for social change and innovation to occur.

International Policy

Most major issues on the development agenda in the last decades still remain as challenges facing the world in the new millennium, and are addressed in the eight Millennium Development Goals adopted by the United Nations in 2000. These reflect the multi-dimensional aspects of poverty and the needs of the poorest and traditionally marginalized groups. They include extreme poverty, low incomes and hunger, lack of primary education, gender inequality, high child and maternal mortality, poor health conditions as shown by the spread of HIV/AIDS, malaria and tuberculosis and the lack of environmental sustainability. These are all challenges, which will benefit from participatory processes of social change. Thus, the importance of communication as an essential element in tackling these issues.

With the emphasis on the poorest, the international community recognises that special measures are required to address the needs of vulnerable groups and minorities. For example, a number of initiatives are being promoted for indigenous people, who are among the most disadvantaged and vulnerable groups of people in the world today. In 1994, the United Nations launched the International Decade for the World's Indigenous People (1995-2004) to promote and protect the rights of indigenous people worldwide. Within the framework of this Decade, in 2000 the UN Economic and Social Council created the Permanent Forum on Indigenous Issues, with indigenous participation and membership. The Forum has a mandate to discuss indigenous issues related to economic and social development, culture, the environment, education, health and human rights. It provides advice and recommendations on indigenous issues to the UN; raises awareness and promotes coordination and integration of activities within the UN system; and disseminates information related to indigenous issues. During its last session in May 2004 the Forum adopted recommendations concerning the education of indigenous people. During the discussions the use of communication and appropriate community media were also raised. Also within the framework of the Decade, The UN Commission on Human Rights is discussing a Universal Declaration on the Rights of Indigenous People. Article 17 deals specifically with communication and states: "Indigenous people have the right to establish their own media in their own languages. They also have the right to equal access to all forms of non-indigenous media. States should take effective measures to ensure that Stateowned media duly reflect indigenous cultural diversity."

The most recent international conference, the World Summit on the Information Society, held in Geneva in 2003 and to be followed up in Tunis in 2005, was devoted to putting the potential of knowledge and ICTs at the service of development, and to promote the use of information and knowledge for the achievement of internationally agreed development goals, including those contained in the Millennium Declaration. The Plan of Action stressed the importance of promoting access and use for all, with emphasis on the special requirements of women and girls, indigenous people, older peoples, persons with disabilities, disadvantaged children, and other vulnerable groups. It called upon Governments and other stakeholders to establish sustainable and multipurpose community public access points, providing affordable or free of charge access to the Internet. It emphasized the importance of socially meaningful content in ICTs to empower local communities. The Plan of Action also called upon Governments to create policies that enhance and promote respect for different cultures, languages and traditions. It urged them to give support to media based in local communities, combining the use of traditional media and new technologies to facilitate the use of local languages, to preserve local heritage and nomadic communities. It invited Governments to respect indigenous knowledge and traditions, to enhance the capacity of indigenous people to develop content in their own languages and to enable them to use and benefit from their traditional knowledge in the information society. 1

Isolated and Marginalized Groups

International development goals now place high priority on reaching the poorest of the poor. Who are they? Small subsistence farmers, women, youth in urban and rural areas, indigenous people, nomads, mountain people, refugees, landless labourers, rural artisans, small fishermen, inhabitants of small islands, to mention just a few. In recent years the international environment has created new social actors such as migrant workers, Diasporas, victims of AIDS, the disabled, and victims of war and conflict situations.

The information revolution has also created a new category: The information poor and the computer illiterates. (Saik Yoon 2000). Isolated and marginalized groups face particular constraints with regard to access to information and communication, and thus have limited participation and voice in the public sphere and in decision-making processes affecting their lives. They belong to the culture of silence. They are on the wrong side of the digital divide, unable to participate in the Information Society and thus risk further marginalization, politically, socially and economically.

What is their profile?

- They are poor, with practically no or little money to spend on access to communication technology.
- They live in isolated rural areas, or in slums in large cities, or in mountain terrains, or on distant small islands, often without electricity, and telephones.
- They are unemployed, or work as unskilled labour or self-employed subsistence farmers or unskilled agricultural labour.
- They are illiterate or semi-literate, with little access to education and training.
- They are part of minority ethno-linguistic groups.
- They often have social, economic, cultural and political customs that are distinct from those of the dominant societies.
- They are powerless, suffer from social discrimination, and lack recognition of their identities and ways of life.
- They are victims of violence, drugs, wars and new pandemics such as HIV/AIDS.
- In the majority of cases they speak minority languages.

Their communication systems include alternative and small media such as video and audio visuals, popular theatre, local and community radio, poetry, proverbs, storytellers, popular songs and music, loudspeakers, in addition to informal meetings in the street, in the market place and at ritual celebrations. They belong primarily to oral cultures. At the same time, globalisation and new information technologies have created new identities, which go beyond the boundaries of the state or geographical communities and traditional institutions. Thus, social movements representing minority and disadvantaged groups make use of new communication networks and information flows to express their concerns, share common interests, and promote social change and action for collective rights. They have created transnational public spheres without boundaries of time and space. These movements are usually based on common issues and interests such as human rights, the environment, labour standards and gender. Examples include women's associations, human rights groups, ethnic minorities, indigenous groups, migrant workers, Diasporas, religious movements, victims of AIDS, environmental activists, and Dalits.

ICTs have been used successfully to give women a voice and to build up networks for social and political advocacy. Examples include global networks such as Women's Net and ISIS International, and regional networks such as Femnet, SANGONet and APC-Africa-Women in Africa; Depth News and Women's Feature Service in Asia; DAWN (Development Alternatives with Women for a new Era) and CAFRA (Caribbean Association for Feminist Research and Action) in the Caribbean.

The Indigenous Media Network brings together indigenous journalists from all parts of the world to disseminate information from an indigenous perspective and to use as a tool to campaign for the rights of indigenous people worldwide. Transnational networks linking small grass root groups were fundamental in co-ordinating actions to dispute water policies in Bolivia, in challenging Brazilian deforestation policies and drug prices in Africa. (Huesca 2001). And, it is well known that the indigenous Zapatista movement in Chiapas was able to survive and promote its agenda thanks to the international backing received through the use of Internet and other media. These social movements and their networks make use of the Internet, bulletins, pamphlets, cartoons, video, street theatre, graffiti, radio and any other media available to them.

Information, Knowledge and Communication

It has been demonstrated that economic and technological inputs will go under-utilised without knowledge, and it is for the sharing of knowledge that communication is indispensable. However, knowledge and communication are essential but not sufficient elements to address poverty. Marginal communities do not exist in isolation from wider contexts of social, political, economic forces and unequal power structures that are barriers to social change. These constraints need to be taken into account. Information and communication can never substitute for structural changes. For example, the extent to which subsistence farmers can benefit from information will vary according to other factors such as ownership of land, proximity of markets, available means of transportation, and their productive resources to respond to the opportunities information sources might provide. (Curtain, 2004). In addition, collecting and disseminating information are not the same as knowledge sharing and communication. Communication is a two way process, and true knowledge is more than information. Knowledge is the meaning that people make of information. And, for societies the world over making sense of information depends on their ability to discuss and debate it. For social change to occur there must be opportunities for dialogue. Only when information helps people communicate, participate and allows them to make informed choices does that information become knowledge. (Panos 1998)

Need for New and Better Directions

As communication practitioners our mission has always been to make life better for the poor, and those at risk. The ultimate test of communication for development will continue to be what impact it has on improving the quality of lives of marginal and vulnerable groups. Yet, there have been many changes since the discipline of communication for development began some 50 years ago. There is need for new directions to respond to a changing environment and new social actors. There is need to create an alternative framework for communication interventions, that is truly people and participation oriented, and not only on paper. It must involve them in assessing the nature of the problem, defining priorities, formulating solutions and managing the processes of change.

At the same time, we also have lessons learned from years of experience and practice, and a variety of approaches developed in the past are still valid. We need to blend the old with the new. The questions this Roundtable should examine are whether current strategies, experience and knowledge are appropriate for working with marginal and vulnerable groups, and how they should be modified or expanded. A new approach to HIV/ AIDS Communication The HIV/AIDS pandemic is the most serious public health issue facing developing countries, creating new vulnerable and marginalized individuals. The epidemic is both a cause and an effect of underdevelopment and the spread of HIV/AIDS is linked to issues of gender inequality, discrimination, poverty and marginalization.

The fight against AIDS has become a top international priority, and has brought communication in the forefront as a critical tool for influencing behaviour and life styles. Apart from a few notable successes, the record of tackling this new development challenge has been poor, and the pandemic continues to spread. There has been overemphasis on short-term results, while AIDS is a long term and complex problem. Past strategies to bring about behaviour change – formulating and disseminating messages to persuade people to be abstinent, faithful or to use a condom – have not been always successful. Thus, while information dissemination and health messages are essential, they are not sufficient and new approaches and strategies are required. The Eighth UN Roundtable on Communication for Development held in Nicaragua in 2001 focused on HIV/AIDS and the communication challenges it presents. It concluded that broader and longer term strategies, with a series of complementary and multisectoral approaches were required to address the social, cultural, political and gender aspects of AIDS. Approaches should move from putting out messages to fostering an environment where the voices of those most affected by the pandemic can be heard, and where dialogue and discussion can flourish. Consultation and negotiation to identify the best way forward in a partnership process should be applied rather than trying to persuade people to change behaviours.

Some Lessons from Experience

Based on what has worked in the past, the following are some principles, which are still valid as guidelines on how participatory communication for social change can best be used to work with marginal and vulnerable groups:

Communication as Process

The Challenge for Change Program's work with the Fogo Islanders in the 1960s has often been seen as a turning point in the development of participatory communication processes. The Fogo Process was one of the first examples of filmmaking and video as a process to obtain social change in a disadvantaged community. It included a series of working practices that have influenced many participatory communication programs throughout the world and that are still very valid. Key ingredients included:

- Communication as a process for empowerment, for conflict resolution, and to negotiate with decision makers to modify policy.
- Communication technology and media only as tools to facilitate the process.
- Programmes planned and produced with and by the poor themselves, about their social problems, and not just produced by outsiders.
- The professional quality of the product becomes secondary to content and process.
- The importance of interpersonal communication and the role of a facilitator, a community worker or a social animator.
- Community input into the editing of the material, and dialogue with decision makers.

The Fogo Process provides evidence of how local communities who have been marginalized by economic and political structures can become empowered through communication to transform conditions of uneven development. (Crocker, 2003)

Starting with the People

Listening to people, learning about their perceived needs and taking into account their knowledge and culture is another essential prerequisite for successful communication with marginal groups. Listening, the capacity to read reality through the ear is an important skill developed by oral cultures. People develop listening skills acutely when they rely exclusively on oral communication. Dialogue also requires the capacity to listen and to be silent. Dialogue only takes place where silence is respected (Hamelink, 2004). Listening goes beyond a simple appraisal of needs. It involves listening to what people already know, what they aspire to, what they perceive as possible and desirable and what they feel they can sustain.

Today, compared to many years ago, there are several participatory research methods which have been developed to enable outsiders and communities rapidly to share experiences and learn together about their realities. For example, the SADC Centre of Communication for Development based in Harare, Zimbabwe, has developed a methodology of participatory rural communication appraisal (PRCA). PRCA enables development workers to involve community members in identifying problems and proposing solutions that will be adopted by the community. Research for the design and production of communication programs becomes an interactive process, allowing the community to express its problems and learn about itself. This ensures that the development processes initiated will reflect the perceptions and realities of the rural community, thus encouraging the sustainability of the development innovation.

Preserving Indigenous Knowledge and Culture

Another basic concept underlying participatory communication is respect for the knowledge, values and culture of indigenous people. Far away from global information highways marginal communities in rural areas contain a wealth of indigenous knowledge and traditional cultural resources, a rich but fragile heritage which risks to be lost with the advent of modern technology.

"The essence of involving rural people in the process of their own development lies in the sharing of knowledge... the outcome of useful sharing of knowledge is not so much the replacement of traditional techniques by modern ones, as a merging of modern and traditional systems to produce a more appropriate hybrid, one that befits the economic and technical capacities of rural populations as well as their cultural values."(FAO, 1987) Traditional subsistence farmers in many cases have known better than the agricultural experts what cultivation methods were appropriate in their own environment. Indigenous groups have access to a large volume of traditional knowledge about their environment and are highly efficient users of available resources that have been crucial for their survival. In Arctic Canada, for example, perceptions on climate change have been essential for the survival of aboriginal groups and they have contributed their traditional knowledge and local observations to scientists and decision makers. (Neil Ford, 2000) The Proderith rural communication system in Mexico has often been cited as an example of communication approaches for participatory planning, peasant empowerment and sharing of knowledge with indigenous people. Respect for their traditional knowledge system, their local culture and indigenous language was an essential ingredient.

Mayan Values

"Proderith staff had little idea of how to spark a dialogue among and with the indigenous, Mayan speaking people. The ingenious solution proved to be video recordings with Don Clotilde Cob, an 82-year-old man who could talk about the problems. He was a proud, ex-revolutionary, who had learned Spanish and taught himself how to read and write as an adult. He was articulate and lucid in both Mayan and Spanish. This charismatic old man, with his white hair and neat beard, sat cross-legged in front of a video camera for hours on end. He held forth about the past, about the revolution, about the greatness of Mayan culture, and about life today. He deplored the decline of such Mayan traditions as the family vegetable plot, explained how he cultivated his own maize, and complained that today's young people did not even know to do that properly. He accused the young of abandoning all that had been good in Mayan culture; they would sell eggs to buy cigarettes and soft drinks, and so it was no wonder that diets were worse than they were in his youth.

Scores of people sat in attentive silence in the villages as these tapes were played. In the evening, under a tree, the words in Mayan flowed from the screen, and the old man's eloquent voice and emphatic gestures spread their spell. For many, it was the first time they had ever heard anyone talk about the practical values of their culture. It was also the first time they had seen themselves on "television", and talking their own language. They frequently asked that the tapes be played again and again. The desired effect was achieved: the people began to take stock of their situation and think seriously about their values, and so the ground was prepared for when Proderith began to discuss development plans to eradicate malnutrition and promote food security." Source: Colin Fraser and Sonia Restrepo-Estrada "Communication for Rural Development in Mexico: in Good Times and in Bad" in Communicating for Development, 1998.

The Knowledge Systems of Pastoralists

"Human Survival has been based entirely on knowledge systems and, while most have changed beyond recognition or perished altogether, some remain and continue to thrive. Pastoralism is one of these, a way of life based on its own indigenous knowledge system, which is highly successful in the practices of preserving the environment, in livestock production, in animal health and in the art of predicting and handling natural disasters. Many advocates of modernisation do not consider these to be knowledge systems – instead they are described as "backward" or "primitive", as falling outside the prism of a certain production and social system. And when pastoralists accept the offer to be "civilised", neither governments nor business communities in the South have been able to harness modernisation for their benefit. So, neither are pastoralists allowed to live as they wish, nor do those who want them to change come up with a meaningful alternative... Knowledge systems other than the dominant discourse need to be recognised not just as knowledge systems per se, but as things that could be pivotal to the preservation of the environment and ensuring means of existence for the great many people who live on the edges of a rapidly modernising world."

Communication and culture are closely interwoven. Communication is a product of culture and culture determines the code, structure, meaning and context of the communication that takes place. Culture and history also play an important role in the social development of a community. For generations, rural populations living in isolated villages without access to modern means of communication have relied on the spoken word and traditional forms of communication as a means of transmitting culture, knowledge, history and customs. "The wealth of proverbs, songs, stories, and other entertaining forms have a special function in an oral culture. Eloquence and subtlety are valued; a well-phrased statement is remembered. People listen for hours to a good storyteller. Elders use proverbs to comment on the happenings of the day, and proverbs are devices for communicating the insights and experiences of the past." (Fugelsang 1987) New information and communication technologies may be used to enhance cultural self-expression or stifle it through what has been variously labelled as cultural imperialism, cultural invasion, cultural synchronisation or cultural homogenisation. (Ansah 2000). One of the effects of digitalisation is the growing concentration of ownership of different media within a very small number of large multinational corporations. The trend now is for powerful multinationals to buy up newspapers, books and magazines, publishing houses, radio and television networks, telecommunication companies and satellite relay facilities. The result is the reduction of communication content, cultural diversity and opportunities for local traditional systems of communication.

Large corporations strive to maximise profits and pursue economies of scale by reducing the varieties in their media offerings and trimming back small-scale community services that are rarely viable within large-scale operations. The mega corporations fall back on the models tested in their home markets – invariably an American, western model. The result is the displacement of local programmes with foreign ones, and a narrowing of rich cultural diversity. (Saik Yoon, 2000) How strong are indigenous communication systems? How fragile? Is cultural diversity threatened by technology? Already we see young people in both urban and rural environments throughout the developing world embracing western models and abandoning pride in the cultural roots of their parents. In today's global world cultures are no longer isolated. They interact and influence each other. Thus, we witness the emergence of new cultural and knowledge systems which blend rural with urban, local with global, traditional with modern customs and values and which generate "hybrid" cultures and practices. (Servaes 2003) "Glocalisation" is the term now used to define the integration of the global with the local.

To be successful, communication efforts must take into account the cultural values of marginal groups as an avenue for their participation, rather than borrowing communication strategies from outside that promote change without due consideration for culture. Preserving cultural diversity, local languages and traditional systems of communication in the face of globalisation is one of the major challenges for communication practitioners in this Information Age.

MEDIA AND APPROACHES

In the past communication specialists relied almost exclusively on alternative media for activities at community level. We must not forget the lessons learned through their experience. But, the advent of new technologies and their convergence now means that new mixes and matches can be made for more effective communication programs with disadvantaged groups. Communication initiatives should make use of all media channels available, both modern and traditional, and there is merit in combining electronic media with other media that people already like, use and know how to control (Ramirez 2003).

Traditional Communication Systems

The preservation of traditional forms of communication and social change are not mutually exclusive. Traditional communication systems can be important channels for facilitating learning, people's participation and dialogue for development purposes. Indigenous media have been successfully adopted to promote issues of relevance to marginal groups. Popular theatre, puppet shows, music and dance have been used, for instance in health care, to discuss family size, female genital mutilation, teenage pregnancies, HIV/AIDS, and unsettling life styles. They have also been applied in literacy programs, environmental protection and in introducing agricultural practices. Traditional forms of communication can also be integrated with other media such as radio, television, video and audiocassettes. What is important is that they should not be produced only by outsiders. The participation of local artists, storytellers, performers and musicians in the production and use of traditional media ensures respect for traditional values, symbols and realities and, at the same time, ensures that such media productions appeal to communities. It also increases the credibility of media programs and thus their effectiveness as vehicles to share knowledge and bring about social change. (Balit 1999)

An offshoot from traditional and popular media, and the popular culture of telenovelas in Latin America, is the use of melodramatic soap operas for radio and television, which use real or fictional "social models" to promote changes in life styles. These programs are adapted to local cultural contexts and integrate entertainment with awareness raising and education (Edutainment). Educational messages and best practices are woven into the fictional narrative, thereby communicating to the audiences how they can tackle specific issues, often health issues, in their everyday life. (Tufte 2003) The experience of Soul City in South Africa is a well-known successful example of this approach, which among other themes, has focused on HIV/AIDS. The radio and television series have been complemented with interpersonal communication, printed materials and educational training packages.

Yasarekomo: Self evaluation of a communication experience by indigenous people in Bolivia In 1994, with assistance from FAO, the Asamblea del Pueblo Guaraní (APG), the main Guaranì organization in Bolivia, established a rural communication unit the *Unidad de Comunicación Guaraní (UCG)*, in the Chaco region of Bolivia. The goal of the unit was to improve the quality of life of isolated and marginalized native communities and support indigenous development initiatives. With training from FAO, the Guaranì villagers applied intercultural communication approaches to share knowledge and information using video training packages and community radio. The UCG received assistance from FAO for three years, and then continued independently for an additional six years, generating income by producing intercultural communication materials and implementing communication for development plans agreed with APG and co-funded by the Government, Municipalities and NGOs. The UCG then decided to carry out a self-evaluation in collaboration with the APG and other indigenous organizations of Bolivia. For the first time, indigenous people themselves documented and analyzed in a systematic manner the use of participatory communication media and messages produced by and for Guarani communities, based on the blending of traditional knowledge and customs with modern knowledge and communication techniques. The results of the self-evaluation confirmed the validity of the participatory and intercultural communication approaches applied to advisory services. The study however underlined problems for the future sustainability of the Uni, these included: The need for continued efforts to strengthen the communication capacity of the APG and other indigenous organizations; the importance of "appropriating" new media and acquiring additional equipment and; the need for a national policy recognizing the right of indigenous people to access and provide information and communication services, with financing from local institutions.

Video

Video has for many years been successfully used for participatory planning, empowerment and sharing of knowledge with disadvantaged individuals and communities. Visual images are powerful tools for communicating with illiterate audiences. Cheaper, easy to use video and audio equipment has enabled communities to master production skills thus giving them access to and control over the tools for information and communication generation and exchange. Video Sewa in Ahmedabad, India is a classic example of the use of participatory video for the empowerment of illiterate rural women. Video programmes produced by rural women associated with SEWA (Self-Employed Women's Association) have been used for income generation, occupational health, wage negotiations, legal interventions, teaching new skills and advocating for policy change. Video based approaches can now take advantage of the digitalisation of video coupled with Internet to facilitate production processes and improve networking and sharing of knowledge and information.

Radio

Radio remains the most widely available and affordable mass medium for disadvantaged groups. In rural areas, it is often the only mass medium available. It can reach large numbers of isolated populations over widespread and geographical areas. In some rural areas it is the only source of information about agricultural innovations, weather and market prices. It is oral and thus corresponds to the culture of poverty, making it more adaptable to many indigenous cultures. Because of low production and distribution costs it can be local. Community radio enables neglected communities, such as women, to be heard and to participate in democratic processes within societies. It reflects their interests, and plays an important role in reinforcing cultural expressions and identity as well as local languages. It can provide timely and relevant information on development issues, opportunities, experiences, skills and public interests. It thus has the ability to involve rural communities, indigenous people and underprivileged sectors of urban societies in an interactive social communication process. (UNESCO, 2000)

TRAINING COMMUNITY RADIO WORKERS FOR EMPOWERMENT

A training approach developed in Ghana for community radio workers takes its name from the Kente traditional hand woven cloth of the Ashanti people. The Kente approach is based on the belief that community radio is a different kind of radio and represents a different theoretical and operational model from public and commercial radio. This implies that community radio requires a new kind of "professional" – a community worker with a specific set of values, skills and standards that are focussed on community empowerment. Thus, the training of community workers is woven into the culture of the community and the process of empowerment. It is a practical hand on approach that integrates theory (development communication, communication and culture, management, etc.) with experience and the practice of broadcasting as it applies to community radio, but context based. The four elements/ modules of the course include: Knowing self; Knowing the community; Knowing development and Knowing media. The empowerment of the trainees is seen as part of the process of community empowerment, which is itself the end-goal of the training. The approach was initially developed for Radio Ada, the first full-fledged radio station in Ghana, but presently has been extended to other member stations of the Ghana Community Radio Network and to Ethiopia.

One of the most interesting developments for communication with marginalized people in recent years has been the convergence of local radio with the Internet, creating new models with potential for providing relevant information and knowledge to the poor. The merging of the two technologies presents many opportunities: Radio can deliver information to many listeners, but the Internet enables them to send back information, to ask questions, to request and seek information, and to communicate with specialists. The Internet enables access to information from both national and international sources, while radio can localise, repackage and translate that knowledge to local audiences. (Bennett, 2003). Experiments have been carried out in Asia, Latin America and Africa. These include projects in different environments and seeking to address different sets of problems: To support radio networking and exchanges, community intermediary projects, and projects that link migrants to their home communities. (Bruce Girard, 2003)

Selling a Buffalo through Hybrid Radio

In the western part of Nepal, a farmer in Madanpokhara village, located 8 hours drive from Kathmandu, needed to sell his buffalo. There was no better means to market his buffalo than to make an announcement through a community radio station in his village by paying a very nominal fee. The farmer made the announcement and sold his buffalo. Radio Madapokhara is a hybrid community radio serving to give a voice to the community, through local radio but also having access to new ICTs. Programs are centred on topics that affect the everyday life of the community. The station is now also using computers, digital recording and editing hardware and software. It uses satellite technology for distributing and receiving audio data and files through its satellite audio channels. It receives news and other development content programs everyday from Radio Sagarmatha, the central hub of a network based in Kathmandu, and distributes its programs to other radio stations in the network through the satellite system. The radio had received support from UNESCO, Panos and the Media Development Loan Fund of the Czech Republic.

Migrant communities are on the increase, and their financial remittances as well as the experience gained abroad are an important contribution to the development of their native communities. Radio can play an important role in linking the migrant communities with their native communities, language and cultures.

The Internet, radio and telephone combined can extend communication and enable communities to keep in touch despite migration. Stations in the home country will broadcast news from the migrant communities. The airwave messages coming from abroad can include simple greetings, information about money transfers and emergency alerts. The messages inform people who remain in the region about relatives who have left, and for migrants they are a means to keep in touch with their place of origin. In some cases migrant communities have obtained a few hours a week on multi-lingual stations in their new home country and broadcast programs with news and cultural content from home mixed with content related to the new environment. They have become an important tool for preserving culture. (Bruce Girard, 2003).

ICTs: Potential and Limitations

With the arrival of the Information Revolution, ICTs are getting most of the attention. Governments have adopted national IT policies and liberalised the telecommunication sector to attract investment. Significant sums are being invested by donors, intergovernmental agencies and NGOs to wire the developing world and provide access to computers and the Internet for alleviation of poverty. There is a vast literature on the benefits and potential of computerised communication to enhance people's daily lives. Experiments with the use of Internet and computers have proven to have positive results in various applications: Improved access to education opportunities, increased transparency and efficiency in government services, increased trade and marketing opportunities for marginalized communities, increased community empowerment through access to information, improved networking and opportunities for women, access to medical information for isolated communities and new employment opportunities are only a few of the examples that have bolstered the belief that these technologies have a key role to play in development. However people engaged in development work have mixed feelings about the impact of these technologies on the alleviation of poverty. The initial enthusiasm is now being replaced by more critical and cautious perspectives, as lessons are drawn from the first years of experience in the field. It is clear, for example, that although the Internet is a powerful tool for sharing information and knowledge, and thus for human development, it is not a remedy for all development problems. Poverty cannot be divorced from the underlying social, economic and political issues as well as existing power structures. The emphasis on access to the technologies, though important, must be shifted to the more important issues of meaningful use and social appropriation. Deploying these technologies in ways that benefit the poor requires regulatory frameworks and enabling policy environments, which reflect the needs of all sectors of society.

Social Dimensions of ICTs

The use of ICTs can also transform the local power structures within communities and disrupt community life. For instance, in Guyana indigenous women were so successful trading their hammocks on the Web, that the power structures were transformed providing women economic independence from their husbands. The impact on the community was so strong that the indigenous women were forced by the male community members to end the trading of the hammocks through the web. This case demonstrates clearly that ICTs also can have negative impacts on communities if their use is not managed properly and the key stakeholders are not supporting their use. Source: Bjorn-Soren Gigler, World Bank, 2004

ICTs and the Poor

In some areas the ICT revolution has served only to widen existing economic and social gaps, as new information gaps threaten to further marginalize the poor. The bulk of information resources and technologies are in the developed countries. By conservative estimates, at least 80 per cent of the world's population still lack the most basic communication technologies to enter the Internet global village. Although Internet growth is accelerating faster in developing countries than anywhere else, it will continue to be available only to a tiny proportion of people in the poorest countries for many years to come. The situation is even more serious for rural areas. The Information Revolution has completely bypassed nearly one billion people. They are the rural poor, who constitute 75 percent of the people who live on less than one dollar a day. In many ways the digital divide just reflects all other inequalities: Disparities between urban and rural communities, men and women and between successful farmers and subsistence farmers. In addition, some argue that poor countries cannot afford the cost of telecommunication infrastructure. Money is scarce for economies crippled by external debt and trying to cut back on social sector spending. It is argued that these countries should address instead basic needs such as education, water, health and roads.

Barriers for the Poor

What are the barriers for poor rural people to access new technologies, and the Internet in particular?

- The rural poor lack infrastructure (electricity, telecommunications). ICTs depend on national policies and regulation for telecommunications and broadcasting licences. ICTs require initial capital investment for hardware and software. ICTs also depend on the skills and capacity necessary to use, manage and maintain the technology effectively.

- The rural poor are probably illiterate or semi-literate, with low levels of education. They would not find much in their local language on the Internet.
- They would not find much information relevant to their daily lives.
- They are not usually offered the opportunity to input their own local knowledge. The Web offers them almost no opportunities for local wealth creation.
- They cannot afford the cost of Internet access, and they cannot afford their own computer.

Public Access Points

There is a movement in the development community pushing for the widespread rollout of public access points as a means of extending access to the Internet and bringing it closer to disadvantaged communities and the intermediary organisations that provide services to these communities.

Multi-media community centres, or telecentres are a typical example. They are usually established in rural areas where individual access is unavailable or unaffordable. They provide a range of information services that are relevant to the needs of the communities and often training. They can be used by communities to create and share their information with outside audiences. The services are free, or subsidised by governments, NGOs and donors. Cybercafés instead are privately owned commercial operations that focus primarily on providing customers with access to the Internet and the World Wide Web. Their clients tend to be more urban, more educated and able to pay for their services. They are an important tool for minority groups in urban societies such as youth, women, migrant workers and Diasporas.

While both cybercafés and telecentres might offer training in computer skills and web use, the telecentre is more likely to offer other kinds of training, including non formal education and distance learning in agriculture, health, education, entrepreneurship and other fields related to community development and poverty alleviation. But, bridging the last mile of connectivity with rural communities still needs to be carried out by development workers, using more traditional forms of communication such as radio. (Colle and Roman 2001) Among the problems faced by telecentres for alleviation of poverty has been their lack of sustainability.

Often they have been parachuted from outside and not adopted from within. Research on the needs of the communities has not been carried out and they do not provide relevant and useful local content.

Often information is not translated into local dialects. Socio-cultural issues have been ignored. Training in communication and management skills has not always been provided to local personnel, who must act as information intermediaries. Participation on the part of marginalized sectors of the communities has been lacking. And finally, financial sustainability has not been achieved.

According to Charles Kenny, "while there is a continued (perhaps growing) role for donors to improve access to a range of ICTs in developing countries, that role probably should not extend to the widespread provision of internet access – at least in the poorer regions of the least developed countries. The nature of extreme poverty in Less Developed Countries-very low incomes, subsistence and unskilled wage labour as the dominant income source, food as the dominant consumption good, low education and high illiteracy, minority language group status and rural location – points to an unsustainably high cost and relatively low benefit of direct internet service provision through telecentres to the very poor.

This might suggest that the push for universal Internet access as a tool for poverty relief is misplaced. Instead the paper argues that access programs focused on the telephone and radio might have a higher benefit-cost ratio and lower overall cost as alternatives to and intermediaries for the Internet in poverty alleviation programs." (Kenny, 2002)

The Mobile Phone

The development of the mobile phone as a relatively cheap and powerful tool has enabled communities, even in remote rural areas to spontaneously and locally appropriate it for use. Mobile and satellite telephony are bringing telecommunications within reach not only of the small entrepreneur in developing countries but also of the rural farmer. The Village Pay Phone sponsored by the Grameen Bank in Bangladesh is a classical example of a scheme promoting income-generating activities for the rural poor. It enables illiterate rural women to earn income by renting out mobile phones to members of the community for a fee. A Canadian evaluation of the program showed that the income derived by operators was on average 24 per cent of their household income – and in some cases it was as high as 40 per cent of household income.

Local Appropriation and Impact

FAO has compiled two studies of the ICT scene to identify whether poor communities and groups had taken ownership of ICTs for their own use. The basis for both papers was to identify examples of community driven and local appropriation of ICTs, to identify what worked and what didn't work, and to contribute to the on-going debate on impact. The studies identify some analytical tools and guiding principles to foster local appropriation of ICTs:

Despite an increase in case studies there is still a need for more empirical evidence to demonstrate impact and understand more about how communities make use of ICTs. Few projects have paid attention to monitoring and evaluation of outcomes, with the result that there is little data to assess the actual impact of these technologies on the poor and therefore little sound evidence to merit further project investment. Donors have failed to devote resources to research outcomes in any depth. And, more qualitative indicators are required. According to UNDP, "There has also been a desire to hide failures on the part of those involved, in many cases. Although many ICT for development initiatives have failed, few failures have been documented. This is due to the lack of incentives in the development system to encourage project managers, development agencies or implementing partners to critically report and make public project shortfalls or failures"(UNDP 2000).

However, donors and development organisations are now beginning to query approaches based only on access to technology, and wish to address how best to use ICTs to achieve development objectives. It is important to note that some valuable studies do exist and these provide an important basis for developing criteria for assessing what is good practice.3

In the rush to "wire" developing countries, little attention has been paid to an ICT conceptual framework or guidelines for ICT utilisation. The design of ICT programs for the poor must take into account the lessons learned over the years by communication for development efforts. There needs to be a focus on the needs of communities and the benefits of the new technologies rather then the quantity of technologies available. The emphasis must be on the use of new technologies as a means of improving the living conditions of the poor, rather than becoming an end in themselves. The real needs of communities must be identified with them and addressed. Successful examples of local appropriation have been those in which ICTs support the priorities and goals of communities, such as increased incomes or capacity building in business management and marketing, improved agricultural productivity or increased employment opportunities. Or where they strengthen existing traditional communication systems to promote networking and advocacy for social change.

Local content and languages are critical to enable the poor to have access to the benefits of the information revolution. The creation of local content requires building on existing and trusted traditional communication systems and methods for collecting and sharing information. These include established community media such as radio, which can be enhanced through connection with the Internet. In addition there are new technologies such as digital video that can also be appropriated for the production of local content. To be effective, external content has to be adapted and translated into vernacular languages, before local audiences can understand it. There is therefore a growing need also to develop the capacity for locally based professionals to download and transform global content for local consumption.

The Role of Donors and Development Agencies

There are dozens of new initiatives to promote digital opportunities, but co-ordination between these initiatives is poorly developed and efforts may be duplicated. There is much greater scope for co-ordination and common effective strategies. Opinions differ on what donor organisations should be doing to support the growth and use of the Internet and other information technologies in developing countries. It is argued that the spread of ICTs is best left to the private sector, since the proliferation of fax machines and mobiles phones, for example, has not come about through a targeted development intervention. If the market is ensuring that access is spreading in terms of physical availability, then donors and NGOs should shift their focus to ensuring an appropriate use of the technologies, that the benefits are maximised and that marginalization is minimised. What is clear is that whereas Internet growth is independent of donor support, access for disadvantaged groups will not grow without support from donors and subsidies from Governments. Without a specific focus by donors on poor, rural and marginal groups, the digital age will bypass these nonprofitable sectors.

8

Practices of Community Work

COMMUNITY OF PRACTICE

A community of practice (CoP) is, according to cognitive anthropologists Jean Lave and Etienne Wenger, a group of people who share an interest, a craft, and/or a profession. The group can evolve naturally because of the members' common interest in a particular domain or area, or it can be created specifically with the goal of gaining knowledge related to their field.

It is through the process of sharing information and experiences with the group that the members learn from each other, and have an opportunity to develop themselves personally and professionally. CoPs can exist online, such as within discussion boards and newsgroups, or in real life, such as in a lunch room at work, in a field setting, on a factory floor, or elsewhere in the environment.

While Lave and Wenger coined the term in the 1990s, this type of learning practice has existed for as long as people have been learning and sharing their experiences through storytelling.

OVERVIEW OF ORIGIN AND DEVELOPMENT

Since the publication of "situated learning: legitimate peripheral participation" in 1991, communities of practice have been the focus of attention, first as a theory of learning and later as part of the field of knowledge management.

Early Years

To understand how learning occurs outside the classroom while at the Institute for Research on Learning, Lave and Wenger studied how newcomers or novices to informal groups become established members of those groups. Lave and Wenger first used the term communities of practice to describe learning through practice and participation, which they named situated learning.

The structure of the community was created over time through a process of legitimate peripheral participation. Legitimation and participation together define the characteristic ways of belonging to a community whereas peripherality and participation are concerned with location and identity in the social world.

Lave and Wenger's research looked at how apprenticeships help people learn. They found that when newcomers join an established group or community, they spend some time initially observing and perhaps performing simple tasks in basic roles as they learn how the group works and how they can participate (an apprentice electrician, for example would watch and learn before actually doing any electrical work; initially taking on small simple jobs and eventually more complicated ones). Lave and Wenger described this socialization process as legitimate peripheral participation.

The term "community of practice" is that group that Lave and Wenger referred to, who share a common interest and a desire to learn from and contribute to the community with their variety of experiences.

Later Years

In his later work (Wenger 1998), Wenger abandoned the concept of legitimate peripheral participation and used the idea of an inherent tension in a duality instead. He identifies four dualities that exist in communities of practice, participation-reification, designed-emergent, identification-negotiability and local-global, although the participation-reification duality has been the focus of particular interest because of its links to knowledge management.

He describes the structure of a CoP as consisting of three interrelated terms: 'mutual engagement', 'joint enterprise' and 'shared repertoire'.

- Mutual Engagement: Firstly, through participation in the community, members establish norms and build collaborative relationships; this is termed mutual engagement. These relationships are the ties that bind the members of the community together as a social entity.
- Joint Enterprise: Secondly, through their interactions, they create a shared understanding of what binds them together; this is termed the joint enterprise. The joint enterprise is (re)negotiated by its members and is sometimes referred to as the 'domain' of the community.
- Shared Repertoire: Finally, as part of its practice, the community produces a set of communal resources, which is termed their shared repertoire; this is used in the pursuit of their joint enterprise and can include both literal and symbolic meanings.

Present Work

For Etienne Wenger, learning is central to human identity. A primary focus of Wenger's more recent work is on learning as social participation – the individual as an active participant in the practices of social communities, and in the construction of his/her identity through these communities.

In this context, a community of practice is a group of individuals participating in communal activity, and experiencing/continuously creating their shared identity through engaging in and contributing to the practices of their communities.

The structural characteristics of a community of practice are again redefined to a domain of knowledge, a notion of community and a practice.

- Domain: A domain of knowledge creates common ground, inspires members to participate, guides their learning and gives meaning to their actions.

- Community: The notion of a community creates the social fabric for that learning. A strong community fosters interactions and encourages a willingness to share ideas.
- Practice: While the domain provides the general area of interest for the community, the practice is the specific focus around which the community develops, shares and maintains its core of knowledge.

In many organizations, communities of practice have become an integral part of the organization structure. These communities take on knowledge stewarding tasks that were formally covered by more formal organizational structures. In some organizations there are both formal and informal communities of practice. There is a great deal of interest within organizations to encourage, support, and sponsor communities of practice in order to benefit from shared knowledge that may lead to higher productivity (Wenger 2004). Communities of practice are now viewed by many in the business setting as a means to capturing the tacit knowledge, or the know-how that is not so easily articulated.

An important aspect and function of communities of practice is increasing organization performance. Lesser & Storck (2001, p. 836) identify four areas of organizational performance that can be affected by communities of practice:

- Decreasing the learning curve of new employees
- Responding more rapidly to customer needs and inquiries
- Reducing rework and preventing "reinvention of the wheel"
- Spawning new ideas for products and services.

EXAMPLES OF COMMUNITIES OF PRACTICE

The communities Lave and Wenger studied were naturally forming as practitioners of craft and skill-based activities met to share experiences and insights. Lave and Wenger observed situated learning within a community of practice among Yucatán midwives, native tailors, navy quartermasters and meat cutters

(Lave & Wenger 1991) as well as insurance claims processors. (Wenger 1998). Other fields have made use of the concept of CoPs. Examples include education (Grossman 2001), sociolinguistics, material anthropology, and second language acquisition.

A famous example of a community of practice within an organization is that which developed around the Xerox customer service representatives who repaired the machines in the field (Brown & Duguid 2000). The Xerox reps began exchanging tips and tricks over informal meetings over breakfast or lunch and eventually Xerox saw the value of these interactions and created the Eureka project to allow these interactions to be shared across the global network of representatives. The Eureka database has been estimated to have saved the corporation 100$ million. Communities of practice compared to functional or project teams:

- A project team differs from a community of practice in several significant ways (McDermott, 1999).
- A project team is driven by deliverables with shared goals, milestones and results.
- A project team meets to share and exchange information and experiences just as the community of practice does, but team membership is defined by task.
- A project team typically has designated members who remain consistent in their roles during the project.
- A project team is dissolved once its mission is accomplished.

By contrast,

- A community of practice is often organically created, with as many objectives as members of that community.
- Community membership is defined by the knowledge of the members. CoP membership changes and members may take on new roles within the community as interests and needs arise.
- A community of practice can exist as long as the members believe they have something to contribute to it, or gain from it.

Communities of Practice versus Communities of Interest

In addition to the distinction between CoP and other types of organizational groupings found in the workplace, in some cases it is useful to differentiate CoP from Communities of Interest (CoI).

Community of Interest:

- A group of people interested in sharing information and discussing a particular topic that interests them.
- Members are not necessarily experts or practitioners of the topic around which the CoI has formed.
- The purpose of the CoI is to provide a place where people who share a common interest can go and exchange information, ask questions, and express their opinions about the topic.
- Membership in a CoI is not dependent upon expertise-one only needs to be interested in the subject.

Community of Practice:

- A CoP, in contrast, is a group of people who are active practitioners.
- CoP participation is not appropriate for non-practitioners.
- The purpose of a CoP, as discussed above, is to provide a way for practitioners to share tips and best practices, ask questions of their colleagues, and provide support for each other.
- Membership is dependent on expertise-one should have at least some recent experience performing in the role or subject area of the CoP.
- Example: Someone who is interested in photography and has some background/training in it finds an online CoP for working photojournalists, who use it to discuss various aspects of their work. Since this community is focused on working photojournalists, it would not be appropriate for an amateur photographer to contribute

to the CoP discussions there. Depending on the CoPs structure non-CoP members may have access to reading the discussions and accessing other materials of the community.

Knowledge Management

Wasko and Faraj (2000) describe three kinds of knowledge: "knowledge as object", "knowledge embedded within individuals", and "knowledge embedded in a community". Communities of Practice have become associated with finding, sharing, transferring, and archiving knowledge, as well as making explicit "expertise", or tacit knowledge. Tacit knowledge is considered to be those valuable context-based experiences that can not easily be captured, codified and stored. Because knowledge management is seen "primarily as a problem of capturing, organizing, and retrieving information, evoking notions of databases, documents, query languages, and data mining", the community of practice, collectively and individually, is considered a rich potential source of helpful information in the form of actual experiences; in other words, best practices. Thus, for knowledge management, a community of practice is one source of content and context that if codified, documented and archived can be accessed for later use.

BENEFIT OF COMMUNITY OF PRACTICE

Social Capital

Social capital is said to be a multi-dimensional concept, with both public and private facets (Putnam 2001). That is, acquiring social capital gives value to both the individual and the group as a whole, in which the social capital is generated. Through informal connections that participants make in their community of practice, and in the formal process of sharing their expertise, learning from others, and participating in the group, members are said to be acquiring social capital-or a trust that members build between themselves and others that can lead to better communication. Thus, CoPs are considered a way to gain social capital, especially to those members who demonstrate expertise and experience.

FACTORS OF A SUCCESSFUL COMMUNITY OF PRACTICE

Members of communities of practice are thought to be more efficient and effective conduits of information and experiences. While organizations tend to provide manuals to meet the training needs of their employees, CoP's help foster the process of storytelling among colleagues which, in turn, helps them strengthen their skills on the job. Studies have shown that workers spend a third of their time looking for information and are five times more likely to turn to a co-worker rather than an explicit source of information. Time is saved by conferring with members of a CoP. Members of the community have tacit knowledge, which can be difficult to store and retrieve outside. For example, one person can share the best way to handle a situation based on his experiences, which may enable the other person to avoid mistakes and shorten the learning curve. In a CoP, members can openly discuss and brainstorm about a project, which can lead to new capabilities. The type of information that is shared and learned in a CoP is boundless (Dalkir 2005). Duguid (2005) clarifies the difference between tacit knowledge, or knowing *how*, and explicit knowledge, or knowing *what*. Performing optimally in a job requires being able to convert theory into practice. Communities of practice help the individual bridge the gap between knowing *what* and knowing *how*. (Duguid 2005)

As members of communities of practice, individuals report increased communication with people (professionals, interested parties, hobbyists), less dependence on geographic proximity, and the generation of new knowledge.

Social Presence

Communicating with others in a community of practice involves creating *social presence*. Tu (2002) defines social presence as "the degree of salience of another person in an interaction and the consequent salience of an interpersonal relationship". It is believed that social presence affects how likely an individual is of participating in a COP (especially in online environments). (Tu 2002) Management of a community of practice often faces many barriers that inhibit individuals from engaging in knowledge exchange. Some of the reasons for these barriers are egos and personal attacks, large overwhelming COP's, and time constraints.

Motivation

Motivation to share knowledge is critical to success in communities of practice. Studies show that members are motivated to become active participants in a CoP when they view knowledge as meant for the public good, a moral obligation and/or as a community interest. Members of a community of practice can also be motivated to participate by using methods such as tangible returns (promotion, raises or bonuses), intangible returns (reputation, self-esteem) and community interest (exchange of practice related knowledge, interaction).

Collaboration

Collaboration is essential to ensuring that communities of practice thrive. Research has found that certain factors can indicate a higher level of collaboration in knowledge exchange in a business network. Sveiby and Simons found that more seasoned colleagues tend to foster a more collaborative culture. Additionally they noted that a higher educational level also predicts a tendency to favor collaboration.

ACTIONS TO CULTIVATE A SUCCESSFUL COMMUNITY OF PRACTICE

What makes a community of practice succeed depends on the purpose and objective of the community as well as the interests and resources of the members of that community. Wenger identified seven actions that could be taken in order to cultivate communities of practice:

1. Design the community to evolve naturally-Because the nature of a Community of Practice is dynamic, in that the interests, goals, and members are subject to change, CoP forums should be designed to support shifts in focus.
2. Create opportunities for open dialog within and with outside perspectives-While the members and their

knowledge are the CoP's most valuable resource, it is also beneficial to look outside of the CoP to understand the different possibilities for achieving their learning goals.

3. Welcome and allow different levels of participation-Wenger identifies 3 main levels of participation. 1) The core group who participate intensely in the community through discussions and projects. This group typically takes on leadership roles in guiding the group 2) The active group who attend and participate regularly, but not to the level of the leaders. 3) The peripheral group who, while they are passive participants in the community, still learn from their level of involvement. Wenger notes the third group typically represents the majority of the community.
4. Develop both public and private community spaces-While CoP's typically operate in public spaces where all members share, discuss and explore ideas, they should also offer private exchanges. Different members of the CoP could coordinate relationships among members and resources in an individualized approach based on specific needs.
5. Focus on the value of the community-CoP's should create opportunities for participants to explicitly discuss the value and productivity of their participation in the group.
6. Combine familiarity and excitement-CoP's should offer the expected learning opportunities as part of their structure, and opportunities for members to shape their learning experience together by brainstorming and examining the conventional and radical wisdom related to their topic.
7. Find and nurture a regular rhythm for the community-CoP's should coordinate a thriving cycle of activities and events that allow for the members to regularly meet, reflect, and evolve. The rhythm, or pace, should maintain an anticipated level of engagement to sustain the vibrancy of the community, yet not be so fast-paced

that it becomes unwieldy and overwhelming in its intensity.

WHAT ARE COMMUNITIES OF PRACTICE?

Communities of practice are formed by people who engage in a process of collective learning in a shared domain of human endeavour: a tribe learning to survive, a band of artists seeking new forms of expression, a group of engineers working on similar problems, a clique of pupils defining their identity in the school, a network of surgeons exploring novel techniques, a gathering of first-time managers helping each other cope. In a nutshell: Communities of practice are groups of people who share a concern or a passion for something they do and learn how to do it better as they interact regularly.

Note that this definition allows for, but does not assume, intentionality: learning can be the reason the community comes together or an incidental outcome of member's interactions. Not everything called a community is a community of practice. A neighborhood for instance, is often called a community, but is usually not a community of practice. Three characteristics are crucial:

The Domain: A community of practice is not merely a club of friends or a network of connections between people. It has an identity defined by a shared domain of interest. Membership therefore implies a commitment to the domain, and therefore a shared competence that distinguishes members from other people. (You could belong to the same network as someone and never know it.) The domain is not necessarily something recognized as "expertise" outside the community. A youth gang may have developed all sorts of ways of dealing with their domain: surviving on the street and maintaining some kind of identity they can live with. They value their collective competence and learn from each other, even though few people outside the group may value or even recognize their expertise.

The Community: In pursuing their interest in their domain, members engage in joint activities and discussions, help each other, and share information. They build relationships that enable them to learn from each other. A website in itself is not a community of practice. Having the same job or the same title does not make for a community of practice unless members interact and learn together. The claims processors in a large insurance company or students in American high schools may have much in common, yet unless they interact and learn together, they do not form a community of practice. But members of a community of practice do not necessarily work together on a daily basis. The Impressionists, for instance, used to meet in cafes and studios to discuss the style of painting they were inventing together. These interactions were essential to making them a community of practice even though they often painted alone.

The Practice: A community of practice is not merely a community of interest—people who like certain kinds of movies, for instance. Members of a community of practice are practitioners. They develop a shared repertoire of resources: experiences, stories, tools, ways of addressing recurring problems—in short a shared practice. This takes time and sustained interaction. A good conversation with a stranger on an airplane may give you all sorts of interesting insights, but it does not in itself make for a community of practice. The development of a shared practice may be more or less self-conscious. The "windshield wipers" engineers at an auto manufacturer make a concerted effort to collect and document the tricks and lessons they have learned into a knowledge base. By contrast, nurses who meet regularly for lunch in a hospital cafeteria may not realize that their lunch discussions are one of their main sources of knowledge about how to care for patients. Still, in the course of all these conversations, they have developed a set of stories and cases that have become a shared repertoire for their practice.

It is the combination of these three elements that constitutes a community of practice. And it is by developing these three elements in parallel that one cultivates such a community.

WHERE DOES THE CONCEPT COME FROM?

Social scientists have used versions of the concept of community of practice for a variety of analytical purposes, but the origin and primary use of the concept has been in learning theory. Anthropologist Jean Lave and I coined the term while studying apprenticeship as a learning model. People usually think of apprenticeship as a relationship between a student and a master, but studies of apprenticeship reveal a more complex set of social relationships through which learning takes place mostly with journeymen and more advanced apprentices.

The term community of practice was coined to refer to the community that acts as a living curriculum for the apprentice. Once the concept was articulated, we started to see these communities everywhere, even when no formal apprenticeship system existed. And of course, learning in a community of practice is not limited to novices. The practice of a community is dynamic and involves learning on the part of everyone.

Where is the Concept being Applied?

The concept of community of practice has found a number of practical applications in business, organizational design, government, education, professional associations, development projects, and civic life.

Organizations. The concept has been adopted most readily by people in business because of the recognition that knowledge is a critical asset that needs to be managed strategically. Initial efforts at managing knowledge had focused on information systems with disappointing results.

Communities of practice provided a new approach, which focused on people and on the social structures that enable them to learn with and from each other. Today, there is hardly any organization of a reasonable size that does not have some form communities-of-practice initiative. A number of characteristics explain this rush of interest in communities of practice as a vehicle for developing strategic capabilities in organizations:

- Communities of practice enable practitioners to take collective responsibility for managing the knowledge they need, recognizing that, given the proper structure, they are in the best position to do this.

- Communities among practitioners create a direct link between learning and performance, because the same people participate in communities of practice and in teams and business units.
- Practitioners can address the tacit and dynamic aspects of knowledge creation and sharing, as well as the more explicit aspects.
- Communities are not limited by formal structures: they create connections among people across organizational and geographic boundaries.

From this perspective, the knowledge of an organization lives in a constellation of communities of practice each taking care of a specific aspect of the competence that the organization needs. However, the very characteristics that make communities of practice a good fit for stewarding knowledge—autonomy, practitioner-orientation, informality, crossing boundaries—are also characteristics that make them a challenge for traditional hierarchical organizations. How this challenge is going to affect these organizations remains to be seen.

Government. Like businesses, government organizations face knowledge challenges of increasing complexity and scale. They have adopted communities of practice for much the same reasons, though the formality of the bureaucracy can come in the way of open knowledge sharing. Beyond internal communities, there are typical government problems such as education, health, and security that require coordination and knowledge sharing across levels of government. There also, communities of practice hold the promise of enabling connections among people across formal structures. And there also, there are substantial organizational issues to overcome.

Education. Schools and districts are organizations in their own right, and they too face increasing knowledge challenges. The first applications of communities of practice have been in teacher training and in providing isolated administrators with access to colleagues. There is a wave of interest in these peer-to-peer professional-development activities. But in the education sector, learning is not only a means to an end: it the end product. The perspective of communities of practice is therefore also relevant at this level. In business, focusing on communities of practice adds a layer of complexity to the organization, but it does not fundamentally change what the business is about. In schools, changing the learning theory is a much deeper transformation. This will inevitably take longer. The perspective of communities of practice affects educational practices along three dimensions:

- *Internally*: How to organize educational experiences that ground school learning in practice through participation in communities around subject matters?
- *Externally*: How to connect the experience of students to actual practice through peripheral forms of participation in broader communities beyond the walls of the school?
- *Over the lifetime of students*: How to serve the lifelong learning needs of students by organizing communities of practice focused on topics of continuing interest to students beyond the initial schooling period?

From this perspective, the school is not the privileged locus of learning. It is not a self-contained, closed world in which students acquire knowledge to be applied outside, but a part of a broader learning system. The class is not the primary learning event. It is life itself that is the main learning event. Schools, classrooms, and training sessions still have a role to play in this vision, but they have to be in the service of the learning that happens in the world.

Associations. A growing number of associations, professional and otherwise, are seeking ways to focus on learning through reflection on practice. Their members are restless and their allegiance is fragile. They need to offer high-value learning activities. The peer-to-peer learning activities typical of communities of practice offer a complementary alternative to more traditional course offerings and publications.

Social sector. In the civic domain, there is an emergent interest in building communities among practitioners. In the non-profit world, for instance, foundations are recognizing that philanthropy needs focus on learning systems in order to fully leverage funded projects. But practitioners are seeking peer-to-peer connections and learning opportunities with or without the support of institutions. This includes regional economic development, with intra-regional communities on various domains, as well as inter-regional learning with communities gathering practitioners from various regions.

International development. There is increasing recognition that the challenge of developing nations is as much a knowledge as a financial challenge. A number of people believe that a communities-of-practice approach can provide a new paradigm for development work. It emphasizes knowledge building among practitioners. Some development agencies now see their role as conveners of such communities, rather than as providers of knowledge.

The web. New technologies such as the Internet have extended the reach of our interactions beyond the geographical limitations of traditional communities, but the increase in flow of information does not obviate the need for community. In fact, it expands the possibilities for community and calls for new kinds of communities based on shared practice.

The concept of community of practice is influencing theory and practice in many domains. From humble beginnings in apprenticeship studies, the concept was grabbed by businesses interested in knowledge management and has progressively found its way into other sectors. It has now become the foundation of a perspective on knowing and learning that informs efforts to create learning systems in various sectors and at various levels of scale, from local communities, to single organizations, partnerships, cities, regions, and the entire world.

SEVEN PRINCIPLES FOR CULTIVATING COMMUNITIES OF PRACTICE

In Silicon Valley, a community of circuit designers meets for a lively debate about the merits of two different designs developed by one of the participants. Huddling together over the circuit diagrams, they analyse possible faults, discuss issues of efficiency, propose alternatives, tease out each other's assumptions, and make the case for their view. In Boston, a group of social workers who staff a help line meet to discuss knotty client problems, express sympathy as they discuss difficulties, probe to understand each other's feelings, and gently offer suggestions. Their meetings are often deeply challenging and sometimes highly emotional. The fact-driven, sometimes argumentative, meetings of the Silicon Valley circuit designers are extremely different from the compassionate meetings of the social workers in Boston. But despite their differences, the circuit designers' and social workers' communities are both vibrant and full of life. Their energy is palpable to both the regular participants and visitors.

Because communities of practice are voluntary, what makes them successful over time is their ability to generate enough excitement, relevance, and value to attract and engage members. Although many factors, such as management support or an urgent problem, can inspire a community, nothing can substitute for this sense of *aliveness*.

How do you design for aliveness? Certainly you cannot contrive or dictate it. You cannot design it in the traditional sense of specifying a structure or process and then implementing it. Still, aliveness does not always happen automatically. Many natural communities never grow beyond a network of friends because they fail to attract enough participants. Many intentional communities fall apart soon after their initial launch because they don't have enough energy to sustain themselves. Communities, unlike teams and other structures, need to invite the interaction that makes them alive. For example, a park is more appealing to use if its location provides a short cut between destinations. It invites people to sit for lunch or chat if it has benches set slightly off the main path, visible, but just out of earshot, next to something interesting like a flower bed or a patch of sunlight. 1 The structure of organizational relationships and events also invite a kind of interaction. Meetings that contain some open time during a break or lunch, with enough space for people to mingle or confer privately, invite one-on-one discussion and relationship building. Just as a good park has varied spaces for neighborhood baseball games, quiet chats, or solitary contemplation, a well-designed community of practice allows for participating in group discussion, having one-on-one conversations, reading about new ideas, or watching experts duel over cutting-edge issues. Even though communities are voluntary and organic, good community design can invite, even evoke, aliveness.

Designing to evoke aliveness is different from most organizational design, which traditionally focuses on creating structures, systems, and roles that achieve relatively fixed organizational goals and fit well with other structural elements of the organization. Even when organizations are designed to be flexible and responsive to their environment, organic growth and aliveness are typically not primary design goals. 2 For communities of practice, however, they are paramount, even though communities also need to contribute to organizational goals. Designing for aliveness requires a different set of design principles. The goal of community design is to bring out the community's own internal direction, character, and energy. The principles we developed to do this focus on the dilemmas at the heart of designing communities of practice. What is the role of design for a "human institution" that is, by definition, natural, spontaneous, and self-directed? How do you guide such an institution to realize itself, to become "alive?" From our experience we have derived seven principles:

1. Design for evolution.
2. Open a dialogue between inside and outside perspectives.
3. Invite different levels of participation.
4. Develop both public and private community spaces.
5. Focus on value.
6. Combine familiarity and excitement.
7. Create a rhythm for the community.

These design principles are not recipes, but rather embody our understanding of how elements of design work together. They reveal the thinking behind a design. Making design principles explicit makes it possible to be more flexible and improvisational.

Design for Evolution

Because communities of practice are organic, designing them is more a matter of shepherding their evolution than creating them from scratch. Design elements should be catalysts for a community's natural evolution. As they develop, communities usually build on preexisting personal networks. For example, when Schlumberger launched a series of communities of practice in its research division, most people were already part of networks connected through the company's extensive bulletin board system. The dynamic nature of communities is key to their evolution. As the community grows, new members bring new interests and may pull the focus of the community in different directions. Changes in the organization influence the relative importance of the community and place new demands on it. For example, an IT community that was only marginally important to an organization suddenly became critical as the company discovered the potential of a few e-business pilots. Changes in the core science or technology of a community constantly reshape it, often bringing in professionals from neighbouring disciplines or introducing technological advances that change their way of working. Because communities are built on existing networks and evolve beyond any particular design, the purpose of a design is not to impose a structure but to help the community develop.

Community design is much more like life-long learning than traditional organization design. "Alive" communities reflect on and redesign elements of themselves throughout their existence. Community design often involves fewer elements at the beginning than does a traditional organization design. In one case, the coordinator and core members had many ideas of what the community could become. Rather than introduce those ideas to the community as a whole, they started with a very simple structure of regular weekly meetings. They did not capture meeting notes, put up a Web site, or speculate with the group on "where this is going." Their first goal was to draw potential members to the community. Once people were engaged in the topic and had begun to build relationships, the core members began introducing other elements of community structure—such as a Web site, links to other communities, projects to define key practices—one at a time.

The key to designing for evolution is to combine design elements in a way that catalyses community development. Physical structures—such as roads and parks—can precipitate the development of a town. Similarly, social and organizational structures, such as a community coordinator or problem-solving meetings, can precipitate the evolution of a community. Which community design elements are most appropriate depends on the community's stage of development, its environment, member cohesiveness, and the kinds of knowledge it shares. But evolution is common to all communities, and the primary role of design is to catalyze that evolution.

Open a Dialogue between Inside and Outside Perspectives

Good community design requires an insider's perspective to lead the discovery of what the community is about. When designing teams, we know a team's output requirements in advance and can design to achieve that output. But effective community design is built on the collective experience of community members. Only an insider can appreciate the issues at the heart of the domain, the knowledge that is important to share, the challenges their field faces, and the latent potential in emerging ideas and techniques. Only an insider can know who the real players are and their relationships. This requires more than community "input." It requires a deep understanding of community issues. Good community design requires an understanding of the community's potential to develop and steward knowledge, but it often takes an outside perspective to help members see the possibilities. Because intentional communities are new for most organizations, members often have a hard time imagining how a more developed community could improve upon their current personal networks or help them leverage dormant capabilities. Good community design brings information from outside the community into the dialogue about what the community could achieve. Sometimes this involves educating community members about the role of communities in other organizations. It might mean bringing an "outsider" into a dialogue with the community leader and core members as they design the community. As a result of this dialogue, the people who understand the issues inside the community and have legitimacy within it are also able to see new possibilities and can effectively act as agents of change.

The well-connected leader of a new community on emerging technology was concerned about how to develop the community when many of the "prima donnas" of the industry were outside his company. When he saw how a similar community in another organization was structured to involve outside experts in multiple ways, he started rethinking the potential structure of his own community. He realized that the key issues in his community were less about technology and more about the business issues involved in developing the technology. This understanding of the business perspective of the other community gave him a sharper sense of the strategic potential of his own.

Invite Different Levels of Participation

Good community architecture invites many different levels of participation. Consider the variety of activities we might find in a city neighborhood on any given day: solitary shoppers, people walking briskly to work, friends out for a casual stroll, couples chatting at an outdoor cafe, a crowd watching a street performer. Others are on the periphery, watching the action from the windows above the street. A community of practice is very similar. People participate in communities for different reasons—some because the community directly provides value, some for the personal connection, and others for the opportunity to improve their skills. We used to think that we should encourage all community members to participate equally. But because people have different levels of interest in the community, this expectation is unrealistic.

Alive communities, whether planned or spontaneous, have a "coordinator" who organizes events and connects community. But others in the community also take on leadership roles. We commonly see three main levels of community participation. The first is a small core group of people who actively participate in discussions, even debates, in the public community forum. They often take on community projects, identify topics for the community to address, and move the community along its learning agenda. This group is the heart of the community. As the community matures, this core group takes on much of the community's leadership, its members becoming auxiliaries to the community coordinator. But this group is usually rather small, only 10 to 15 percent of the whole community. At the next level outside this core is the active group. These members attend meetings regularly and participate occasionally in the community forums, but without the regularity or intensity of the core group. The active group is also quite small, another 15 to 20 percent of the community.

A large portion of community members are peripheral and rarely participate. Instead, they keep to the sidelines, watching the interaction of the core and active members. Some remain peripheral because they feel that their observations are not appropriate for the whole or carry no authority. Others do not have the time to contribute more actively. In a traditional meeting or team we would discourage such half-hearted involvement, but these peripheral activities are an essential dimension of communities of practice. Indeed, the people on the sidelines often are not as passive as they seem. Like people sitting at a cafe watching the activity on the street, they gain their own insights from the discussions and put them to good use. They may have private conversations about the issues being discussed in the public forum. In their own way, they are learning a lot. In one community, a peripheral member attended nearly all meetings for two years, but almost never contributed. Then he was transferred to another division and, to everyone's surprise, started a similar community there.

Finally, outside these three main levels are people surrounding the community who are not members but who have an interest in the community, including customers, suppliers, and "intellectual neighbors." Community members move through these levels. Core members often join the sideline as the topic of the community shifts. Active members may be deeply engaged for a month or two, then disengage. Peripheral members drift into the center as their interests are stirred. Because the boundaries of a community are fluid, even those outside the community can become quite involved for a time, as the focus of the community shifts to their areas of interest and expertise. The key to good community participation and a healthy degree of movement between levels is to design community activities that allow participants at all levels to feel like full members. Rather than force participation, successful communities "build benches" for those on the sidelines. They make opportunities for semiprivate interaction, whether through private discussion rooms on the community's Web site, at a community event, or in a one-on-one conversation. This keeps the peripheral members connected. At the same time, communities create opportunities for active members to take limited leadership roles, such as leading a development project that requires a minimal time commitment. To draw members into more active participation, successful communities build a fire in the center of the community that will draw people to its heat.

Develop both Public and Private Community Spaces

Like a local neighborhood, dynamic communities are rich with connections that happen both in the public places of the community—meetings, Web site—and the private space—the one-on-one networking of community members. Most communities have public events where community members gather—either face-to-face or electronically—to exchange tips, solve problems, or explore new ideas, tools, and techniques. These events are public in that they are open to all community members, though they are often closed to people outside the community. Sometimes they include formal presentations, but most often they are informal discussions of current problems and issues. Public community events serve a ritualistic as well as a substantive purpose. Through such events, people can tangibly experience being part of the community and see who else participates. They can appreciate the level of sophistication the community brings to a technical discussion, how it rallies around key principles, and the influence it has in the organization.

As we've emphasized before, communities are much more than their calendar of events. The heart of a community is the web of relationships among community members, and much of the day-to-day occurs in one-on-one exchanges. Thus, a common mistake in community design is to focus too much on public events. A community coordinator needs to "work" the private space between meetings, dropping in on community members to discuss their current technical problems and linking them with helpful resources, inside or outside the community. These informal, "back channel" discussions actually help orchestrate the public space and are key to successful meetings. They ensure that the spontaneous topics raised at the meetings are valuable to the whole and that the people attending will have something useful to add. The one-on-one networking creates a conduit for sharing information with a more limited number of people, using the coordinator's discretion as a gate. Every phone call, e-mail exchange, or problem-solving conversation strengthens the relationships within the community.

The public and private dimensions of a community are interrelated. When the individual relationships among community members are strong, the events are much richer. Because participants know each other well, they often come to community events with multiple agendas: completing a small group task, thanking someone for an idea, finding someone to help with a problem. In fact, good community events usually allow time for people to network informally. Well-orchestrated, lively public events foster one-on-one connections. As one coordinator said, "I like to see who walks out of the room together, who hangs around and talks. The more new connections I see, the better the meeting was." The key to designing community spaces is to orchestrate activities in both public and private spaces that use the strength of individual relationships to enrich events and use events to strengthen individual relationships.

Focus on Value

Communities thrive because they deliver value to the organization, to the teams on which community members serve, and to the community members themselves. Value is key to community life, because participation in most communities is voluntary. But the full value of a community is often not apparent when it is first formed. Moreover, the source of value often changes over the life of the community. Frequently, early value mostly comes from focusing on the current problems and needs of community members. As the community grows, developing a systematic body of knowledge that can be easily accessed becomes more important.

Rather than attempting to determine their expected value in advance, communities need to create events, activities, and relationships that help their potential value emerge and enable them to discover new ways to harvest it. A group of systems engineers thought that sharing project proposals would be useful. Once they began, however, they discovered that the proposals themselves were not that helpful. What they needed was the engineers' logic for matching that software with that hardware and that service plan. This logic, of course, was not explicit in the proposal. These engineers needed to meet, discuss their proposals, and unveil the logic that held their systems together.

Many of the most valuable community activities are the small, everyday interactions—informal discussions to solve a problem, or one-on-one exchanges of information about a tool, supplier, approach, or database. The real value of these exchanges may not be evident immediately. When someone shares an insight, they often don't know how useful it was until the recipient reports how the idea was applied. The impact of applying an idea can take months to be realized. Thus, tracing the impact of a shared idea takes time and attention.

In fact, a key element of designing for value is to encourage community members to be explicit about the value of the community throughout its lifetime. Initially, the purpose of such discussion is more to raise awareness than collect data, since the impact of the community typically takes some time to be felt. Later, assessments of value can become more rigorous.

Several months after it started one community made discussing value part of its monthly teleconferences. Most community members were not able to identify any particular value when these discussions began, even though they all felt participation was useful. Soon, however, one community member was able to quantify the value his team gained by applying a new technique he learned from another member. Another said the real value of the community was more personal and less quantifiable; he knew who to contact when he had a problem. Once these examples surfaced, other community members were better able to identify the specific value they derived from participation. Although people often complain about the difficulty of assessing community value, such early discussions greatly help community members as well as potential members and other stakeholders understand the real impact of the community.

Combine Familiarity and Excitement

Successful communities offer the familiar comforts of a hometown, but they also have enough interesting and varied events to keep new ideas and new people cycling into the community. As communities mature, they often settle into a pattern of regular meetings, teleconferences, projects, Web site use, and other ongoing activities. The familiarity of these events creates a comfort level that invites candid discussions. Like a neighborhood bar or café, a community becomes a "place" where people have the freedom to ask for candid advice, share their opinions, and try their half-baked ideas without repercussion. They are places people can drop by to hear about the latest tool, exchange technical gossip, or just chat about technical issues without fear of committing to action plans. Communities of practice are what Ray Oldenberg calls "neutral places," separate from the everyday work pressures of people's jobs. Unlike team members, community members can offer advice on a project with no risk of getting entangled in it; they can listen to advice with no obligation to take it. These are reasons why a group of scientists in a pharmaceutical company, driven by urgency to develop new products, see their community as a place to think, reflect, and consider ideas too "soft" for the development teams.

Like a well-planned, challenging conference, vibrant communities also supply divergent thinking and activity. For example, a community of immunologists invites a controversial speaker to their annual conference, a Nobel Prize winner whose ideas are respected by the community but controversial enough to challenge their normal way of thinking. P&G invites its communities to its science fair, where the latest ideas and inventions are displayed and discussed. Conferences, fairs, and workshops such as these bring the community together in a special way and thus facilitate a different kind of spontaneous contact between people. They can provide novelty and excitement that complements the familiarity of everyday activities.

Lively communities combine both familiar and exciting events so community members can develop the relationships they need to be well connected as well as generate the excitement they need to be fully engaged. Routine activities provide the stability for relationship-building connections; exciting events provide a sense of common adventure.

Create a Rhythm for the Community

Our everyday lives have a rhythm: waking up and preparing for work, commuting, checking e-mail, attending meetings, commuting home, engaging with kids' activities, enjoying quiet time. Although there are different rhythms for different people, most of our lives do have a rhythm, which contributes to its sense of familiarity. Towns also have a rhythm. Take the college town of Boulder, Colorado. Throughout the year it has a series of monthly festivals: a river festival, a road race, an arts festival, a Fourth of July celebration, a World Affairs Conference, and a few festivals whose occasion hardly anyone remembers. Like most towns, it also sponsors numerous projects—an arts fund drive, clothing for the homeless. These events and community projects give residents an opportunity to assemble, converse, share opinions, spout off, and have fun together in a way that punctuates the life of the town. They give the town a beat.

Vibrant communities of practice also have a rhythm. At the heart of a community is a web of enduring relationships among members, but the tempo of their interactions is greatly influenced by the rhythm of community events. Regular meetings, teleconferences, Web site activity, and informal lunches ebb and flow along with the heartbeat of the community. When that beat is strong and rhythmic, the community has a sense of movement and liveliness. If the beat is too fast, the community feels breathless; people stop participating because they are overwhelmed. When the beat is too slow, the community feels sluggish. A community of library scientists had an annual meeting and a Web site with a threaded discussion. Not surprisingly, six months after the conference there was very little activity on the Web. An engineering community, on the other hand, held a biweekly teleconference as well as several focused, face-to-face meetings during the year. In this community there is typically a flurry of activity on the Web site just before and after the teleconferences and meetings. The events give the community a beat around which other activities find their rhythm. Sometimes key projects and special events create milestones for the community, breaking up the regular rhythm. Members of a community on team development at the Veterans Benefits Administration travelled to regional offices around the country. They gave workshops and coached local team members and managers. These office visits made the community's contribution to the organization visible and marked a major step in the community's development.

The rhythm of the community is the strongest indicator of its aliveness. There are many rhythms in a community—the syncopation of familiar and exciting events, the frequency of private interactions, the ebb and flow of people from the sidelines into active participation, and the pace of the community's overall evolution. A combination of whole-community and small-group gatherings creates a balance between the thrill of exposure to many different ideas and the comfort of more intimate relationships. A mix of idea-sharing forums and tool-building projects fosters both casual connections and directed community action. There is no right beat for all communities, and the beat is likely to change as the community evolves. But finding the right rhythm at each stage is key to a community's development.

9

Information and Community Mobilization in Rural India

Given the poor quality of many schools in developing countries (with high teacher absence, large class sizes, low levels of achievement and limited inputs) there is considerable policy interest in alternative approaches to making the education system better and more accountable. One much debated approach to improving social service delivery is to provide communities with information that will motivate them to mobilize and demand better services. This project evaluates the effect on education of providing people with information on: the resources that should be available to them, the mechanisms through which they can produce change, and current functioning of local schools.

Three interventions, designed jointly by Pratham, an NGO working on primary education in India, the Abdul Latif Jameel Poverty Action Lab at MIT and the World Bank, have been randomly assigned in about 300 villages in eastern Uttar Pradesh, India, a populous region with low educational outcomes.

Intervention One: A team of three people visits various communities within villages and starts a conversation about education that covers the following issues: the current status of schools and education in the village, the quality of local schools, state mandated provisions for schools (such as pupil teacher ratios), infrastructure, midday meals, scholarships, and local funds available for education. People are asked if they know about the Village Education Committee and its membership, role and responsibilities. After two days of meetings in smaller communities around the village, people are asked to attend a village-wide meeting including the head of the village council, the head teacher of the primary school, members of the Village Education Committee. People are encouraged to ask for information from the local village leadership (any gaps in information are filled in by the Pratham worker) and to discuss issues that are constraining improvements in the schools.

Intervention Two: In addition to all the steps outlined above, villages are actively encouraged to participate in testing to see if children can read simple text and solve simple arithmetic problems. Volunteers put together a "report card" for each community, which is presented at the village-wide meeting.

Intervention Three: In addition to the above two interventions, community volunteers are trained to teach children how to read using an accelerated reading technique developed by Pratham, with the goal of teaching illiterate children to read in 3 months. This evaluation will test the effectiveness of this reading program as well as examine whether giving communities a concrete way to address a specific problem makes them more likely to mobilize on other dimensions as well.

Results

We find that these interventions had no impact on community involvement in public schools and no impact on teacher effort or learning outcomes in those schools. However, we do find that the intervention that trained volunteers to teach children to read had a large impact on activity outside public schools—local youths volunteered to be trained to teach, and children who attended these camps substantially improved their reading skills. These results suggest that citizens face substantial constraints in participating to improve the public education system, even when they care about education and are willing to do something to improve it.

COMMUNITY MOBILIZATION FOR SOCIAL CHANGE IN INDIA

Description: Examples of how you can support Community Development in India:

* Help secure access to safe drinking water and assist in finding employment for local community members through watershed management and community capacity-building initiatives.
* Draft impact assessments on past projects such as solutions for displacement, farmer education initiatives, obtaining access to governmental programs, models for demanding rights, and improving literacy.
* Support a capacity building program by setting up management systems, preparing training modules, offering workshops, and undertaking research studies related to understanding the social actors of governance.
* Assist promotion of renewable energy technology such as smokeless woodstoves, bio-gas plants, solar stoves and lamps in rural communities.
* Help local industries develop industrial greenbelts and start recycling bio-degradable wastes.
* Support an organization's migrant labor programs by providing shelter, health and financial services for migrant groups in destination centers.
* Research successes of local, grassroots development organizations and propose collaborative networks that may attack common problems in the communities.

About FSD

The Foundation for Sustainable Development (FSD) is a non-profit 501(c)(3) organization founded in 1995 to support underserved, international communities in a collaborative and sustainable manner. Our model incorporates three overlapping programs:

Sustainable Development Training Programs

FSD provides comprehensive training and immersion

programs for interns and volunteers seeking hands-on experience in Africa, Asia, and Latin America. Program participants come from countless professions and more than 300 universities worldwide to collaborate with our partner organizations on community-driven projects that reflect sustainable practices.

Partner Organizations

Donations and grants given to FSD are used to support projects and initiatives implemented by our partner organizations, site teams, interns, and volunteers.

Community-Based Organizations

Our professional field staff, consultants, and program participants provide on-site technical training and capacity building to more than 200 community-based organizations.

COMMUNITY ISSUES ADDRESSED BY FSD IN INDIA

Following independence, India created a strong centralized federal government. However, over three quarters of the Indian population continue to live in rural villages-all diverse communities separated by geography, religion, and language. The large, bureaucratic federal government struggled to coordinate and manage these communities, creating a huge gap between the state and its citizens. This has led to problems with the quality of such things as healthcare, schooling, and labor rights in many rural communities.

Forms of local governance have emerged to ensure that justice and equality are afforded to all Indian citizens. Success in grassroots governance is largely due to the work of many NGOs that focus on community development in rural areas. Road construction, rights for migrant laborers, and improvements in waste management are all examples of recent achievements that village community groups were recently afforded after collaboration with local organizations.

Interns in Rajasthan will have the opportunity to work directly on community development in a place where many remain ignorant about their legal rights and isolated from their political system. FSD works to empower local communities by assisting grassroots organizations to form village level seminars, provide training programs, and organize rallies. These organizations work in the communities to establish local management committees, which generate awareness and encourage political and social change. These non-governmental organizations are extremely effective agents for change, but continue to need help with public relations, impact-assessment reports, and facilitation of educational workshops within these communities.

Minimum Education: High School

Intern Types: Communications, Counseling, Development, Economics, Family and Home Studies, Fourth World Studies, Human Resources, Humanities, International Relations, Labor & Industrial Relations, Political Science/Politics, Public Admin, Public Pol, Govt, Urban & Regional Planning and Women's Studies

Languages: English and Hindi

Cost in US$: Varies

Cost Includes: Emergency evacuation services, Excursions, Food, Housing, In-country orientation/Training, In-country staff support, International travel, Language instruction, Living stipend, Medical insurance, Pre-departure orientation/Training, Registration fees, Travel while in host country, Written materials abroad and Written materials pre-departure

Your contribution fee covers all program costs (excluding airfare) and is 100% tax deductible for U.S. residents. Included in the fee is: a one-week orientation; family homestay will all meals provided; language lessons (not available in Latin America); development trainings and workshops; group sessions; midterm retreat (9+ weeks only); final debriefing session; on-going in-country support from FSD site team and U.S. staff; USD 200 mini-grant; eligibility for additional project funding up to USD 500, medical evacuation and limited health insurance; and pick-up from the airport.

Experience Required: no

Typical Volunteer Projects: AIDS, building schools, community centers, community development, community health, community organizing, conflict resolution, counseling, economic development, education, energy, family planning, feasibility studies, grassroots organization, health, health education, human rights, income-generation, nutrition, peace, playgrounds, popular education, population issues, primary education, professional services, public education, public policy, secondary education, small business development, strategic planning, street kids, teaching, volunteering, women, youth and youth development.

Typical Volunteer: FSD supports participants who boldly wish to initiate the change they believe is necessary in the developing world. Interns are passionate about sharing their practical knowledge, heart-felt enthusiasm, and economic resources with communities abroad that suffer unnecessary hardship. They wish to gain hands-on, grassroots development experience because they believe change is most powerfully cultivated on a community level. The aim is to experientially learn how their work can empower the community toward applying sustainable development solutions, rather than increasing reliance on foreign aid. Participants choose FSD because the program structure enables them to design and implement their own sustainable projects in collaboration with their host organization. They are able to test their ideas and theories in the most direct way possible, giving them the experience and knowledge they seek. The flexibility of the host organizations allows for participants at all stages and levels of experience in international development to participate, thus opening the programs to a diverse group of capable applicants.

Age Range: 18-75

This Program is open to Worldwide Participants..

Typical Living Arrangement: Home-stays.

Participants Travel to India Independently.

Typically Participants Work Independently Or in Groups of 3-10.

Application Process Involves:

- Letters of Reference
- Phone Interview
- Resume
- Written Application.

Typically The Application Process Time Is 1 months

Post Services Include:

- Alumni Network
- Exit Debriefing Abroad
- Job and Internship Network.

Foundation for Sustainable Development's Mission Statement: Founded in 1995, the Foundation for Sustainable Development (FSD) supports the efforts of more than 300 grassroots, community-based partner organizations throughout Africa, Asia, and Latin America. FSD's programs provide multi-faceted support that relies on active community participation to mobilize lasting solutions. FSD programs include:

- Capacity Building: Our professional field staff provides on-site training and networking opportunities to more than 300 community-based organizations worldwide.
- Training Programs Abroad: FSD provides comprehensive training and immersion programs for interns and volunteers who seek hands-on development experience.
- Grantmaking: Donations and grants given to FSD are used to support sustainable projects led by our partner organizations.
- Engaged Philanthropy: FSD Giving Circles organize groups of donors who pool their time, talent, and resources to make international grants to our partner organizations.

ORGANIZING A COMMUNITY HEALTH ADVOCACY COALITION

Community health coalitions must be "dedicated to recognizing the autonomy of its members while promoting and maintaining a forum whereby its members can join together to collectively plan, share resources, develop strategies[, and] assist in the implementation of programs to address the health needs of all citizens in the community."

WHAT IS A COALITION?

Often used interchangeably with community organizations or neighborhood organizations, the concept of coalitions tends to be ambiguous. Early definitions of coalition, such as an "organization of organizations" or as a "time-limited organization in which there is a convergence of interest in the part of a number of actors... and an interaction around furthering these common interests," are obviously vague. Due to the number of different definitions, one consistent meaning of coalition should be provided for the sake of clarity. Accordingly, coalition will be defined as "a temporary alliance of groups and individuals who band together to achieve both political and nonpolitical objectives." In this chapter, the political and nonpolitical objectives converge to address the same issue: community health promotion.

Health Promotion

The World Health Organization (WHO) defines health as "a state of complete physical, mental and social well-being and not merely the absence of disease or infirmity." In order to reach this goal, the WHO recognizes several factors as essential for health. These factors include peace, shelter, education, food, income, a stable eco-system, sustainable resources, social justice, and equity. Since these basic conditions will not be met until increased attention is given to healthcare, the WHO, in the Ottawa Charter of 1986, emphasizes the need for health promotion. Health promotion refers to the design and implementation of programs and processes that will enable individuals "to increase control over, and to improve, their health." Guided by the three principles of enabling, mediating, and advocating, health promotion activities include:

- building healthy public policies
- creating supportive environments

- strengthening community action
- developing personal skills
- reorienting health services.

With their strong emphasis on collective action, health promotion activities highlight the need for individuals and organizations within a community to work collaboratively as advocates and activists for health.

Advocacy or Activism: Is there a difference?

According to the Merriam-Webster On-line Collegiate Dictionary, advocacy is "the act or process of advocating or supporting a cause or proposal." Activism, on the other hand, is defined as a "doctrine or practice that emphasizes direct vigorous action especially in support of or opposition to one side of a controversial issue." So while activism employs direct, often confrontational actions, advocacy simply implies pleading or arguing in favor of a cause, idea, or policy. Essentially, all activism is advocacy but not all advocacy is activism.

Change can be the result of either advocacy or activism. Moreover, both spontaneous and planned actions can lead to an alteration in the status quo. It would be negligent to ignore the various contributions that spontaneous, confrontational grass-roots citizen responses to community issues have yielded. For the purposes of this chapter, however, only systematic and planned change through the broader area of coalition advocacy will be explored.

PURPOSES AND FUNCTIONS OF A COMMUNITY HEALTH COALITION

Community health coalitions do not and need not exist for the sole purpose of achieving better health indicators in the community. Rather, their reasons for existence can be as varied as the means by which they are formed. Some coalitions are formed primarily to exchange information between various organizations while others focus on building relationships within the community. Improvements in health communication and awareness are important components of creating 'social-well-being.' Moreover, as the case study described later will indicate, different organizations joining together (strength in numbers) with a common voice can often create 'community power' or a sense of empowerment. Targeting this power towards healthcare sends a clear message to outsiders that the community is concerned about the well being of its citizens.

Health care coalitions can also encompass one of several primary functions, such as service delivery, planning and policy development, surveillance and assessment, and education and outreach. Therefore, coalitions that do focus on improving the quality of healthcare can have varied campaigns, from the improvement of healthcare delivery through information gathering, to the lobbying of public officials for different health policies, to the actual operation of health service programs to fill existing gaps in health care. Whatever the reason for formation, the need for community health advocacy coalitions should be apparent from preceding chapters. Without once again describing the various problems in public health, the number of uninsured Americans, the inequalities in access, and the disparities in treatment should highlight a few of the reasons why community health coalitions are so vital. After all, as aforementioned, their existence at the very least demonstrates that the community is concerned about the health of its citizens and will monitor issues impacting that health. Health care providers, health related entities, community leaders, and private citizens could all become members of the coalition and help fulfill that function.

The process of forming a community health advocacy coalition is hardly simple. After all, not only is every community different, but every individual situation may also differ in slight, but significant, ways. Therefore, it is difficult to have one unified umbrella theory of coalition formation. Regardless, certain processes are both common and vital in every situation. This section will describe those essential steps of forming a community health advocacy coalition. The reader should be warned however that in the real-world setting, the order of the steps may need to change or emphasis may need to be placed on different parts. Indeed, the information offered here is just one of many ways a health care coalition could be formed.

For the sake of simplicity, several assumptions have been made in the writing of this section. First, parties interested in forming a coalition have been identified or have made initial contact with each other. Second, the coalition's focus is community health advocacy, be it creating health interventions or demanding legislative change. Third, the coalition is interested in gauging its effectiveness and success in the community. In a real-world setting, the first assumption may not always hold true. A problem or need in the community may have become apparent and one organization therefore decides to create a coalition around the issue.

Organizing a community health advocacy coalition requires that several important components be addressed. Those organizations or individuals who will be involved in planning and implementing the coalition goals need to be identified. These partnering groups must agree upon on an organizational framework best suited to the coalition's objectives. Both the community's needs and readiness to address those needs must be assessed. The coalition must clearly define, plan, and design their health care advocacy strategies. Lastly, the coalition must monitor the implementation of those strategies and also work to ensure its sustainability within the community.

FIVE-STAGE COMMUNITY ORGANIZING PROCESS FOR HEALTH PROMOTION

"Community organization is a planned process to activate a community to use its own social structures and any available resources (internal or external) to accomplish community goals, decided primarily by community representatives and consistent with local values. Purposive social change interventions are organized by individuals, groups, or organizations from within the community to attain and then sustain community improvements and/or new opportunities."

COMMUNITY ANALYSIS

The central components of community analysis are "assessing community capacity to support a project, potential barriers that exist, and community readiness for involvement."

First, the community that the coalition will target or hopes to impact must be clearly defined. A web site sponsored by the University of Minnesota (2000) suggests three components of defining a community: space and geopolitical boundaries, networks of social relations, and systems of power and influence. Space and geopolitical boundaries refer to the idea that a person's "community" may best be defined broadly, as more than cities or counties. The area in which a person lives, works, plays, shops, and socializes may hold the most merit when considering what area to serve with a coalition. Networks of social relations suggest the location of religious services and civic functions, for example, be considered when implementing an intervention. Finally, an important issue for public health planners is identifying the institutions, organizations, and leaders that if involved in a coalition will increase its chance for success. Overall, by considering the definition of the community, organizers of a coalition can be better prepared for obstacles they may face.

Second, data concerning the needs of the community must be collected. Need is defined as "a discrepancy or gap between 'what is,' or the present state of affairs in regard to the group and situation of interest, and 'what should be,' or a desired state of affairs." A needs assessment or "a systematic set of procedures undertaken for the purpose of setting priorities and making decisions about program or organizational improvement and allocation of resources" utilize a variety of data collection techniques. These techniques include, but are not limited to, interviews with key community people, focus groups, public meetings or forums, and surveys. Qualitative data obtained can be analyzed by looking for common themes in responses, while numerous statistical methods can analyse the quantitative data.

Third, the community capacity, barriers, and readiness for change must be assessed. The resources, in terms of key organizations, individuals, and finances, need to be identified. In addition, community characteristics that would limit the effectiveness of the coalition must also be understood. Lastly, the coalition organizers must determine the level of interest for the coalition in the community and whether the identified needs are urgent or crucial enough to warrant a coalition effort. All these factors can be determined through a properly designed needs assessment. It might be useful to also examine the history of health advocacy coalitions in this community and their level of effectiveness.

Once this information is obtained, the data must be synthesized and priorities for intervention need to be set. All coalition members must agree upon the chosen priorities.

DESIGN AND INITIATION

After having a basic sense of the community needs and coalition priorities, the actual core-planning group of the coalition must be established. Composed of a handful of interested members who are willing to make a commitment to the coalition, this group must guide the actions of the coalition until a formal leader or board is chosen. Hence, their main responsibilities are to assist in the processes of community analysis and priority setting. The core-planning group should also decide upon a mission statement, as well as developing some short-term and long-term goals.

After having fulfilled those responsibilities, the core-planning group should decide on a coalition coordinator and organizational structure. Since the coalition will quickly increase in number, adopting an official framework for operation from the very beginning is recommended. After all, power struggles and hidden agendas should be revealed during the early parts of coalition formation, not later.

A variety of organizational structures can be used in coalitions. Dluhy (1990) suggests a classic model, which emphasizes clarity of tasks and the coordination of these tasks. Not only can this structure be used for different types of coalitions, but as coalitions move toward permanence in organizational structure, this model continues to be accommodating.

In addition to this classic model, the University of Minnesota describes two other structures and they should be considered when planning coalition framework. The first such framework is the lead agency model. This approach involves identifying an existing organization that is able to develop, coordinate, and implement the coalition goals. By letting the group be mainly run by a lead agency, the coalition may gain credibility (based on the previous reputation of the lead agency) and influence (based on the lead agency's relationship with community leaders and public officials). In addition, lead agencies can often provide their own resources, in terms of volunteers, staff time, money, etc, to the coalition. If choosing a lead agency model, it is important to keep in mind that in the same fashion the lead agency's reputation and connections can help, they can also hinder the coalition if those factors are poor. In addition, lead agencies may be members of multiple coalitions or be in charge of multiple projects – it is important to get a commitment of time and resources from them. Lastly, lead agencies may try to push their own agendas or programs unto the coalition. If the need for the lead agency's membership and resources is strong, then the coalition may be susceptible to this pressure.

The second framework is the advisory group model. This approach involves forming an advisory board composed of important community groups. Similar to the lead agency model, if the members of the advisory board are well connected, some of that credibility and influence may extend over to the coalition. Unlike the lead agency model though, this framework offers much more flexibility; board members can be rotated on a periodic basis so that all coalition members feel as if they are equal partners. Even with these strengths, the advisory group model too has its share of potential weaknesses. Power struggles may emerge within the board members and certain groups may be devoting more time and resources than others. Secondly, key community leaders may not wish to join the organization because they desire more power than offered by an advisory board model.

Ultimately, the degree to which a model works for a given coalition is dependent on the coalition leaders, the issue at hand, and the community itself. Therefore, the type of organizational framework one chooses must be appropriate to "the conditions of leadership, influence, and decision-making" in a given community. After an organizational structure is selected, additional coalition members should be identified and recruited. The membership of the coalition should reflect the major organizations and groups in the community. It is recommended to contact organizations or groups that can offer technical expertise/capacity, are regarded in the community with credibility, and have an agency culture of partnership and collaboration. In addition, when the community group becomes a coalition member, the organizer must ensure that the organization representative has the authority to speak for his or her group. The new members must agree to the mission statement and goals.

Once these new members are added to the coalition, training and education should be provided to them. "Training helps members increase confidence about their abilities and contributions to community projects and builds understanding of the extent of the health problem being addressed, the consequences of that problem, and alternative solutions."

Lastly, the roles and responsibilities of coalition partners, staff, volunteers, and even the board itself should be clearly defined. These job descriptions may prevent against any future misunderstandings or power struggles.

IMPLEMENTATION

The combination of the first two steps, community analysis and design-initiation, lays the groundwork for developing a step-by-step work-plan. The community analysis provided information about the pressing needs of the community and the areas that deserved priority. That data was then utilized in the design-initiation stage to form a mission statement and coalition goals. The implementation stage requires that those abstract goals be translated into clearly defined points of action.

The strategies developed should not be "one-shot" deals, or actions without reflection. After all, few public health problems are solved with short-term intervention. Effective coalition work requires multiple programs that are woven in a thorough and integrated manner. In addition, even though formal members for the coalition have already been recruited, it is advisable to continue generating citizen support. Community members should be encouraged to volunteer or participate in coalition activities.

MAINTENANCE AND CONSOLIDATION

Such encouragement will help ensure the sustainability of the coalition in the long run. Bracht outlines three primary ways of strengthening coalition work: "integrate intervention activities into community networks; establish a positive organizational culture; and establish an ongoing recruitment plan." Coalitions, unlike most social agencies and business firms, must continue to strive for clarity and purpose as well as reassure their members that their participation is having practical, tangible, and positive impacts on their community.

DISSEMINATION AND REASSESSMENT

As the coalition's work progresses, it is useful to conduct a new community analysis and check for any differences in needs, resources, etc. In addition, updating the community analysis may help identify additional members for the coalition, who are either new to the community or were previously not interested.

Secondly, the effectiveness of coalition programs should be assessed. Victory is not the only possible outcome measure of value here. The coalition can also analyse whether the number of participants increased at events, whether the coalition membership grew, whether there is an increased awareness on healthcare issues, etc. These results should be summarized and made available to the community. The University of Minnesota suggests two possible ways of 'getting the word out.' First, an annual campaign emphasizing the goals and accomplishments of the coalition thus far can be an effective way to remind the community of the coalition. This is especially beneficial when a coalition has made great progress in an immediate response to a problem, but would like the community to recognize its commitment to long-term improvement as well. Secondly, the University of Minnesota (2000) suggests coalition leaders simply "spread the message." Engaging the media and encouraging coalition members to grant interviews helps alert the public to the coalition.

Lastly, the coalition should determine modifications to existing strategies and future directions. It is important to constantly examine the mission statement and current programs to make sure the two are in line.

Funding

In the end, no matter how strong a coalition or how vital a need, the lack of funding could spell disaster. Fundraising is an inevitability of coalition work, unless a member organization donates the necessary resources as an in-kind contribution. If no such generous organization pulls through, then it is recommended that the coalition organizer take a crash course in grant writing. Grants are often the way many coalitions receive funding. Coalitions can also charge organizations for membership, but that might potentially dissuade certain groups from joining. In addition, coalition can organize various fundraising events, such as dinners, auctions, etc.

ADVANTAGES AND DISADVANTAGES OF A COALITION

Researchers over the years have noted various strengths and weaknesses of having a coalition. Therefore, before implementing a coalition of any type, it would be advantageous to carefully consider these factors.

Criticisms of coalitions often begin with the idea that small-targeted groups with narrow objectives can garner change in certain circumstances. Indeed, they can be quite effective and if and when successful, do not need to share the payoffs with any other groups.

Moreover, coalitions can divert energy and resources from an organization. They also may take positions contrary to or unsupportive of an individual organization's interests or policies. In addition, coalitions may use a "slow, consensus-building process for decision making resulting in a weakened position on some issues." After all, the differences among the organizations that comprise the coalition may prevent it from taking strong stands on particular matters or moving as quickly as desired. These disadvantages though should not negate the desirability of joint action by groups under certain conditions. Indeed, in situations where an individual organization is powerless to effectuate change, coalitions may be better equipped to successfully resolve the issue.

Thus, an individual or organization needs to find the proper balance between working alone and collaborating with other groups. Moreover, coalitions allow individual members to become involved in new and broader issues without concerns of total development or management. Ultimately, coalitions provide its members with a greater number of resources and a wider variety of strategies from which to tackle an issue.

Founded in 1987, Jobs with Justice (JwJ) is a nationwide organization committed to improving and protecting workers' rights. At the heart of JwJ's philosophy is the belief that success can only be attained when the struggle for workers' rights is a part of larger campaigns for social and economic justice. With that end in mind, JwJ has created a network of local coalitions "in over 40 cities in 29 states in all regions of the country."

These local coalitions are comprised of labor unions, faith-based, community, and student organizations. Ultimately, JwJ hopes that "by creating strategic alliances locally and among organizations nationally and developing a broad base of support, Jobs with Justice coalitions are re-building the infrastructure that gives communities a sense of their own power."

The Jobs with Justice coalition in Cleveland, Ohio was formed in 1992 and has almost 60 member organizations that cover the full range aforementioned. In 2001, during Cleveland JwJ's first annual strategic planning retreat, the member organizations decided that they wanted a specific sub-committee, termed "working group," to address healthcare issues. While JwJ was already active in a number of healthcare campaigns, the coalition felt problems in the field were significant enough to warrant a separate effort. Indeed, at that time (and still today), the healthcare indicators of Ohio were both dismal and staggering in their magnitude. In 1998, eleven percent of Ohioans were uninsured and over four hundred thousand Ohioans lost health coverage that year. In addition, the number of Ohioans without prescription drug coverage was estimated to be 2.2 million. With these numbers in mind, the JwJ coalition approved the formation of a HealthCare Working Group.

The membership of the Healthcare Working Group reflects the diversity and community relationship-building that is at the core of Jobs with Justice. Athena Godet-Calogeras, Associate Director of Universal Health Care Action Network of Ohio (UHCAN Ohio), serves as chair of the group.

While her professional role gives her health expertise, many of the other members of the group have never been involved in health care issues before. These members represent various community and faith-based organizations in Cleveland, as well as a number of labor unions. It is their common conviction to protect the rights of working class people, whether that involves advocating for a living wage law or health care, that binds them together.

The mission or strategy of the Healthcare Working is: 1) To educate JwJ membership on health care issues; and 2) To work on issues related to the need for and/or achievement of universal health care. The group wants to get involved in statewide legislation that affects working people and in the local struggles of JwJ member organizations — and the community at large — where health care is an issue.

With those goals in mind, the Healthcare Working Group advocated for statewide Medicaid expansion to working parents in 2002-2001 and affordable prescription drugs for Ohioans through the Prescription Drug Fair Pricing Act in 2001-2002. These issues required the group to get involved in various letter-writing campaigns to legislators, public rallies and demonstrations, meetings with public officials, and petition drives. The group has also engaged in numerous activities supporting St. Michael Hospital and the MetroHealth Clinics.

Obviously, the Healthcare Working Group has not (yet) managed to guarantee universal healthcare for all Americans but it has won small, but significant, steps. Many local politicians now know of the group, the media (both television and newspaper) have covered all of their public events, and the members of Jobs with Justice themselves feel better aware of healthcare issues.

These successes led the Cleveland Jobs with Justice coalition in its second annual strategic retreat to once again approve having a Healthcare Working Group.

Bibliography

Agar, Mahlon: *New Perspectives on Community Development*, England (UK) : McGraw – Hill Book Com., 1981.

Bajpai, P.K. : *Social Work Perspectives on Health*, Rawat, Delhi, 1998.

Bedi, M.S. : *Social Development and Social Work* , Himanshu, Delhi, 1994.

Berger, P. L. : *The Sacred Canopy, Elements of a Sociological Theory of Religion*, Garden City, Doubleday & Company, 1967.

Bhaskaran, Vanila : *Research Methods for Social Work,* Rawat, Delhi 2008.

Bhattacharya, Sanjay : *Social Work* : Psycho-Social and Health Aspects : Deep and Deep, Delhi 2008.

Butcher, Hugh & others : *Community Groups in Action*, London : Rutledge ad Kegan Paul., 1988.

Cox Fred: *Community Organization*, Michigan : F.E. Peacock Publishers, 1987.

Das, D.K. Lal : *Practice of Social Research : Social Work* Perspective, Rawat, 2000.

Dhama, O. P & Bhatnager, O.P.: *Education and Communication for Development,* New Delhi : Oxford & IBG Pub. Co. Pvt; Ltd., 1994.

Dunham Arthur: *Community Welfare Organization: Principles and Practice*, New York : Thomas Crowell, 1962.

Elisabeth Relchert: *Social Work and Human Rights : A Foundation for Policy and Practice*, Rawat, Delhi, 2003.

Frederic G. Reamer : *Social Work Values and Ethics,* Rawat, Delhi, 2005.

Friedlander, W.A.: *Concepts and Methods in Social Work*, Eaglewood Cliffs, New Delhi : Bentice Hall International Inc., 1978.

Iqbal, Shaikh Azhar : *Principles and Practices of Social Work*, Sublime, Delhi, 2005.

Jha, Jainendra Kumar : *Social Welfare and Social Work*, Anmol, Delhi, 2002

Khan, M A : *Social Work and Social Policy, Concepts and Methods*, Book Enclave, Delhi, 2007.

Kohli, A S : *Human Rights and Social Work, Issues, Challenges and Response*, Kanishka, Delhi, 2004.

Kumar, Hajira : *Social Work, Social Development and Sustainable Development*, Regency, Delhi, 1997.

Milson Fred: *An Introduction to Community Work*, Rutledge & Kegan Paul, New Delhi : London OXFORD & IBH Publishing Co. Pvt. Ltd, 1973.

Milton Reimer : *Christian Perspectives on Sociology,* Grand Rapids, Mich., Zondervan, 1982.

Murli Desai : *Ideologies and Social Work, Historical and Contemporary Analyses*, Rawat Pub, Delhi, 2002.

Peter Romanofsky: *Community Organizing for Urban Social Change, A Historical Perspective,* Greenwood Press, Delhi, 1981.

Pratima Chaturvedi : *Social Work : Theories and Practices,* Book Enclave, Delhi, 2005.

Profulla C Sarker : *Issues and Perspectives on Social Work and Social Development*, Serials Pub, Delhi, 2008.

Raj Bala Mathur : *Modernisation of Social Work, Planning and Administration*, Book Enclave, Delhi, 2007.

Ramachandran, S.P. : *Social Work for Minorities*, Sumit Enterprises, Delhi, 2008.

Ranjna K. Devi : *Social Work, Philosophy, Concepts and Dimensions*, Omega, Delhi, 2009.

Rizwi, A K : *Social Policy and Social Work*, Mohit Pub, Delhi, 2008.

Ross, Murray & Lappin, Ben: *Community Organization; Theory, Principles, and Practice*, New York : Harper & Row, 1967.

Sanoff, Henry: *Community Participation Methods in Design and Planning*, London : John Wiley and Sons, 2000.

Sen, S K : *Social Work Practices*, Book Enclave, Delhi, 2007.

Shirley, Dennis : *Community Organizing for Urban School Reform,* Austin, University of Texas Press, 1997.

Siddique, H.Y.: *Social Work and Social Action*, New Delhi : Harnam Publications, 1984.

Sinha, Debotosh : *Aspects of Industry and Occupational Social Work*, Abhijeet Pub, Delhi, 2007.

Somesh Kumar: *Methods for Community Participation*, New Delhi : Sage Publication (Vistaar), 2002.

Subheda, I.S. : *Fieldwork Training in Social Work,* Rawat, Delhi, 2001.

Subhedar, I.S. : *Social Work Perspectives,* Om Pub, Delhi, 2006.

Vijendra Kumar : *Problems and Perspectives on Social Work and Social Welfare,* ABD Pub, Delhi, 2002.

Wendy Bowles : *Research for Social Workers : An Introduction to Methods*, Rawat, Delhi, 2003.

Index

R

S

T

U

V

Y

❑❑❑